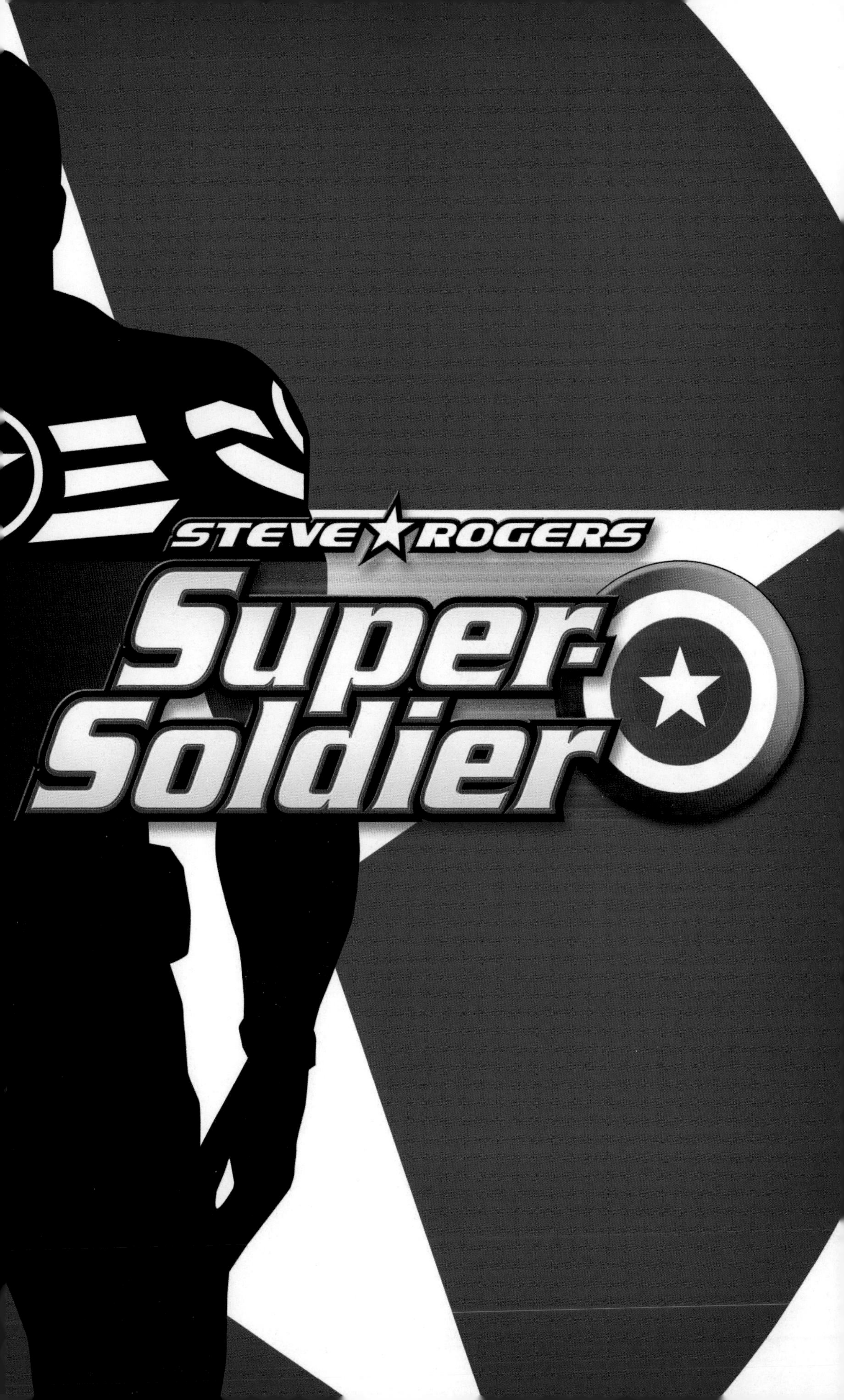

STEVE ROGERS

Super-Soldier

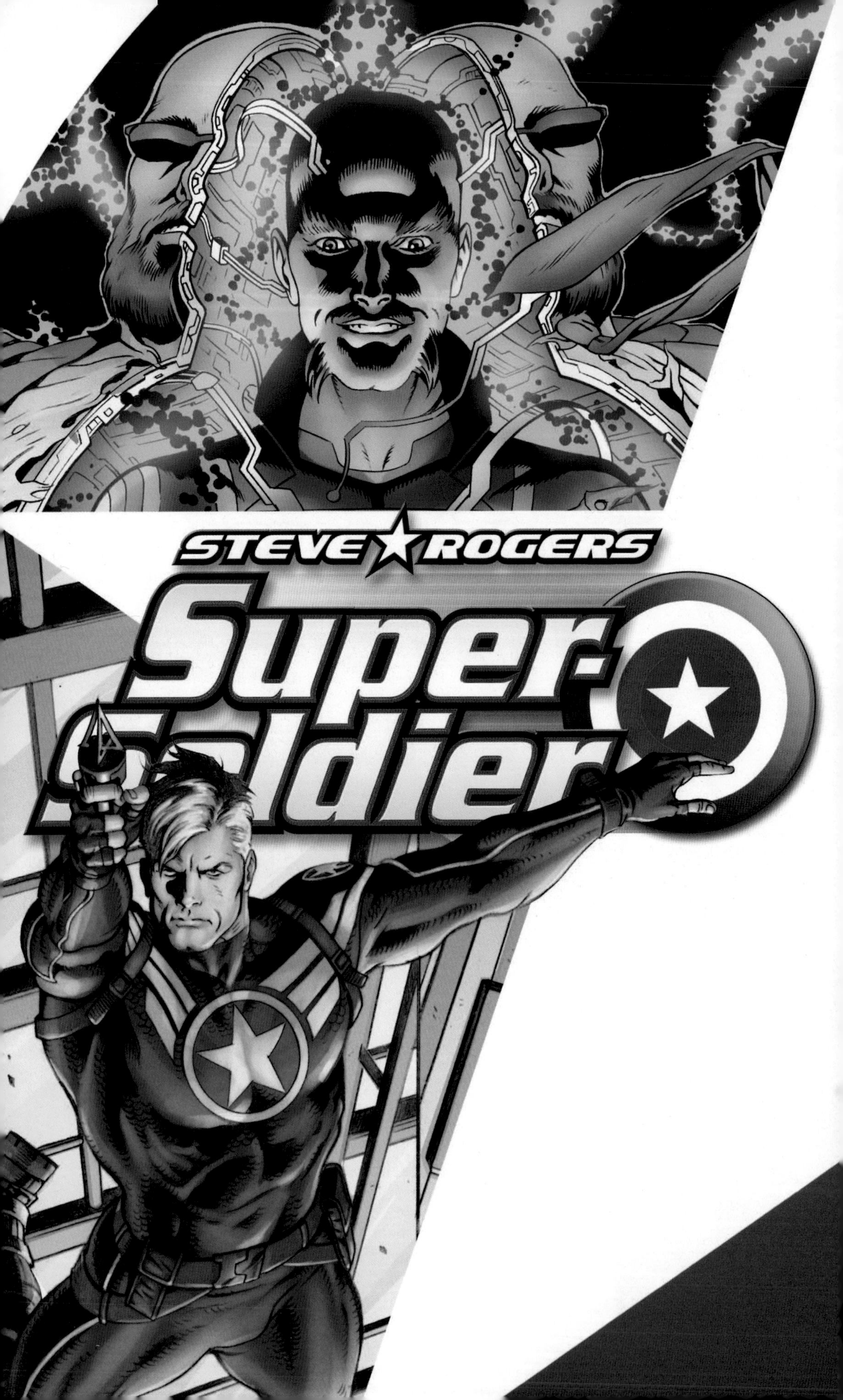
STEVE ROGERS
Super-Soldier

ED BRUBAKER

Artist
DALE EAGLESHAM

Letterer: VC'S JOE CARAMAGNA

Cover Art: CARLOS PACHECO, TIM TOWNSEND & FRANK D'ARMATA

Associate Editor: LAUREN SANKOVITCH

Editor: TOM BREVOORT

Captain America created by **JOE SIMON** & **JACK KIRBY**

Collection Editor: **JENNIFER GRÜNWALD**

Editorial Assistants: **JAMES EMMETT** & **JOE HOCHSTEIN**

Assistant Editors: **ALEX STARBUCK** & **NELSON RIBEIRO**

Editor, Special Projects: **MARK D. BEAZLEY**

Senior Editor, Special Projects: **JEFF YOUNGQUIST**

Senior Vice President of Sales: **DAVID GABRIEL**

Book Designer: **RODOLFO MURAGUCHI**

Editor in Chief: **JOE QUESADA**

Publisher: **DAN BUCKLEY**

Executive Producer: **ALAN FINE**

STEVE ROGERS: SUPER-SOLDIER. Contains material originally published in magazine form as STEVE ROGERS: SUPER-SOLDIER #1-4 and CAPTAIN AMERICA COMICS #1. First printing 2011. ISBN# 978-0-7851-4878-4. Published by MARVEL WORLDWIDE, INC., a subsidiary of MARVEL ENTERTAINMENT, LLC. OFFICE OF PUBLICATION: 135 West 50th Street, New York, NY 10020. **Printed in the U.S.A.** ALAN FINE, EVP - Office of the President, Marvel Worldwide, Inc. and EVP & CMO Marvel Characters B.V.; DAN BUCKLEY, Chief Executive Officer and Publisher - Print, Animation & Digital Media; JIM SOKOLOWSKI, Chief Operating Officer; DAVID GABRIEL, SVP of Publishing Sales & Circulation; DAVID BOGART, SVP of Business Affairs & Talent Management; MICHAEL PASCIULLO, VP Merchandising & Communications; JIM O'KEEFE, VP of Operations & Logistics; DAN CARR, Executive Director of Publishing Technology; JUSTIN F. GABRIE, Director of Publishing & Editorial Operations; SUSAN CRESPI, Editorial Operations Manager; ALEX MORALES, Publishing Operations Manager; STAN LEE, Chairman Emeritus. For information regarding advertising in Marvel Comics or on Marvel.com, please contact Ron Stern, VP of Business Development, at rstern@marvel.com. For Marvel subscription inquiries, please call 800-217-9158. **Manufactured between 12/6/10 and 1/5/11 by R.R. DONNELLEY, INC., SALEM, VA, USA.**

10 9 8 7 6 5 4 3 2 1

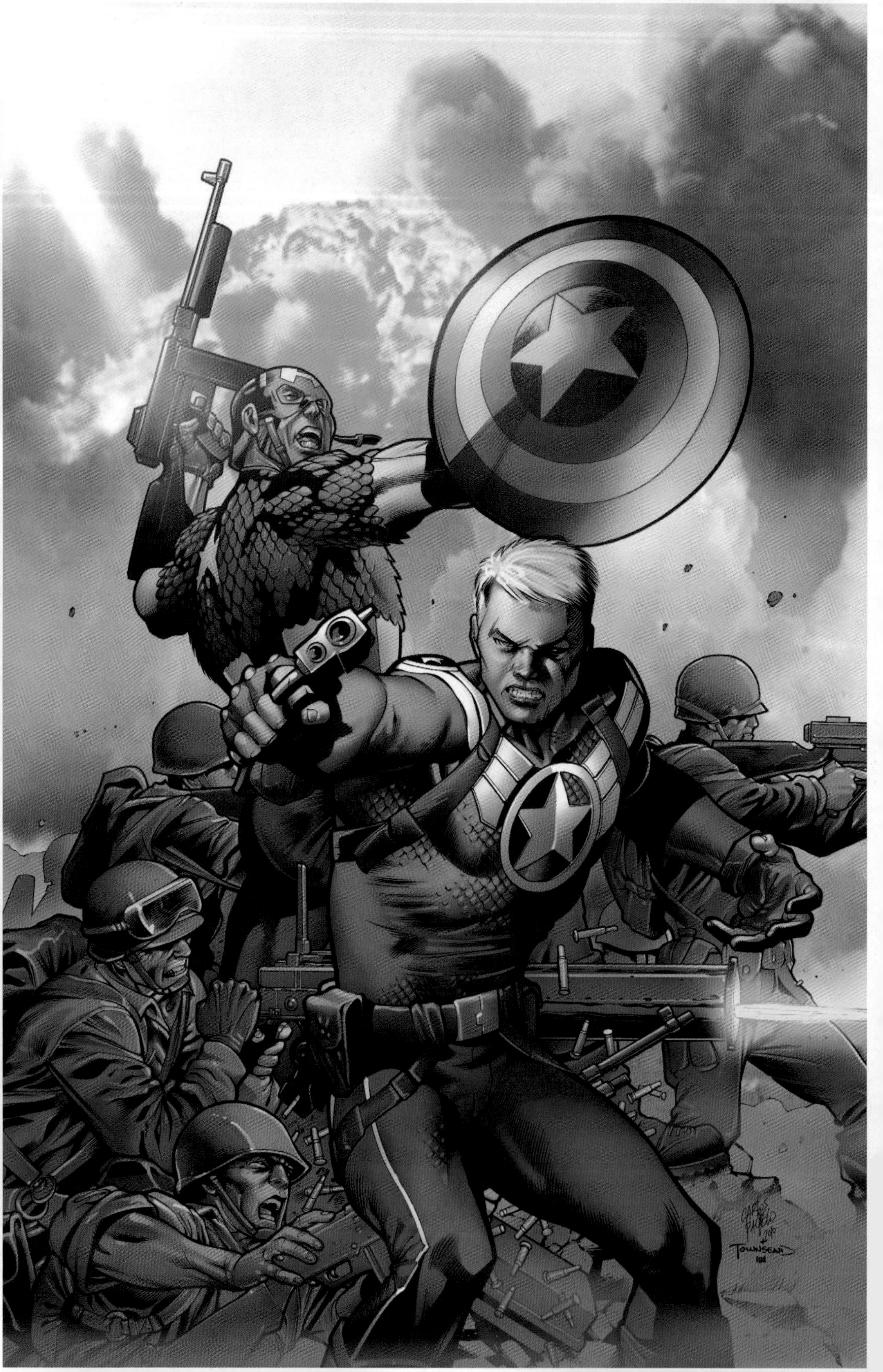

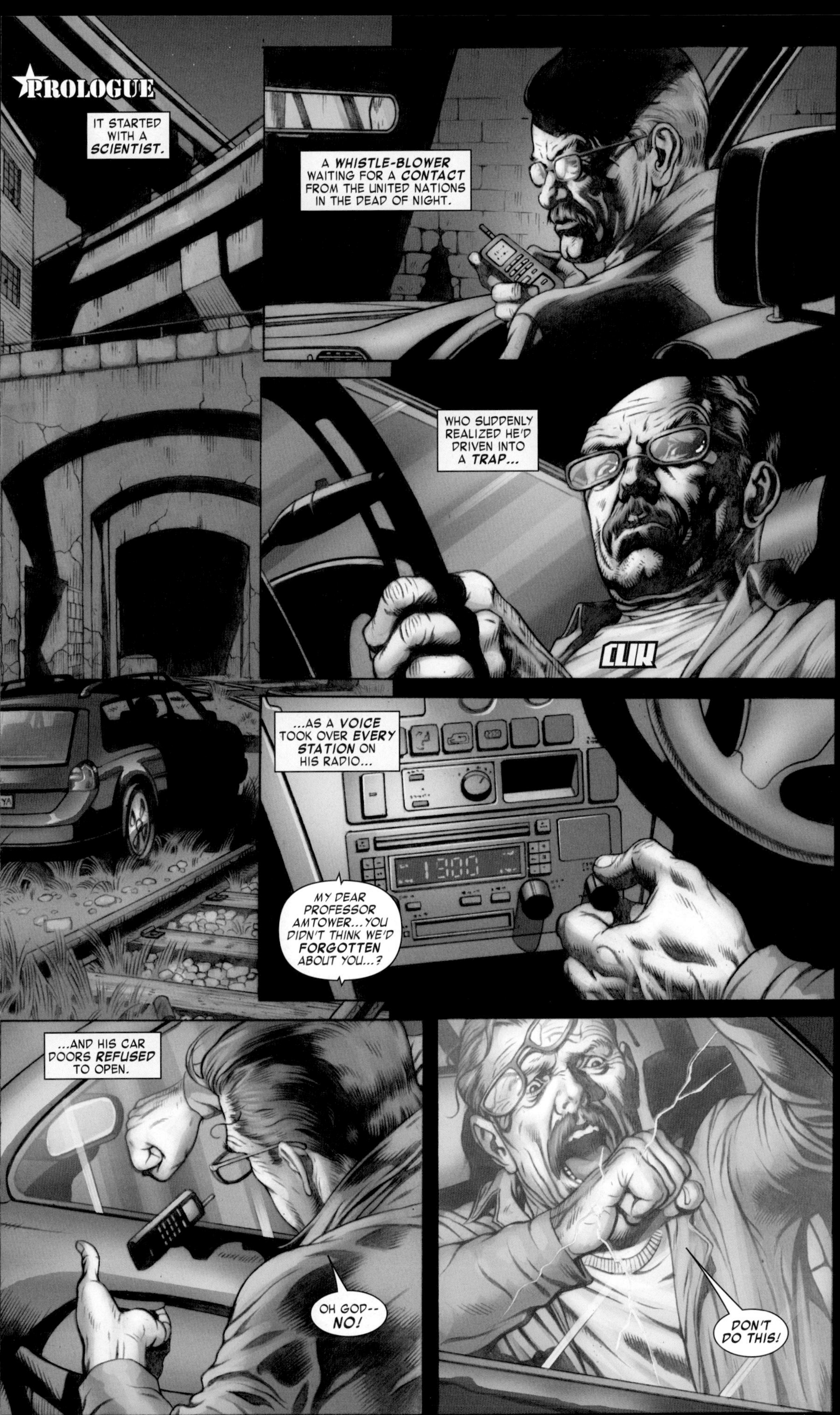
PROLOGUE
IT STARTED WITH A SCIENTIST.
A WHISTLE-BLOWER WAITING FOR A CONTACT FROM THE UNITED NATIONS IN THE DEAD OF NIGHT.
WHO SUDDENLY REALIZED HE'D DRIVEN INTO A TRAP...
CLIK
...AS A VOICE TOOK OVER EVERY STATION ON HIS RADIO...
MY DEAR PROFESSOR AMTOWER...YOU DIDN'T THINK WE'D FORGOTTEN ABOUT YOU...?
...AND HIS CAR DOORS REFUSED TO OPEN.
OH GOD-- NO!
DON'T DO THIS!

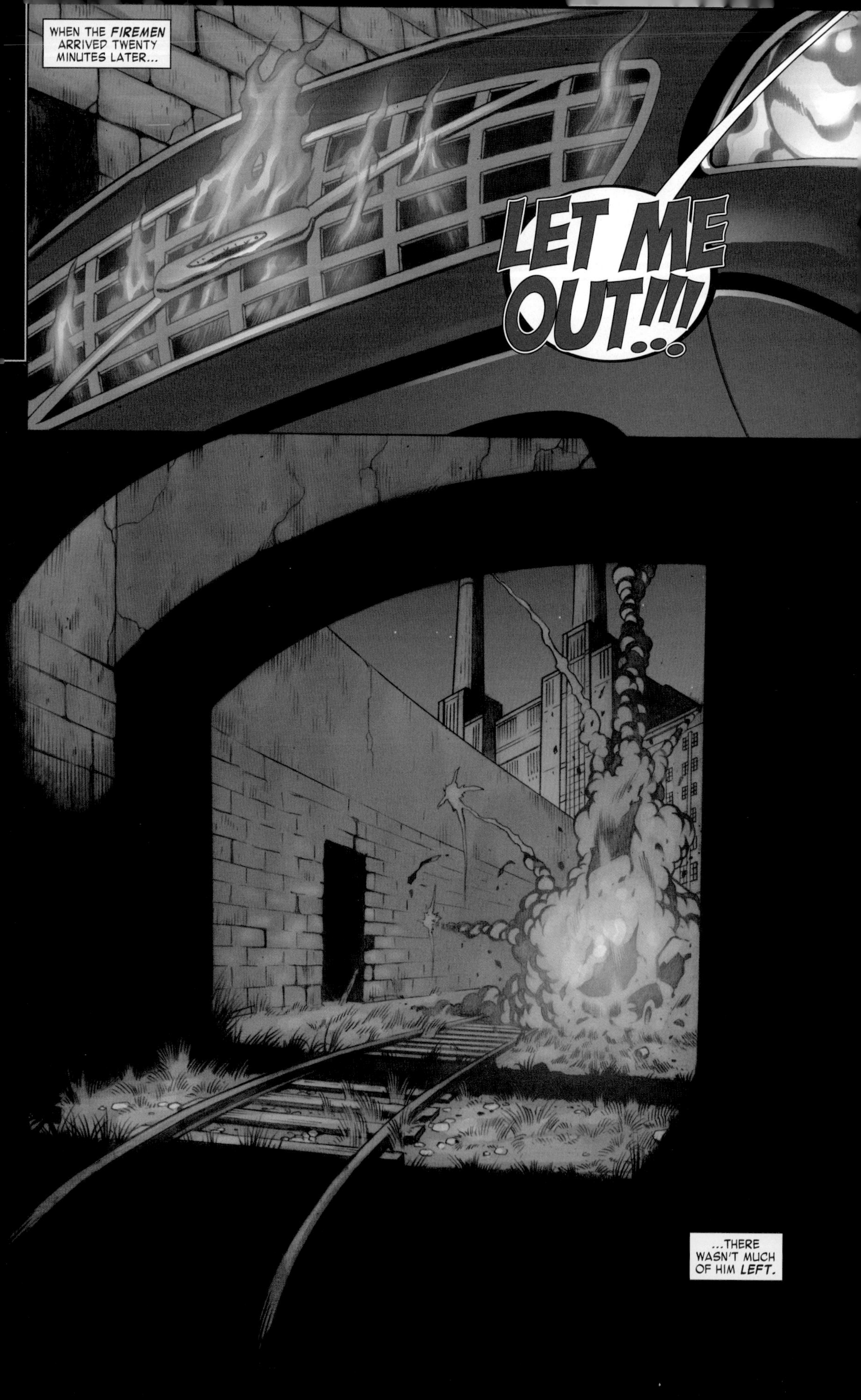
WHEN THE FIREMEN ARRIVED TWENTY MINUTES LATER...
LET ME OUT!!!
...THERE WASN'T MUCH OF HIM LEFT.

IN THE DARK DAYS OF THE EARLY 1940s,
STEVE ROGERS,
A STRUGGLING YOUNG ARTIST FROM THE
LOWER EAST SIDE OF MANHATTAN,
FOUND HIMSELF HORRIFIED BY THE WAR RAGING OVERSEAS.
DESPERATE TO HELP, HE WAS REJECTED BY THE
U.S. ARMY
AS UNFIT FOR SERVICE WHEN HE TRIED TO ENLIST.

UNDETERRED, CONVINCED THIS WAS WHERE HE NEEDED TO BE,
HE WAS SELECTED TO PARTICIPATE IN
A COVERT MILITARY PROJECT CALLED
OPERATION: REBIRTH.
THERE, HE WAS CHOSEN BY SCIENTIST ABRAHAM ERSKINE
AS THE FIRST HUMAN TEST SUBJECT, AND OVERNIGHT WAS
TRANSFORMED INTO
**AMERICA'S FIRST SUPER-SOLDIER,
CAPTAIN AMERICA.**

NOW, DECADES LATER, STEVE ROGERS CARRIES ON THE
BATTLE FOR FREEDOM AND DEMOCRACY AS
**AMERICA'S TOP
LAW-ENFORCEMENT OPERATIVE
AND COMMANDER OF
THE MIGHTY AVENGERS.**

STEVE ROGERS:
SUPER-SOLDIER

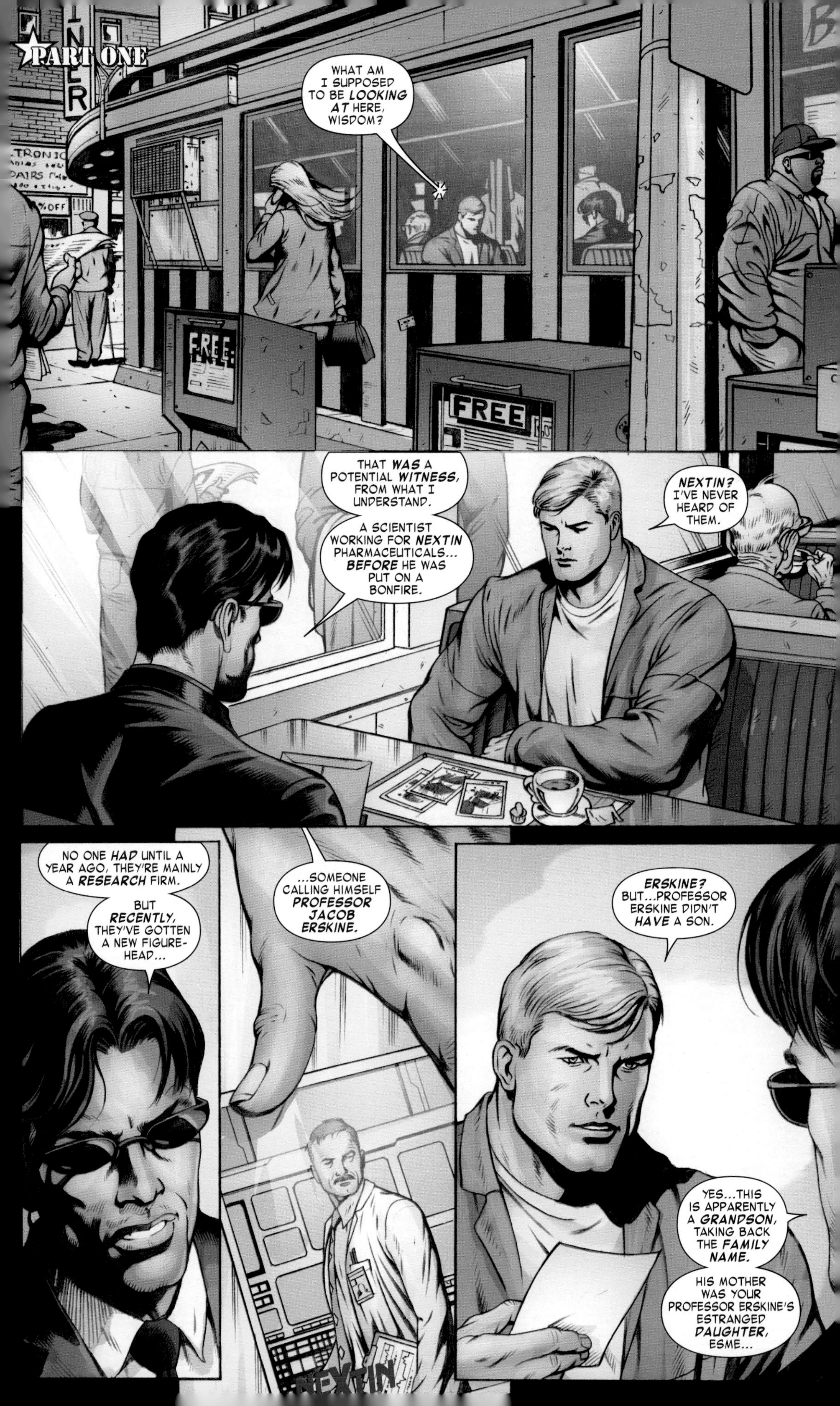
PART ONE
WHAT AM I SUPPOSED TO BE LOOKING AT HERE, WISDOM?
FREE
FREE
THAT WAS A POTENTIAL WITNESS, FROM WHAT I UNDERSTAND.
A SCIENTIST WORKING FOR NEXTIN PHARMACEUTICALS... BEFORE HE WAS PUT ON A BONFIRE.
NEXTIN? I'VE NEVER HEARD OF THEM.
NO ONE HAD UNTIL A YEAR AGO, THEY'RE MAINLY A RESEARCH FIRM.
BUT RECENTLY, THEY'VE GOTTEN A NEW FIGURE-HEAD...
...SOMEONE CALLING HIMSELF PROFESSOR JACOB ERSKINE.
NEXTIN
ERSKINE? BUT...PROFESSOR ERSKINE DIDN'T HAVE A SON.
YES...THIS IS APPARENTLY A GRANDSON, TAKING BACK THE FAMILY NAME.
HIS MOTHER WAS YOUR PROFESSOR ERSKINE'S ESTRANGED DAUGHTER, ESME...

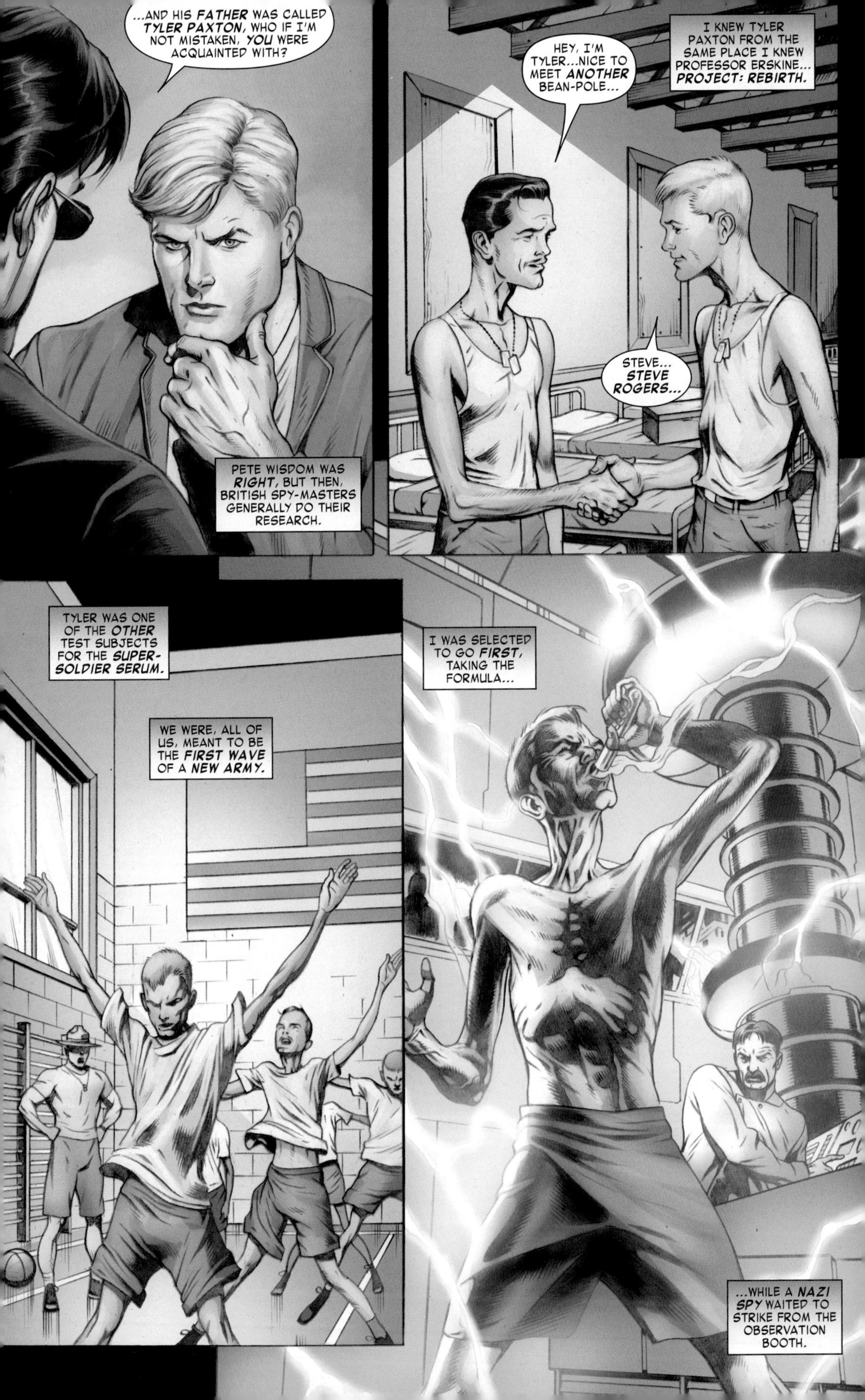
...AND HIS FATHER WAS CALLED TYLER PAXTON, WHO IF I'M NOT MISTAKEN, YOU WERE ACQUAINTED WITH?
PETE WISDOM WAS RIGHT, BUT THEN, BRITISH SPY-MASTERS GENERALLY DO THEIR RESEARCH.
I KNEW TYLER PAXTON FROM THE SAME PLACE I KNEW PROFESSOR ERSKINE... PROJECT: REBIRTH.
HEY, I'M TYLER...NICE TO MEET ANOTHER BEAN-POLE...
STEVE... STEVE ROGERS...
TYLER WAS ONE OF THE OTHER TEST SUBJECTS FOR THE SUPER-SOLDIER SERUM.
WE WERE, ALL OF US, MEANT TO BE THE FIRST WAVE OF A NEW ARMY.
I WAS SELECTED TO GO FIRST, TAKING THE FORMULA...
...WHILE A NAZI SPY WAITED TO STRIKE FROM THE OBSERVATION BOOTH.

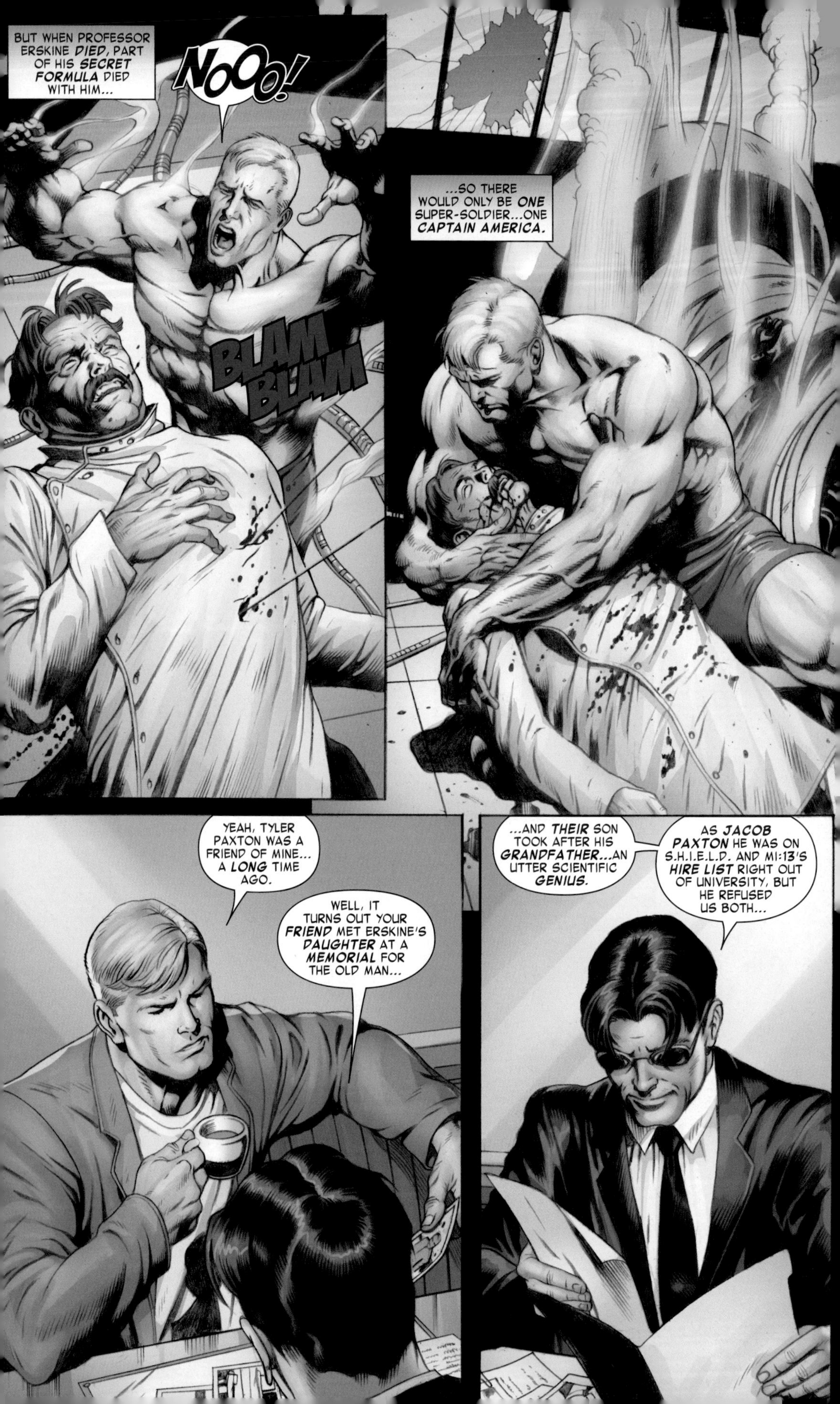

BUT WHEN PROFESSOR ERSKINE DIED, PART OF HIS SECRET FORMULA DIED WITH HIM...
NOOOO!
BLAM BLAM
...SO THERE WOULD ONLY BE ONE SUPER-SOLDIER...ONE CAPTAIN AMERICA.
YEAH, TYLER PAXTON WAS A FRIEND OF MINE... A LONG TIME AGO.
WELL, IT TURNS OUT YOUR FRIEND MET ERSKINE'S DAUGHTER AT A MEMORIAL FOR THE OLD MAN...
...AND THEIR SON TOOK AFTER HIS GRANDFATHER...AN UTTER SCIENTIFIC GENIUS.
AS JACOB PAXTON HE WAS ON S.H.I.E.L.D. AND MI:13'S HIRE LIST RIGHT OUT OF UNIVERSITY, BUT HE REFUSED US BOTH...

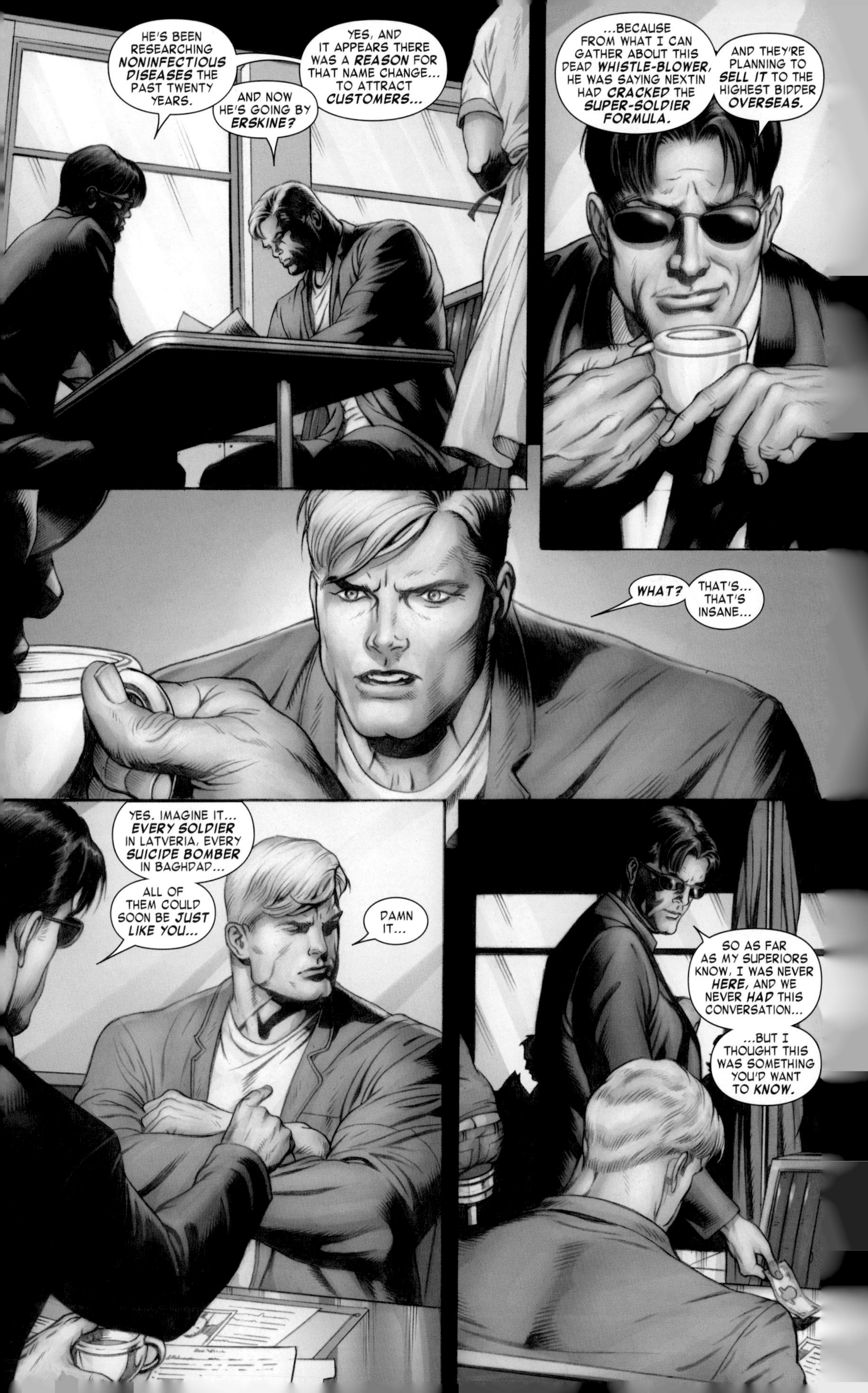

HE'S BEEN RESEARCHING NONINFECTIOUS DISEASES THE PAST TWENTY YEARS.
AND NOW HE'S GOING BY ERSKINE?
YES, AND IT APPEARS THERE WAS A REASON FOR THAT NAME CHANGE... TO ATTRACT CUSTOMERS...
...BECAUSE FROM WHAT I CAN GATHER ABOUT THIS DEAD WHISTLE-BLOWER, HE WAS SAYING NEXTIN HAD CRACKED THE SUPER-SOLDIER FORMULA.
AND THEY'RE PLANNING TO SELL IT TO THE HIGHEST BIDDER OVERSEAS.
WHAT?
THAT'S... THAT'S INSANE...
YES. IMAGINE IT... EVERY SOLDIER IN LATVERIA, EVERY SUICIDE BOMBER IN BAGHDAD...
ALL OF THEM COULD SOON BE JUST LIKE YOU...
DAMN IT...
SO AS FAR AS MY SUPERIORS KNOW, I WAS NEVER HERE, AND WE NEVER HAD THIS CONVERSATION...
...BUT I THOUGHT THIS WAS SOMETHING YOU'D WANT TO KNOW.

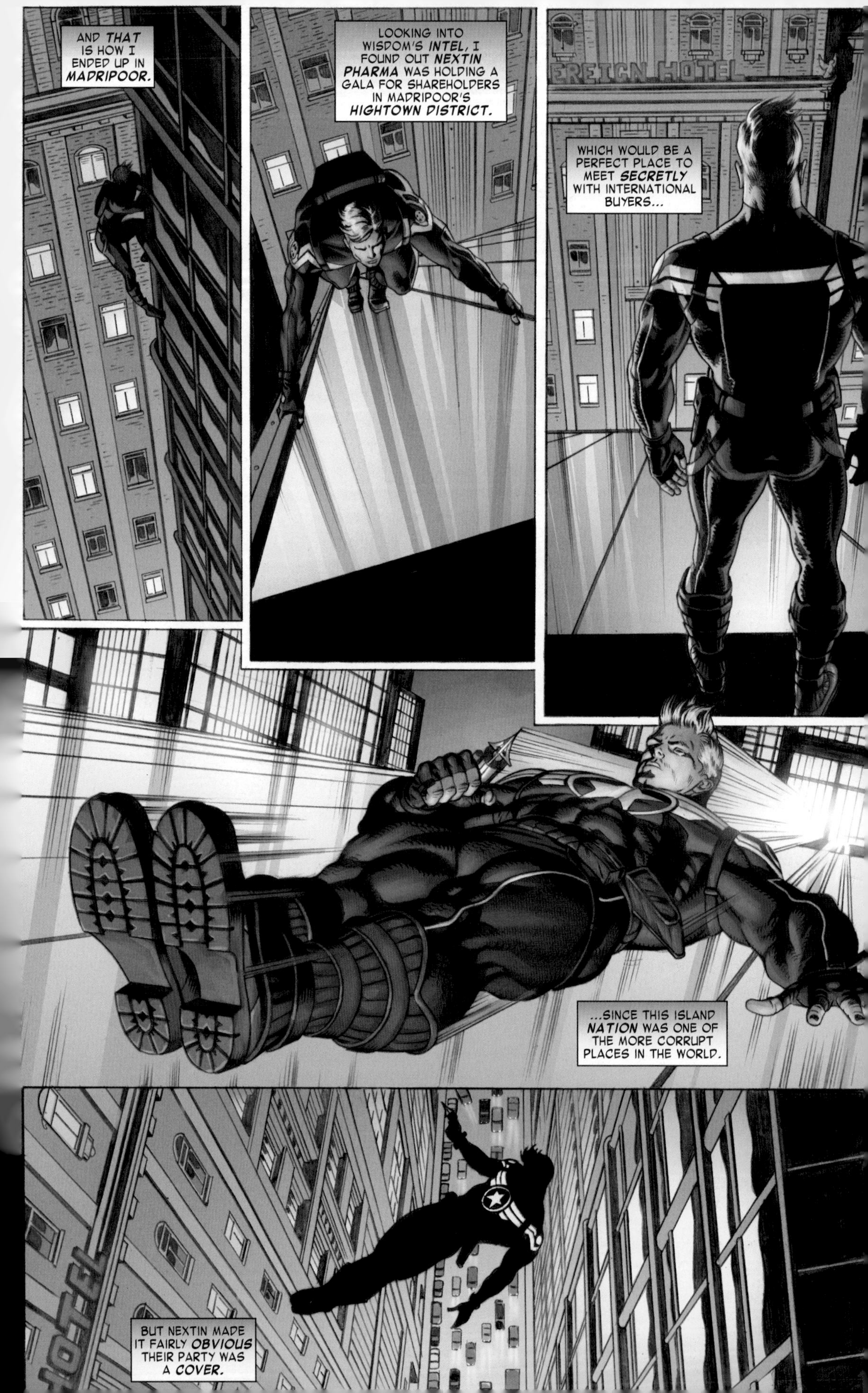
AND THAT IS HOW I ENDED UP IN MADRIPOOR.
LOOKING INTO WISDOM'S INTEL, I FOUND OUT NEXTIN PHARMA WAS HOLDING A GALA FOR SHAREHOLDERS IN MADRIPOOR'S HIGHTOWN DISTRICT.
WHICH WOULD BE A PERFECT PLACE TO MEET SECRETLY WITH INTERNATIONAL BUYERS...
...SINCE THIS ISLAND NATION WAS ONE OF THE MORE CORRUPT PLACES IN THE WORLD.
BUT NEXTIN MADE IT FAIRLY OBVIOUS THEIR PARTY WAS A COVER.

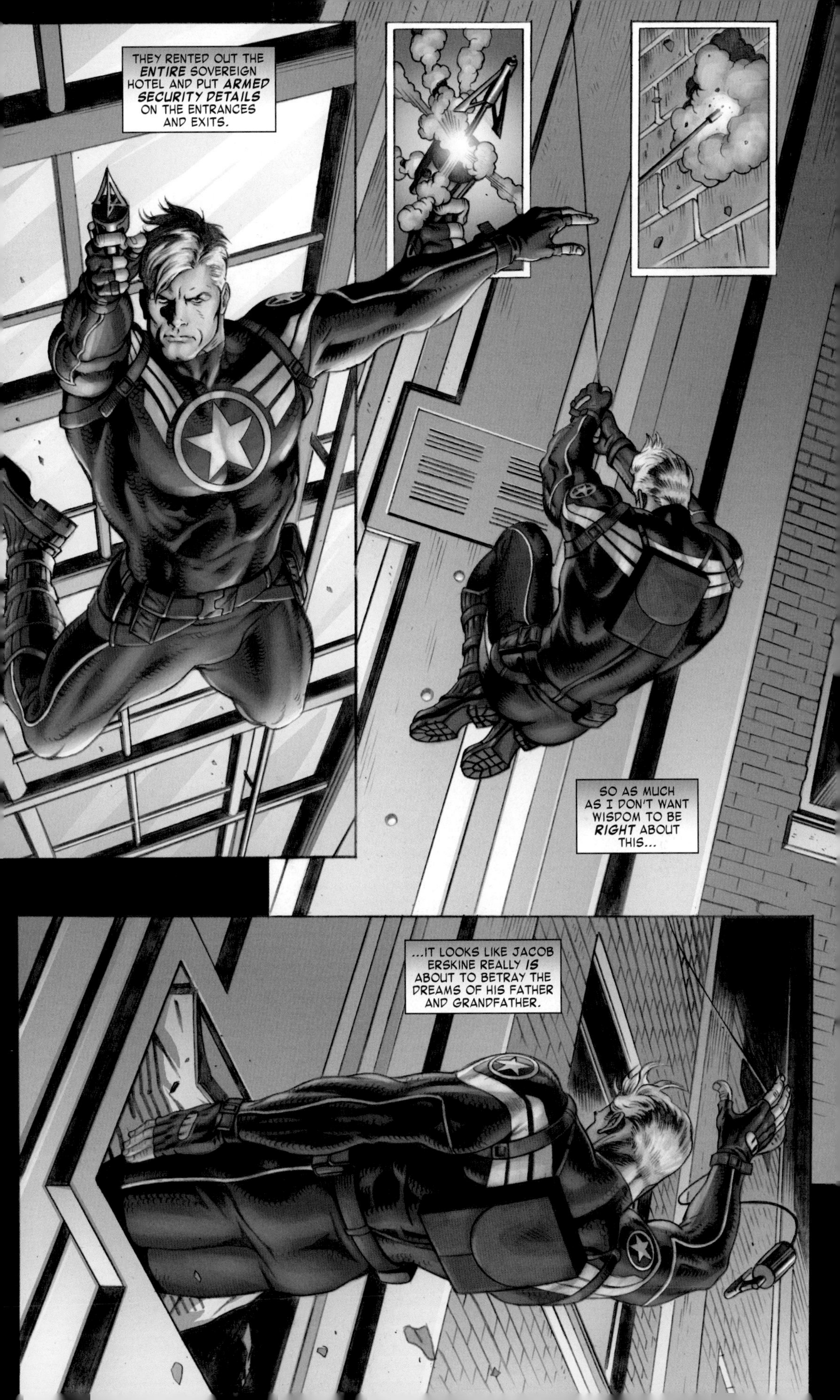
THEY RENTED OUT THE ENTIRE SOVEREIGN HOTEL AND PUT ARMED SECURITY DETAILS ON THE ENTRANCES AND EXITS.
SO AS MUCH AS I DON'T WANT WISDOM TO BE RIGHT ABOUT THIS...
...IT LOOKS LIKE JACOB ERSKINE REALLY IS ABOUT TO BETRAY THE DREAMS OF HIS FATHER AND GRANDFATHER.

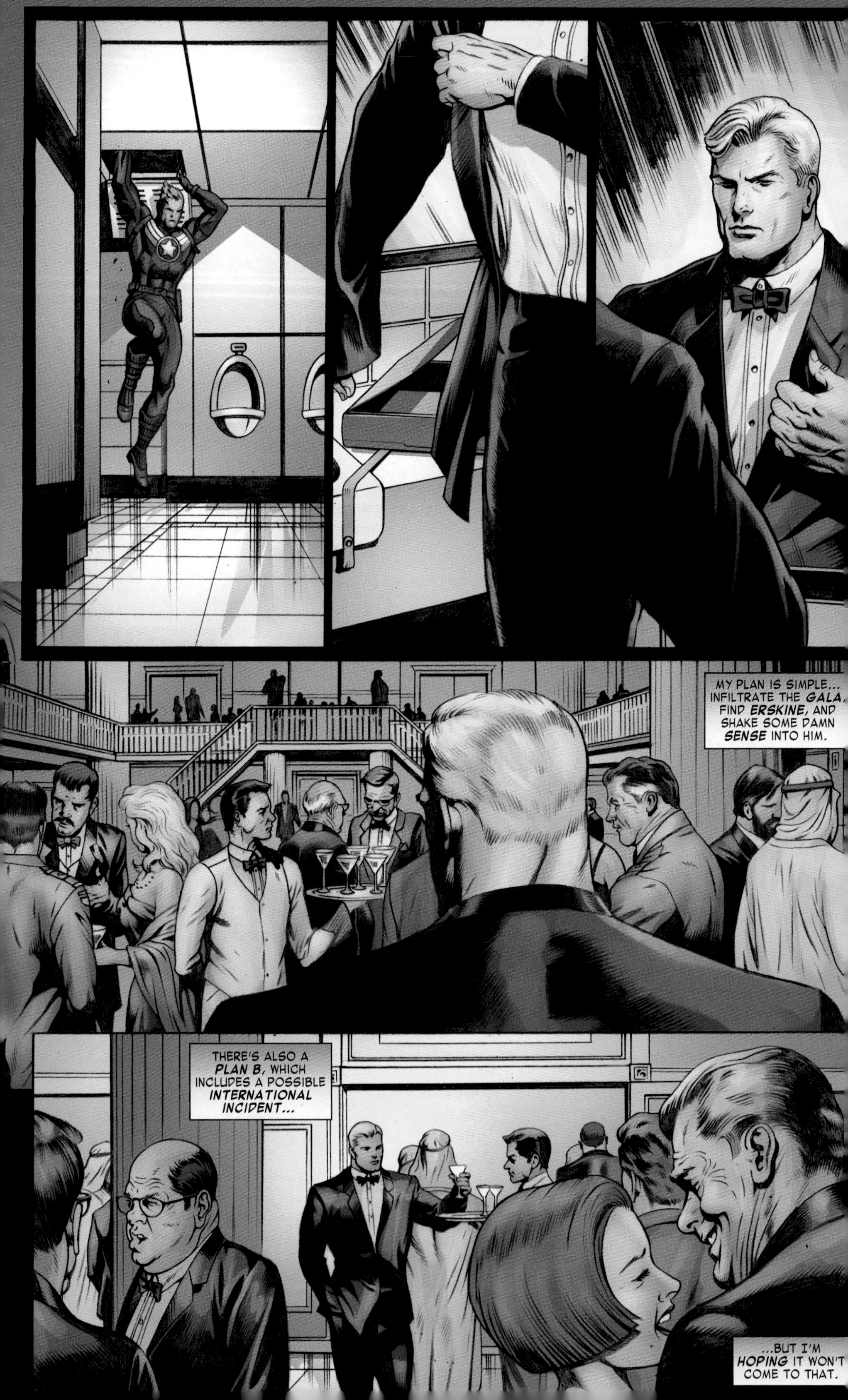
MY PLAN IS SIMPLE... INFILTRATE THE GALA, FIND ERSKINE, AND SHAKE SOME DAMN SENSE INTO HIM.
THERE'S ALSO A PLAN B, WHICH INCLUDES A POSSIBLE INTERNATIONAL INCIDENT...
...BUT I'M HOPING IT WON'T COME TO THAT.

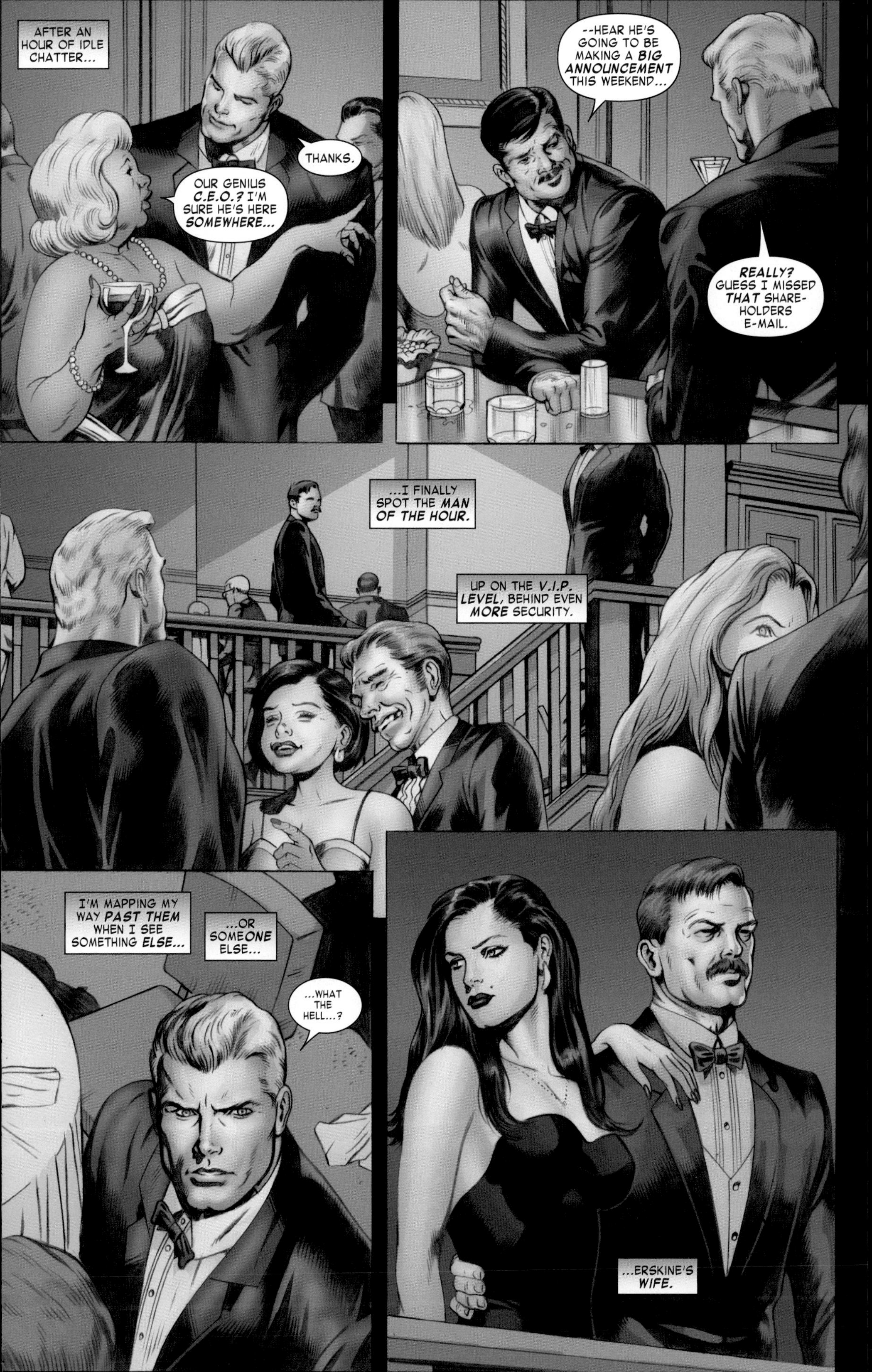
AFTER AN HOUR OF IDLE CHATTER...
OUR GENIUS C.E.O.? I'M SURE HE'S HERE SOMEWHERE...
THANKS.
--HEAR HE'S GOING TO BE MAKING A BIG ANNOUNCEMENT THIS WEEKEND...
REALLY? GUESS I MISSED THAT SHARE-HOLDERS E-MAIL.
...I FINALLY SPOT THE MAN OF THE HOUR.
UP ON THE V.I.P. LEVEL, BEHIND EVEN MORE SECURITY.
I'M MAPPING MY WAY PAST THEM WHEN I SEE SOMETHING ELSE...
...OR SOMEONE ELSE...
...WHAT THE HELL...?
...ERSKINE'S WIFE.

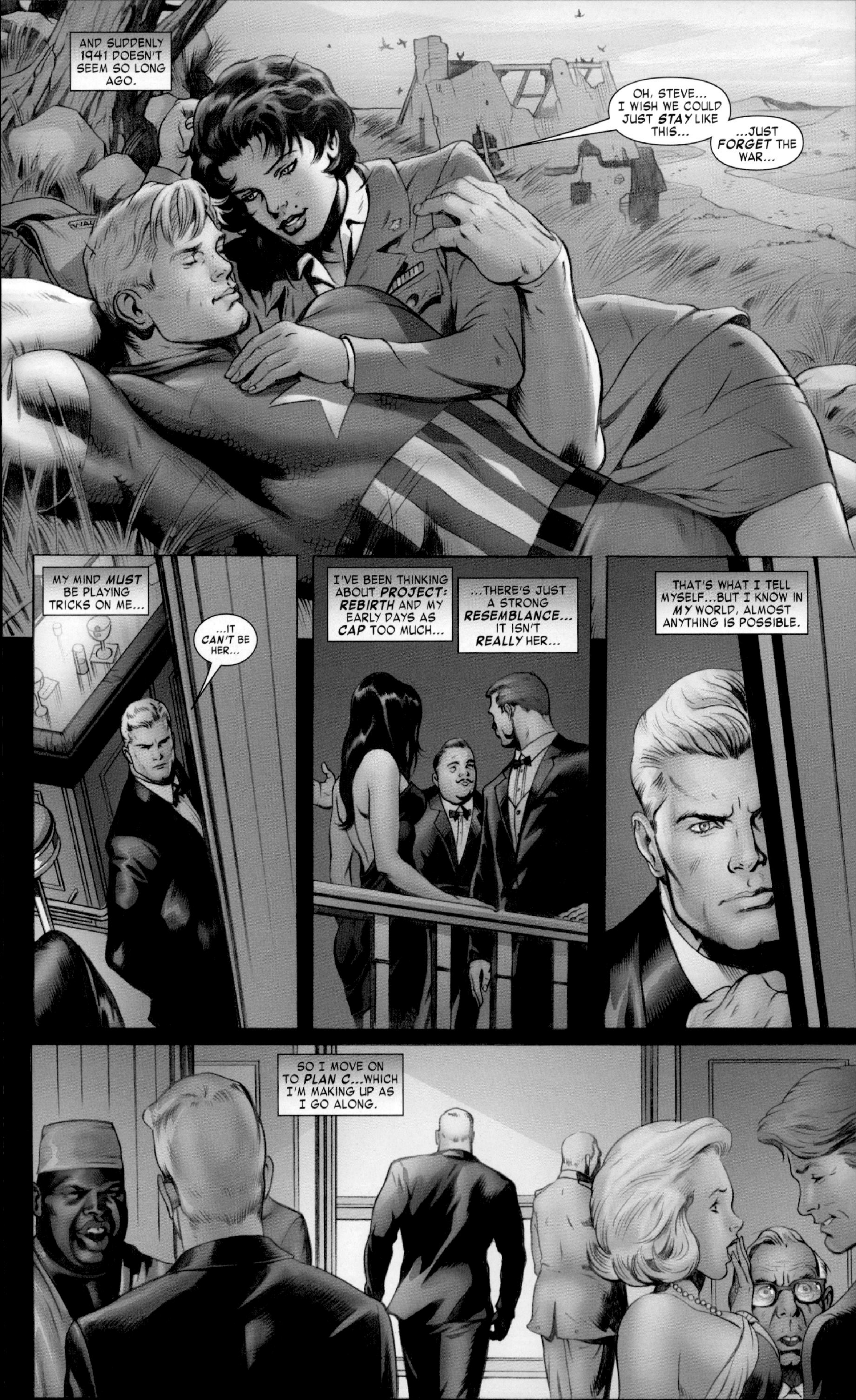
AND SUDDENLY 1941 DOESN'T SEEM SO LONG AGO.
OH, STEVE... I WISH WE COULD JUST STAY LIKE THIS...
...JUST FORGET THE WAR...
MY MIND MUST BE PLAYING TRICKS ON ME...
...IT CAN'T BE HER...
I'VE BEEN THINKING ABOUT PROJECT: REBIRTH AND MY EARLY DAYS AS CAP TOO MUCH...
...THERE'S JUST A STRONG RESEMBLANCE... IT ISN'T REALLY HER...
THAT'S WHAT I TELL MYSELF...BUT I KNOW IN MY WORLD, ALMOST ANYTHING IS POSSIBLE.
SO I MOVE ON TO PLAN C...WHICH I'M MAKING UP AS I GO ALONG.

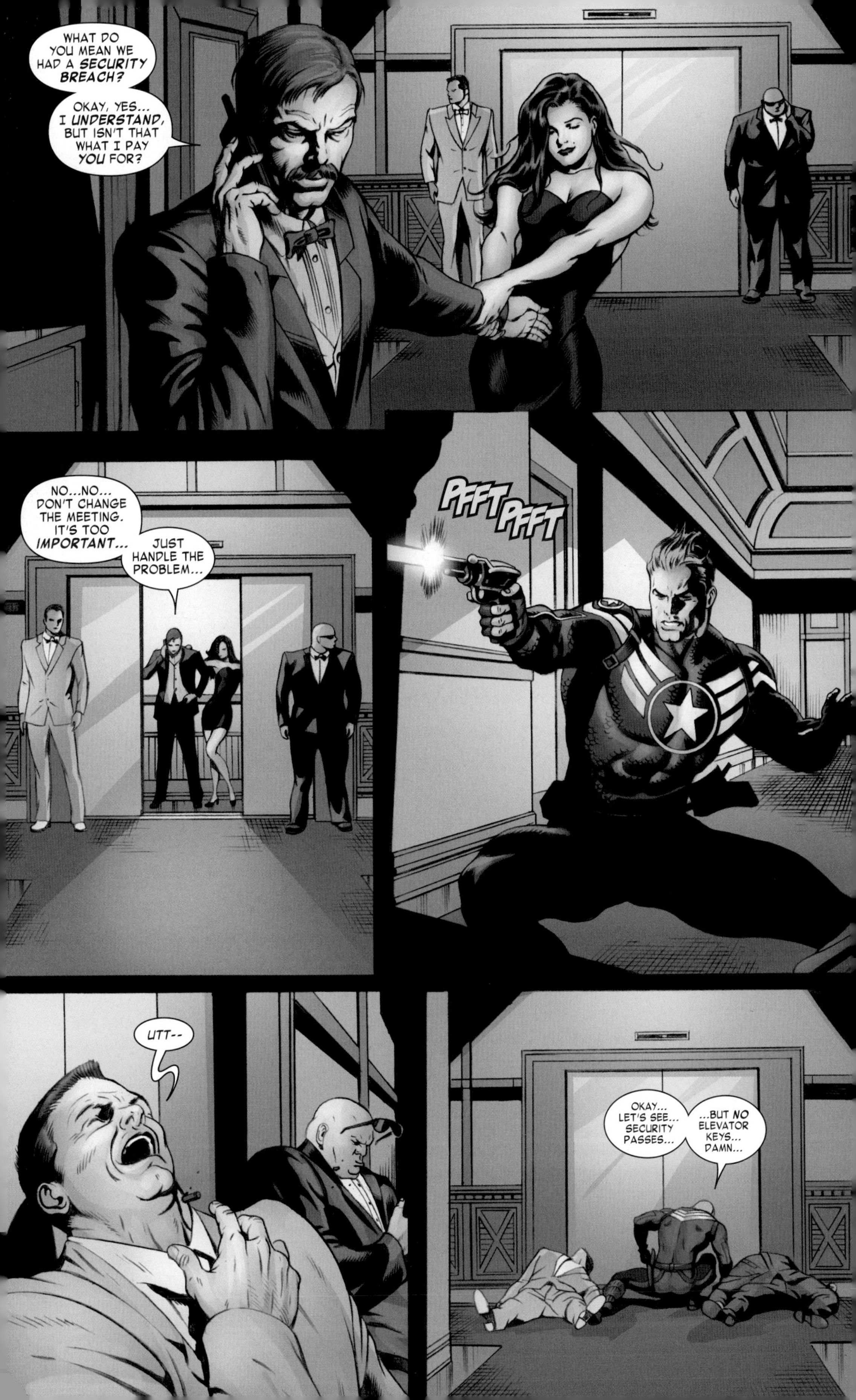
WHAT DO YOU MEAN WE HAD A SECURITY BREACH?
OKAY, YES... I UNDERSTAND, BUT ISN'T THAT WHAT I PAY YOU FOR?
NO...NO... DON'T CHANGE THE MEETING. IT'S TOO IMPORTANT...
JUST HANDLE THE PROBLEM...
PFFT PFFT
UTT--
OKAY... LET'S SEE... SECURITY PASSES...
...BUT NO ELEVATOR KEYS... DAMN...

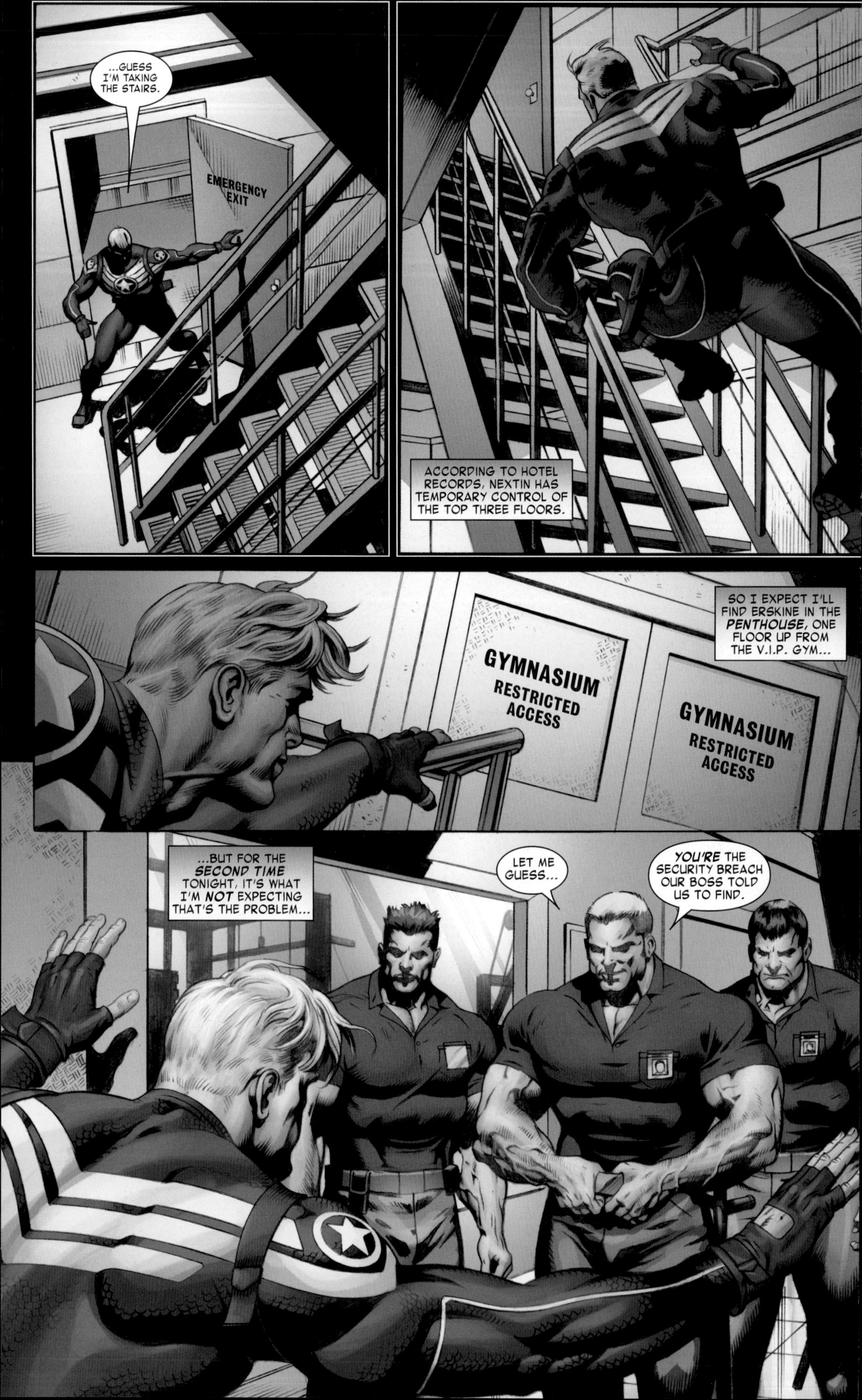
...GUESS I'M TAKING THE STAIRS.
EMERGENCY EXIT
ACCORDING TO HOTEL RECORDS, NEXTIN HAS TEMPORARY CONTROL OF THE TOP THREE FLOORS.
SO I EXPECT I'LL FIND ERSKINE IN THE PENTHOUSE, ONE FLOOR UP FROM THE V.I.P. GYM...
GYMNASIUM RESTRICTED ACCESS
GYMNASIUM RESTRICTED ACCESS
...BUT FOR THE SECOND TIME TONIGHT, IT'S WHAT I'M NOT EXPECTING THAT'S THE PROBLEM...
LET ME GUESS...
YOU'RE THE SECURITY BREACH OUR BOSS TOLD US TO FIND.

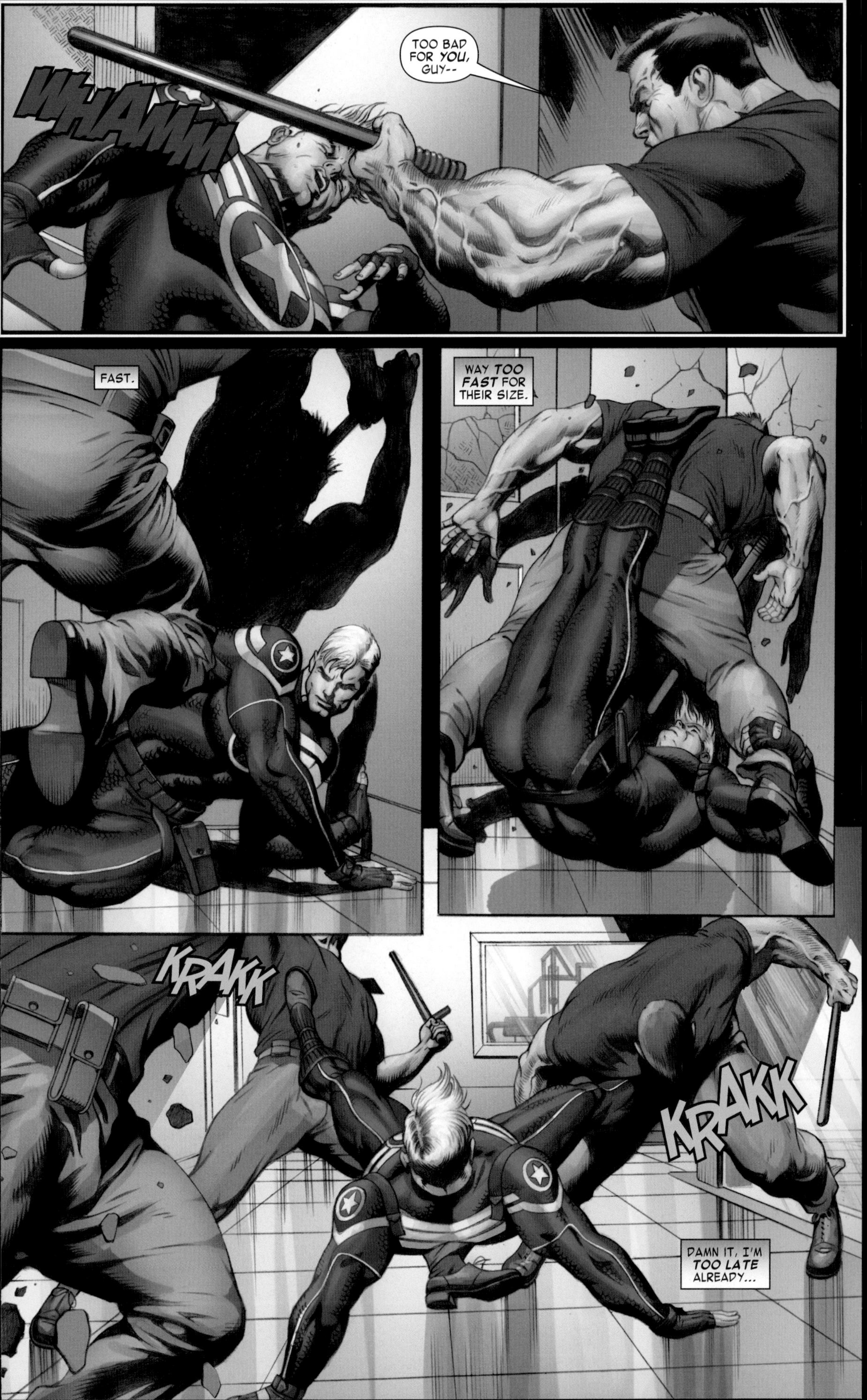
WHAMM
TOO BAD FOR YOU, GUY--
FAST.
WAY TOO FAST FOR THEIR SIZE.
KRAKK
KRAKK
DAMN IT, I'M TOO LATE ALREADY...

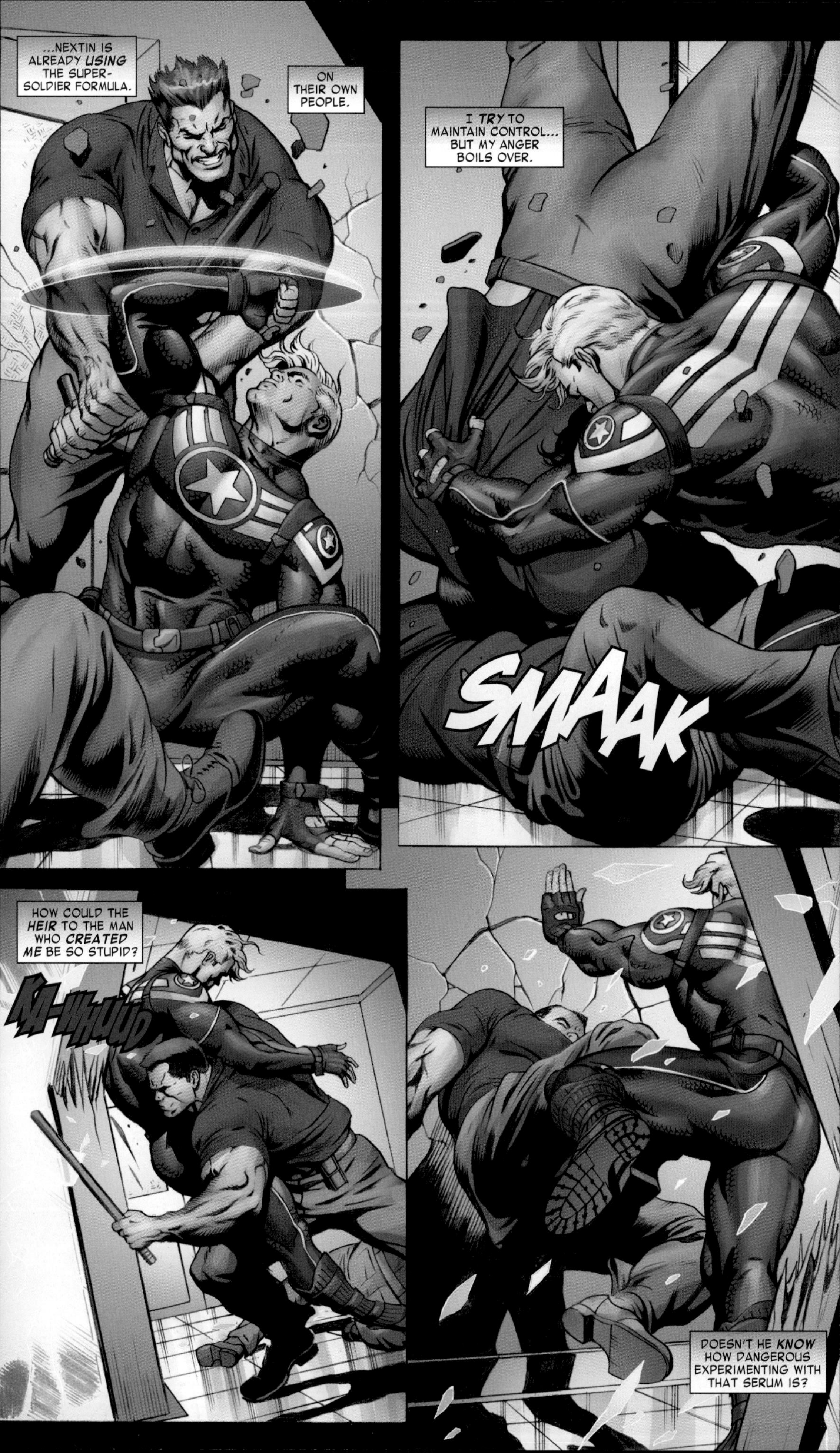
...NEXTIN IS ALREADY USING THE SUPER-SOLDIER FORMULA.
ON THEIR OWN PEOPLE.
I TRY TO MAINTAIN CONTROL... BUT MY ANGER BOILS OVER.
SMAAK
HOW COULD THE HEIR TO THE MAN WHO CREATED ME BE SO STUPID?
KA-WHUUD
DOESN'T HE KNOW HOW DANGEROUS EXPERIMENTING WITH THAT SERUM IS?

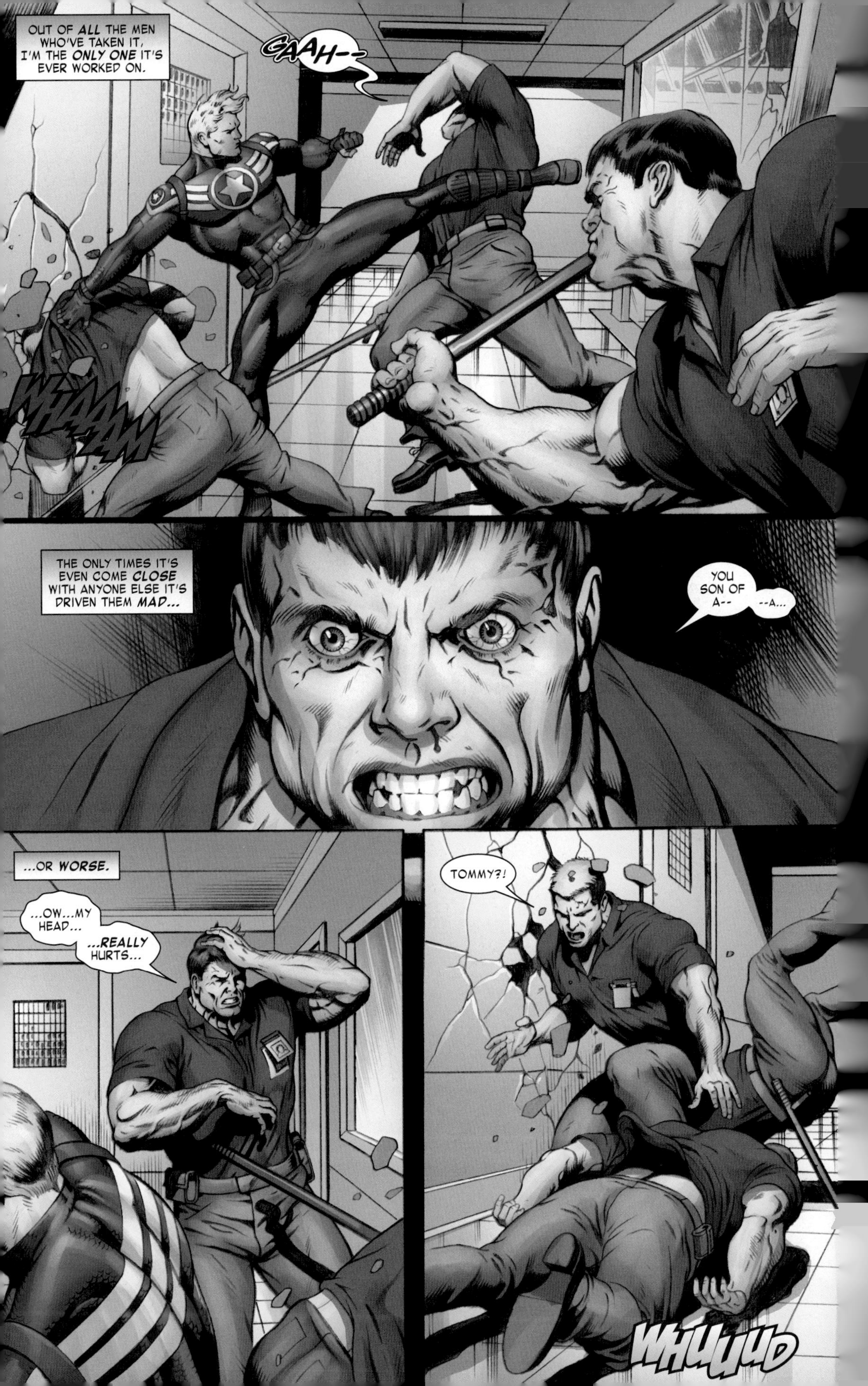
OUT OF ALL THE MEN WHO'VE TAKEN IT, I'M THE ONLY ONE IT'S EVER WORKED ON.
GAAH--
WHAAAM
THE ONLY TIMES IT'S EVEN COME CLOSE WITH ANYONE ELSE IT'S DRIVEN THEM MAD...
YOU SON OF A--
--A...
...OR WORSE.
...OW...MY HEAD...
...REALLY HURTS...
TOMMY?!
WHUUUD

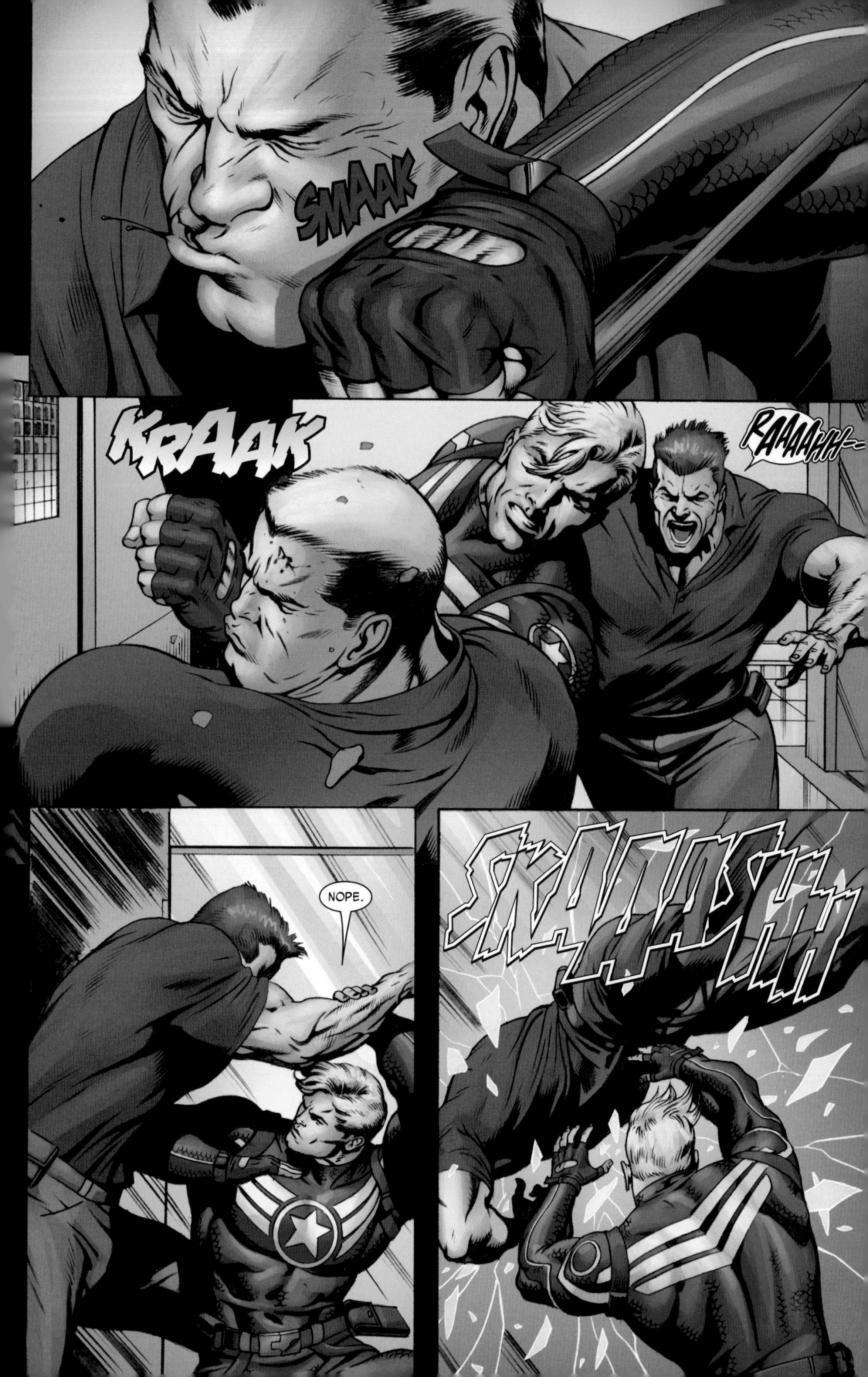
SMAAK
KRAAK
RAAAAHH--
NOPE.
SKRAASH

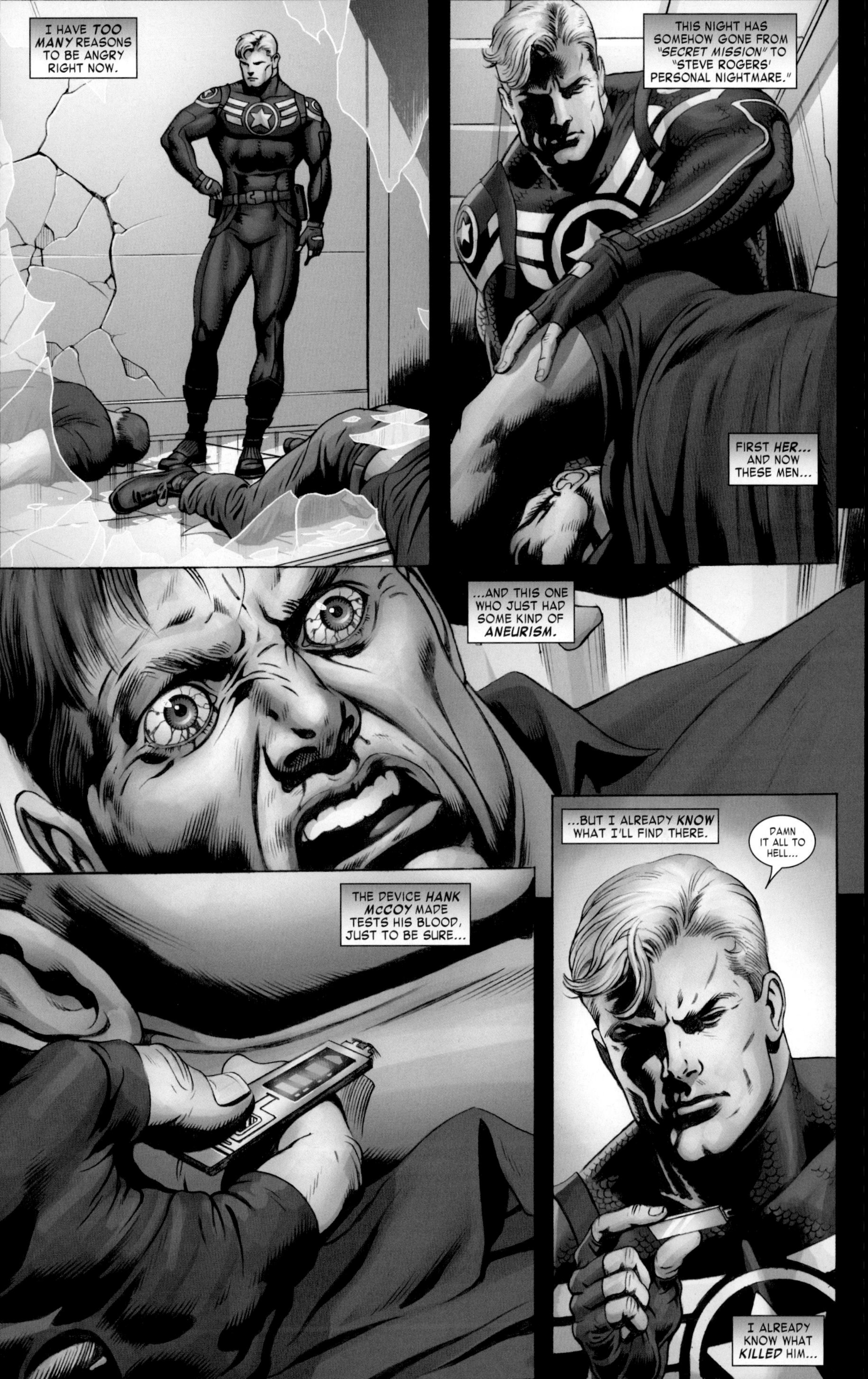
I HAVE TOO MANY REASONS TO BE ANGRY RIGHT NOW.
THIS NIGHT HAS SOMEHOW GONE FROM "SECRET MISSION" TO "STEVE ROGERS' PERSONAL NIGHTMARE."
FIRST HER... AND NOW THESE MEN...
...AND THIS ONE WHO JUST HAD SOME KIND OF ANEURISM.
THE DEVICE HANK McCOY MADE TESTS HIS BLOOD, JUST TO BE SURE...
...BUT I ALREADY KNOW WHAT I'LL FIND THERE.
DAMN IT ALL TO HELL...
I ALREADY KNOW WHAT KILLED HIM...

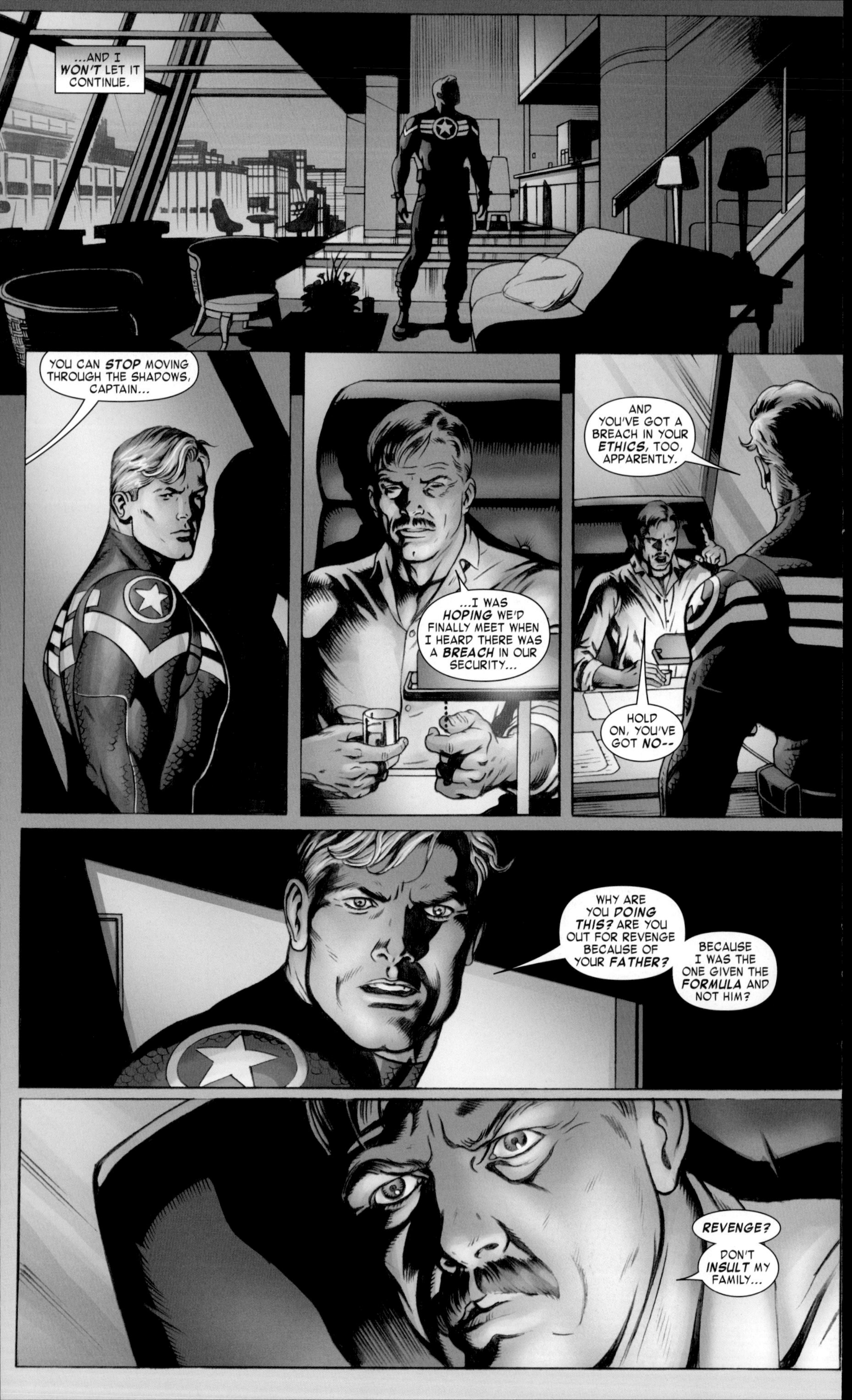
...AND I WON'T LET IT CONTINUE.
YOU CAN STOP MOVING THROUGH THE SHADOWS, CAPTAIN...
...I WAS HOPING WE'D FINALLY MEET WHEN I HEARD THERE WAS A BREACH IN OUR SECURITY...
AND YOU'VE GOT A BREACH IN YOUR ETHICS, TOO, APPARENTLY.
HOLD ON, YOU'VE GOT NO--
WHY ARE YOU DOING THIS? ARE YOU OUT FOR REVENGE BECAUSE OF YOUR FATHER?
BECAUSE I WAS THE ONE GIVEN THE FORMULA AND NOT HIM?
REVENGE?
DON'T INSULT MY FAMILY...

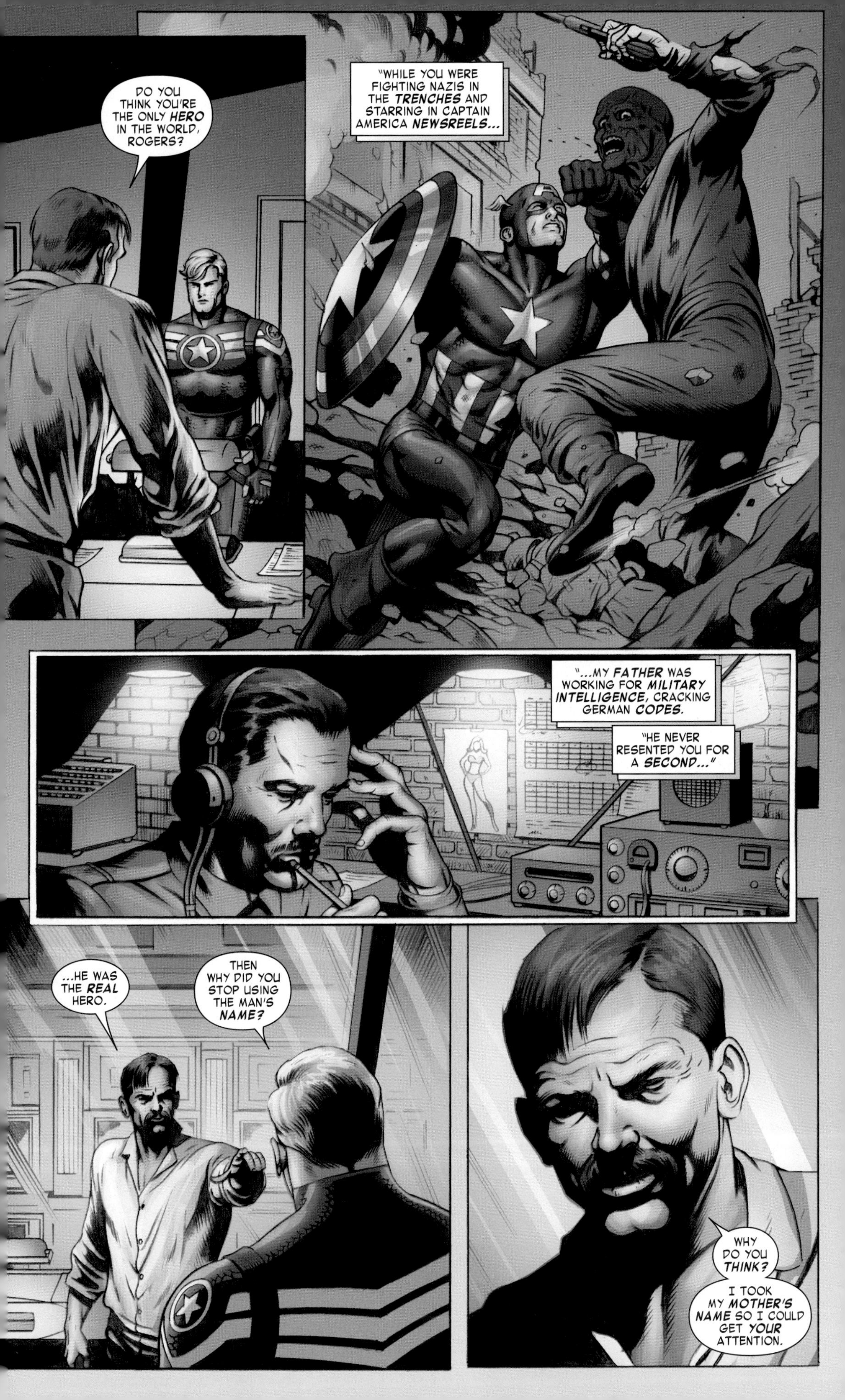
DO YOU THINK YOU'RE THE ONLY HERO IN THE WORLD, ROGERS?
"WHILE YOU WERE FIGHTING NAZIS IN THE TRENCHES AND STARRING IN CAPTAIN AMERICA NEWSREELS...
"...MY FATHER WAS WORKING FOR MILITARY INTELLIGENCE, CRACKING GERMAN CODES.
"HE NEVER RESENTED YOU FOR A SECOND..."
...HE WAS THE REAL HERO.
THEN WHY DID YOU STOP USING THE MAN'S NAME?
WHY DO YOU THINK?
I TOOK MY MOTHER'S NAME SO I COULD GET YOUR ATTENTION.

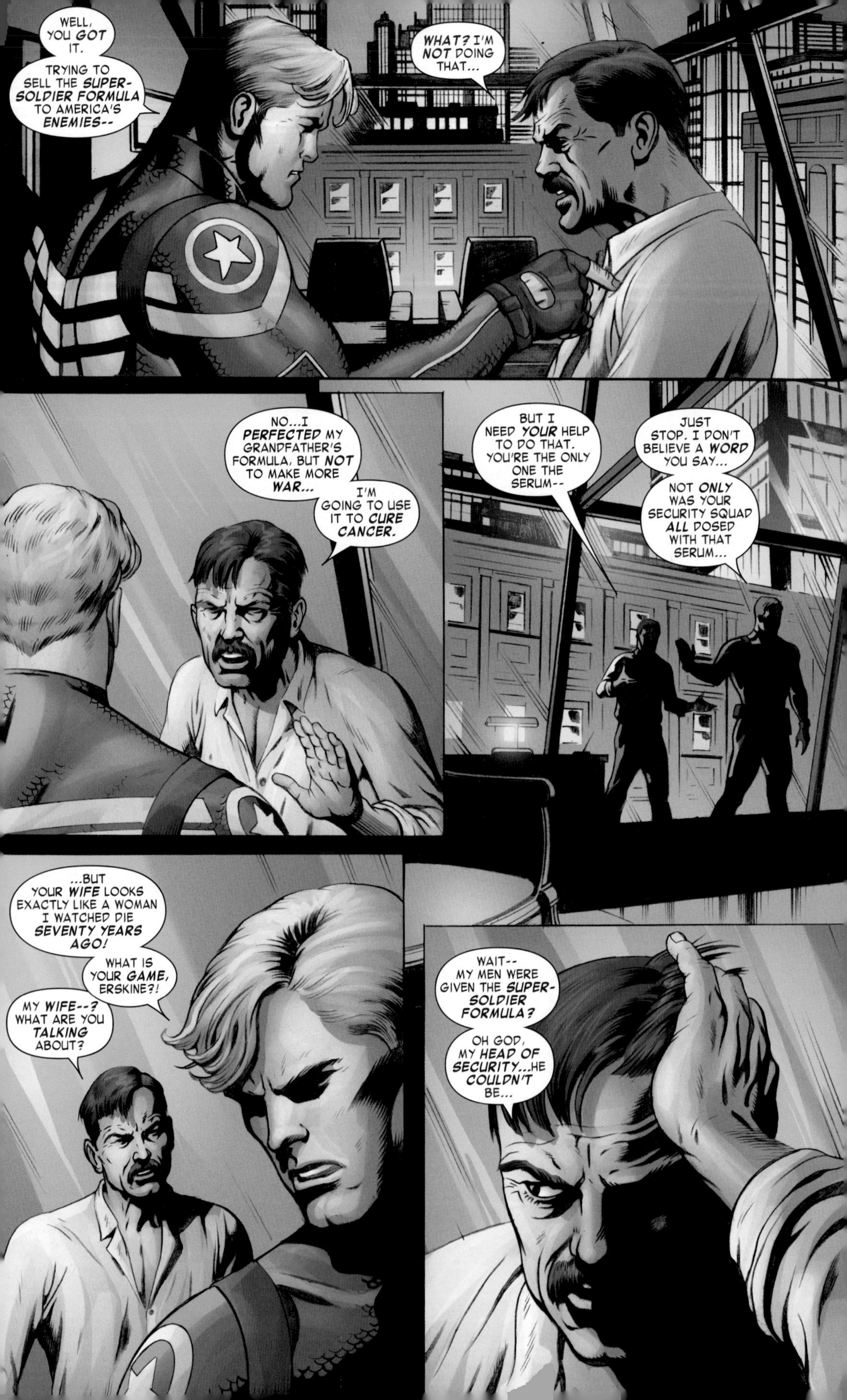
WELL, YOU GOT IT.
TRYING TO SELL THE SUPER-SOLDIER FORMULA TO AMERICA'S ENEMIES--
WHAT? I'M NOT DOING THAT...
NO...I PERFECTED MY GRANDFATHER'S FORMULA, BUT NOT TO MAKE MORE WAR...
I'M GOING TO USE IT TO CURE CANCER.
BUT I NEED YOUR HELP TO DO THAT. YOU'RE THE ONLY ONE THE SERUM--
JUST STOP. I DON'T BELIEVE A WORD YOU SAY...
NOT ONLY WAS YOUR SECURITY SQUAD ALL DOSED WITH THAT SERUM...
...BUT YOUR WIFE LOOKS EXACTLY LIKE A WOMAN I WATCHED DIE SEVENTY YEARS AGO!
WHAT IS YOUR GAME, ERSKINE?!
MY WIFE--? WHAT ARE YOU TALKING ABOUT?
WAIT-- MY MEN WERE GIVEN THE SUPER-SOLDIER FORMULA?
OH GOD, MY HEAD OF SECURITY...HE COULDN'T BE...

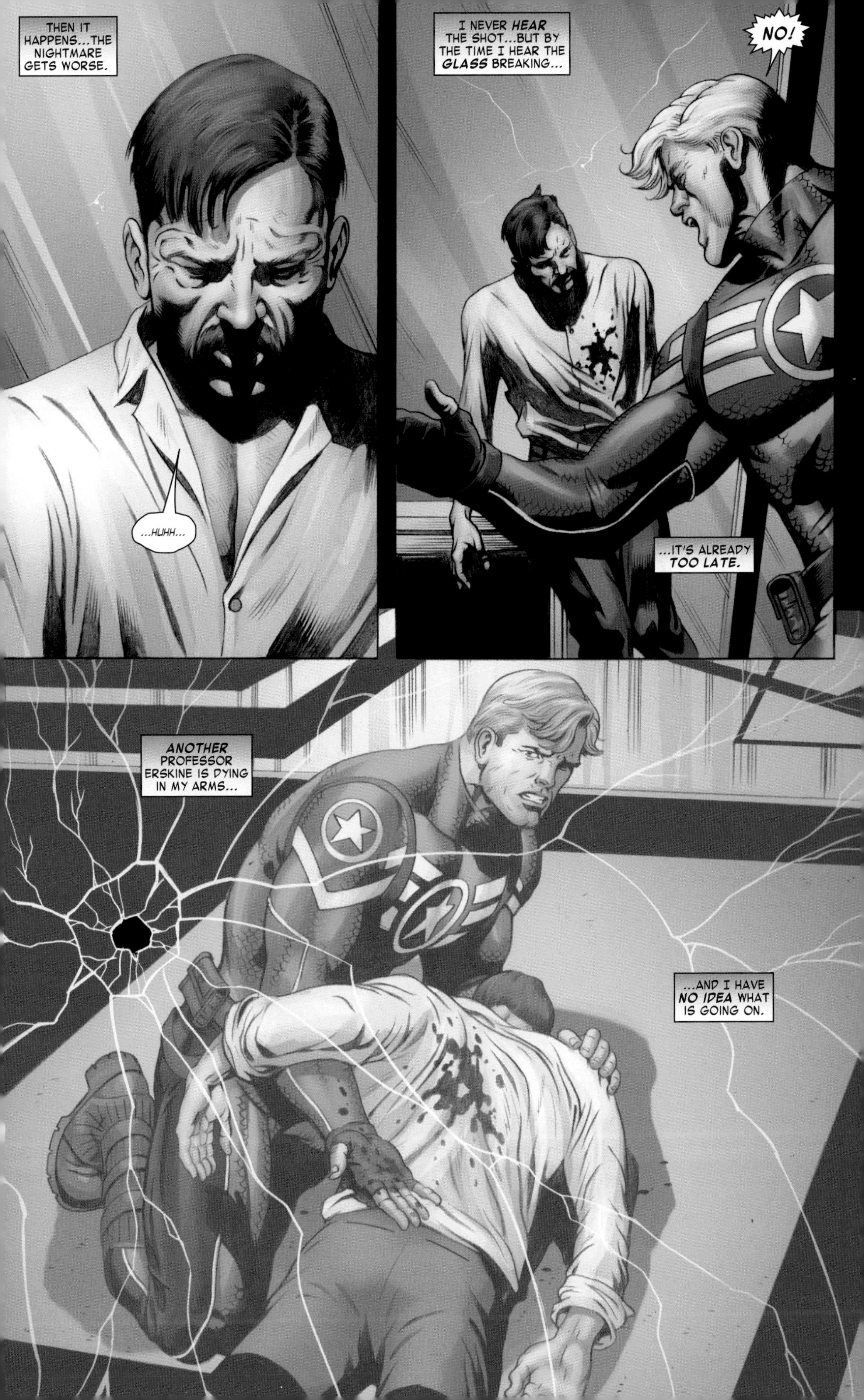
THEN IT HAPPENS...THE NIGHTMARE GETS WORSE.
...HUHH...
I NEVER HEAR THE SHOT...BUT BY THE TIME I HEAR THE GLASS BREAKING...
NO!
...IT'S ALREADY TOO LATE.
ANOTHER PROFESSOR ERSKINE IS DYING IN MY ARMS...
...AND I HAVE NO IDEA WHAT IS GOING ON.

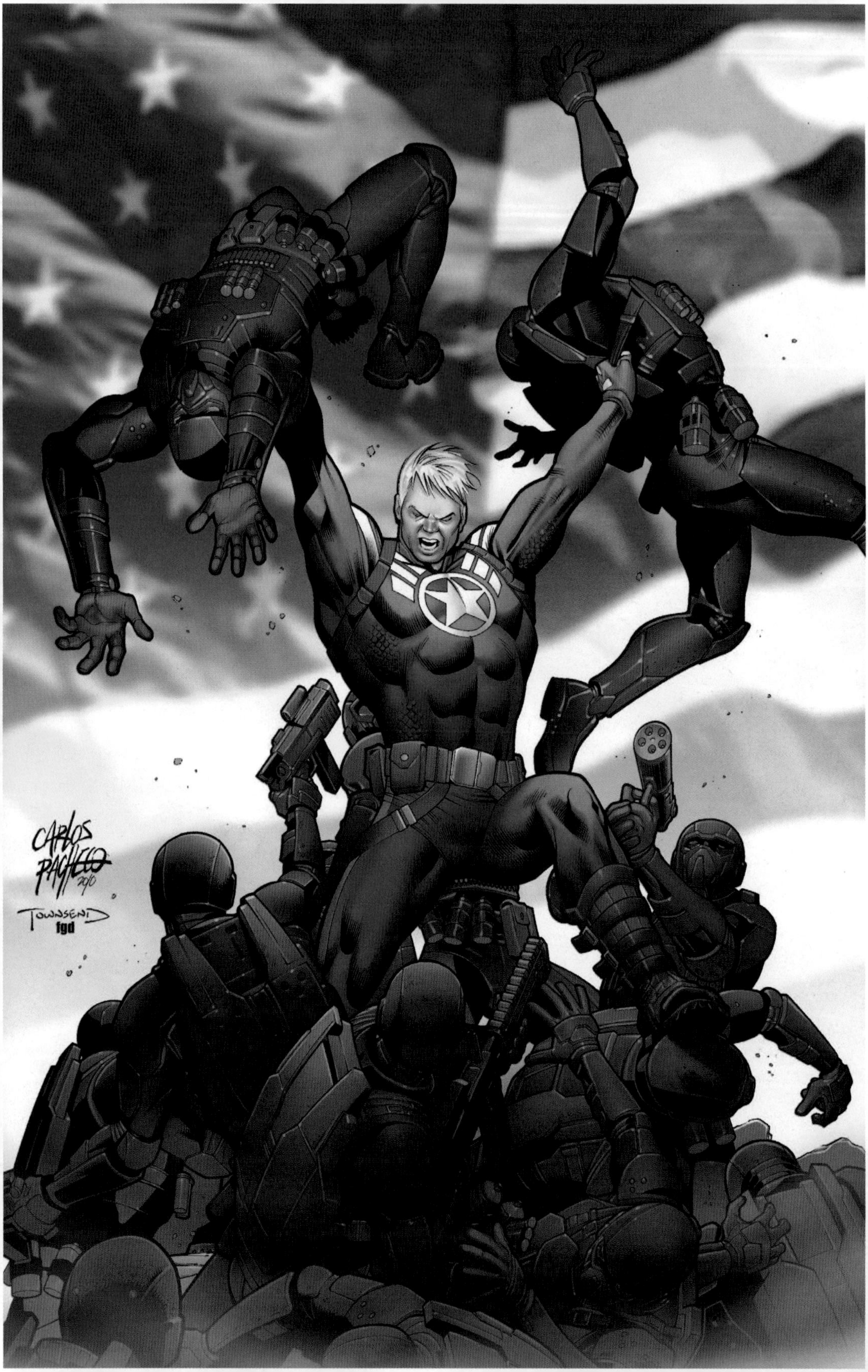
CARLOS PACHECO
TOWNSEND
fgd

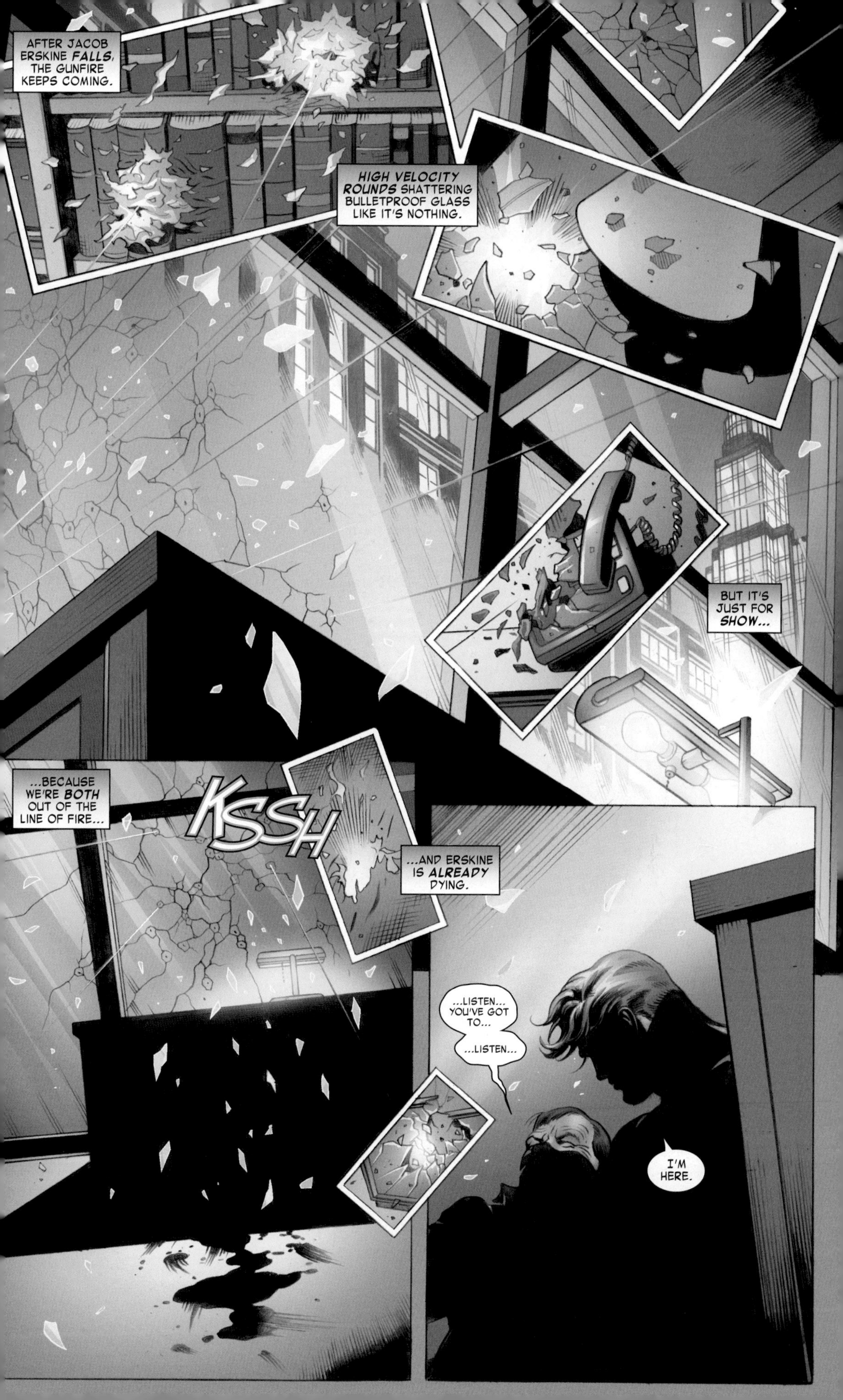
AFTER JACOB ERSKINE FALLS, THE GUNFIRE KEEPS COMING.
HIGH VELOCITY ROUNDS SHATTERING BULLETPROOF GLASS LIKE IT'S NOTHING.
BUT IT'S JUST FOR SHOW...
...BECAUSE WE'RE BOTH OUT OF THE LINE OF FIRE...
KSSH
...AND ERSKINE IS ALREADY DYING.
...LISTEN... YOU'VE GOT TO...
...LISTEN...
I'M HERE.

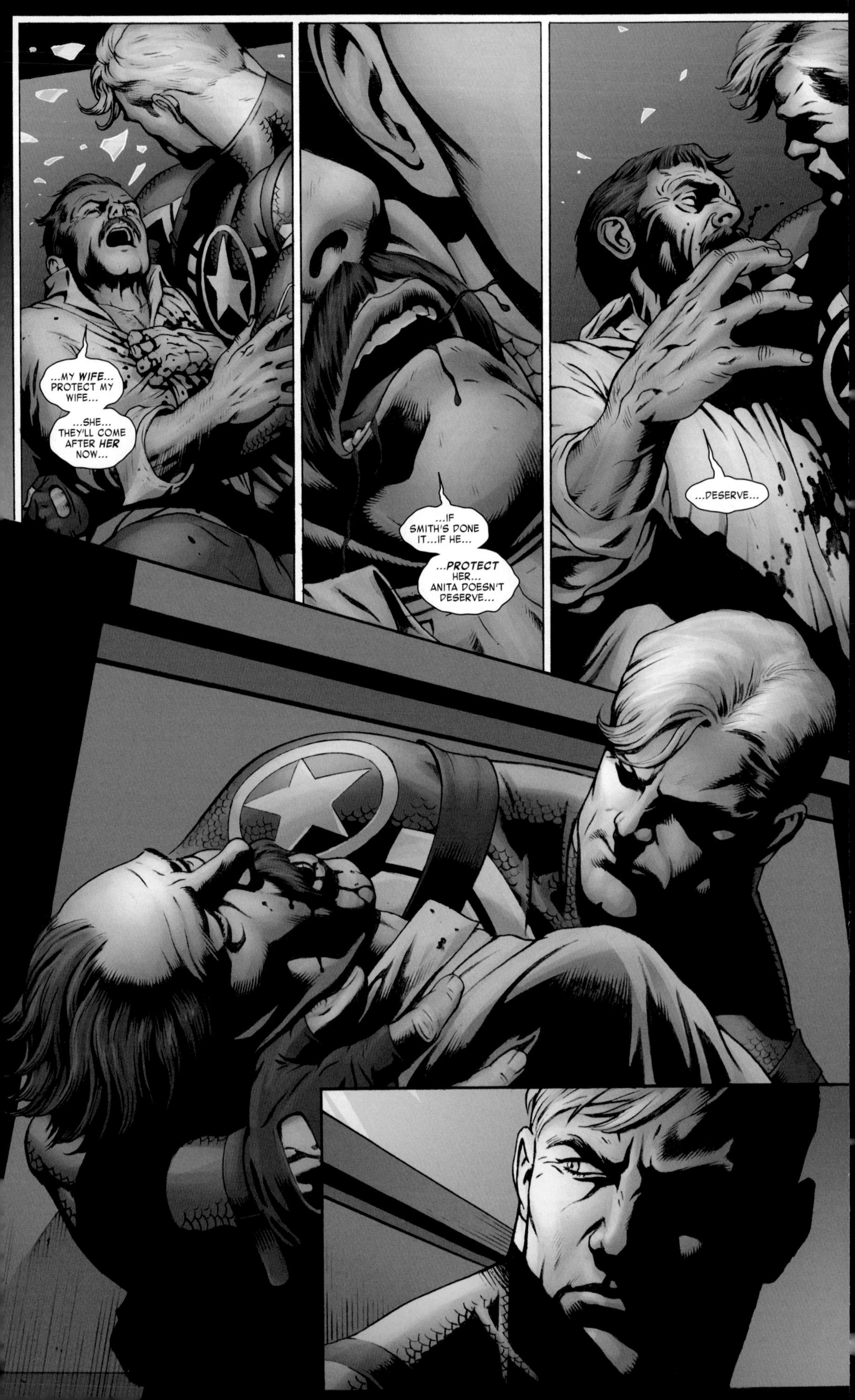
...MY WIFE... PROTECT MY WIFE...
...SHE... THEY'LL COME AFTER HER NOW...
...IF SMITH'S DONE IT...IF HE...
...PROTECT HER... ANITA DOESN'T DESERVE...
...DESERVE...

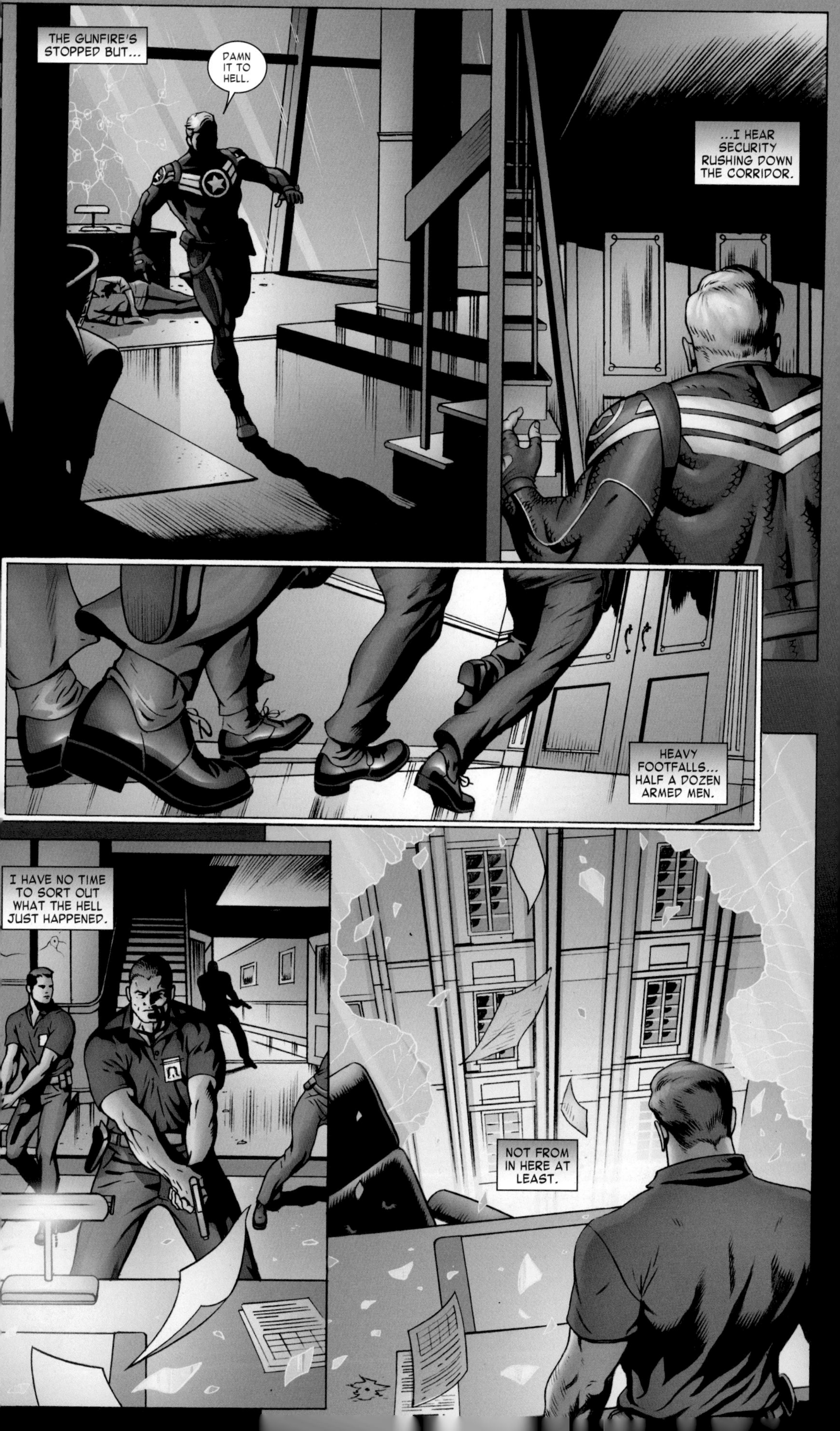
THE GUNFIRE'S STOPPED BUT...
DAMN IT TO HELL.
...I HEAR SECURITY RUSHING DOWN THE CORRIDOR.
HEAVY FOOTFALLS... HALF A DOZEN ARMED MEN.
I HAVE NO TIME TO SORT OUT WHAT THE HELL JUST HAPPENED.
NOT FROM IN HERE AT LEAST.

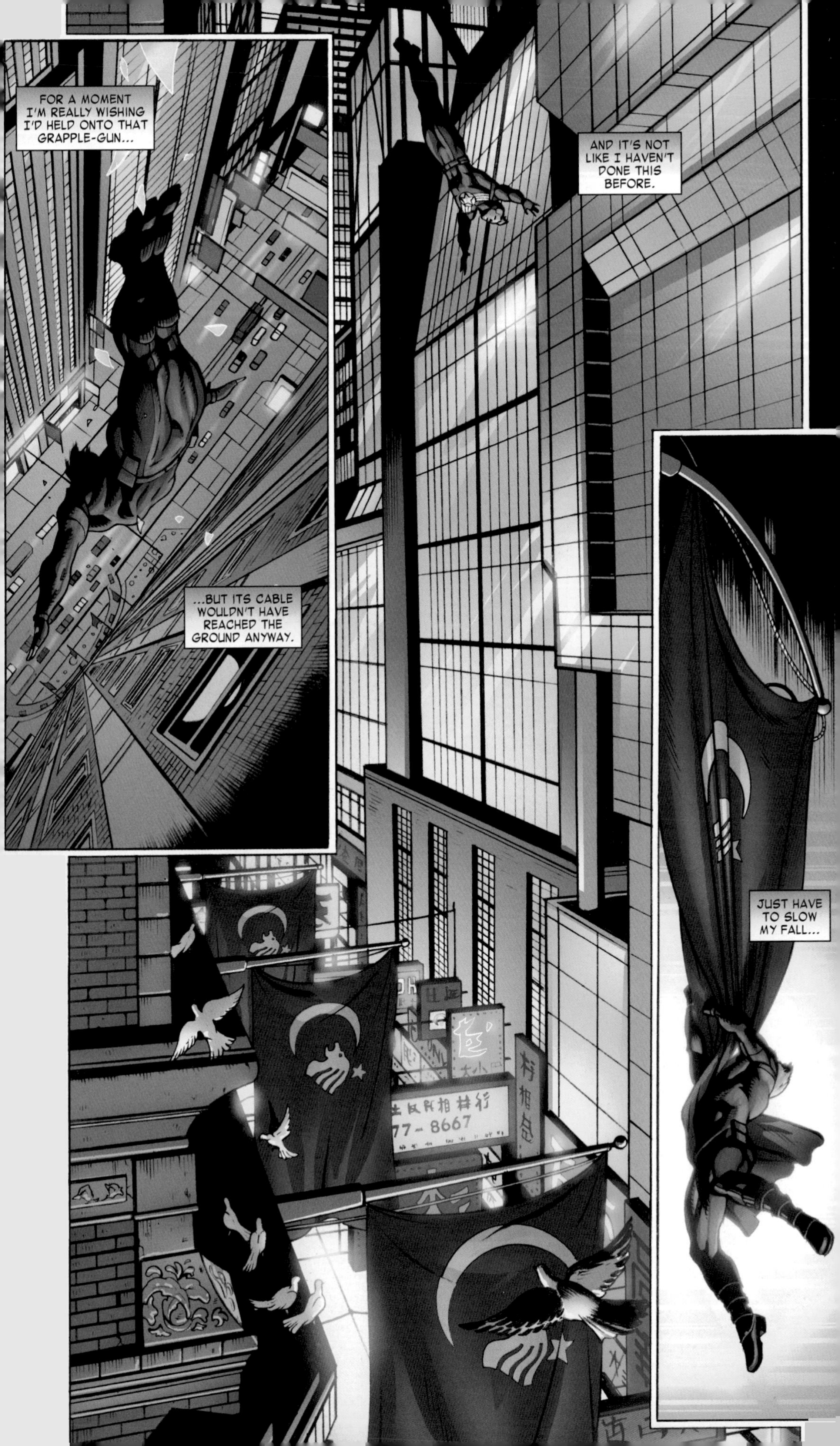
FOR A MOMENT I'M REALLY WISHING I'D HELD ONTO THAT GRAPPLE-GUN...
...BUT ITS CABLE WOULDN'T HAVE REACHED THE GROUND ANYWAY.
AND IT'S NOT LIKE I HAVEN'T DONE THIS BEFORE.
JUST HAVE TO SLOW MY FALL...

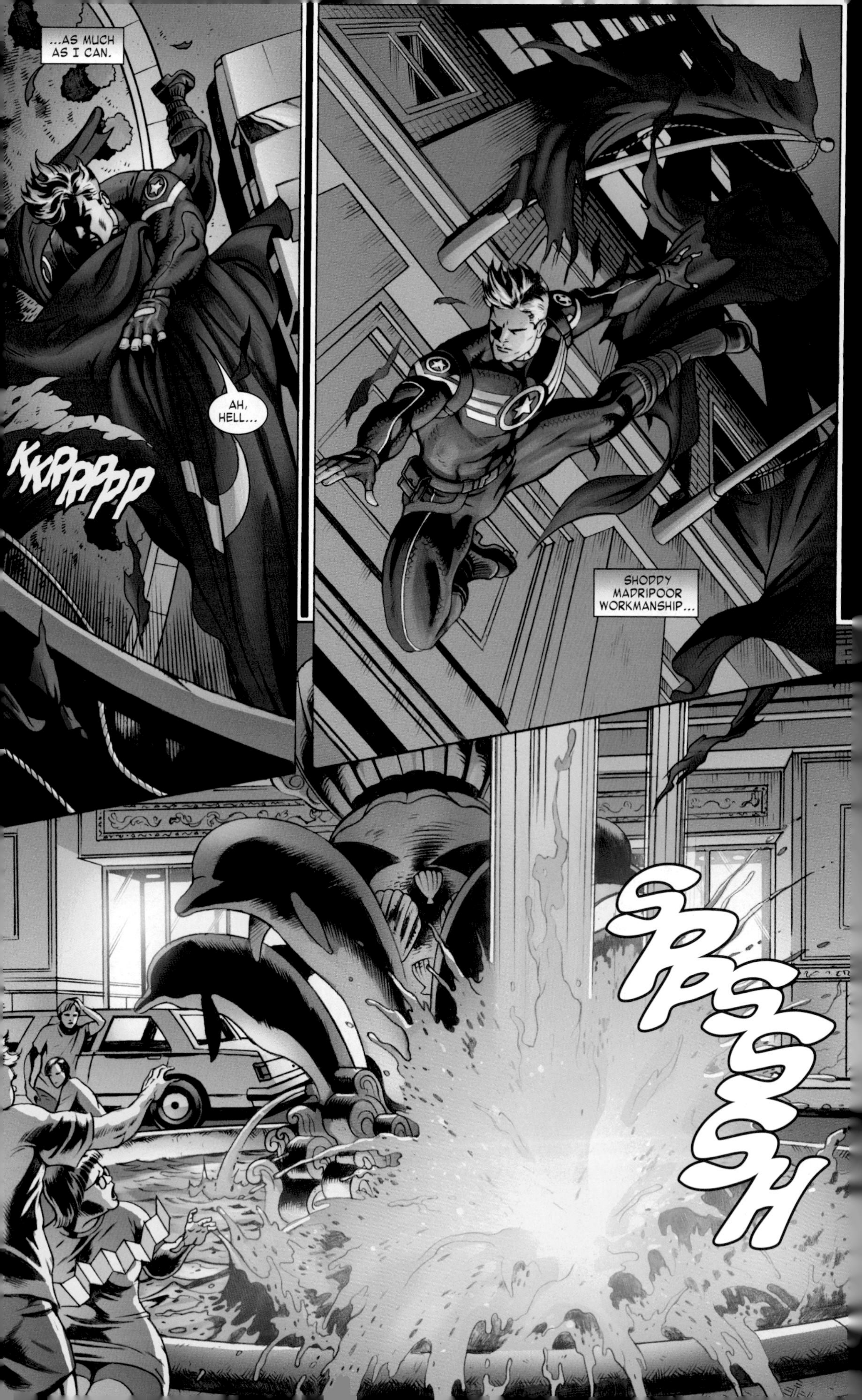
...AS MUCH AS I CAN.
AH, HELL...
KKRRPPP
SHODDY MADRIPOOR WORKMANSHIP...
SPASSSH

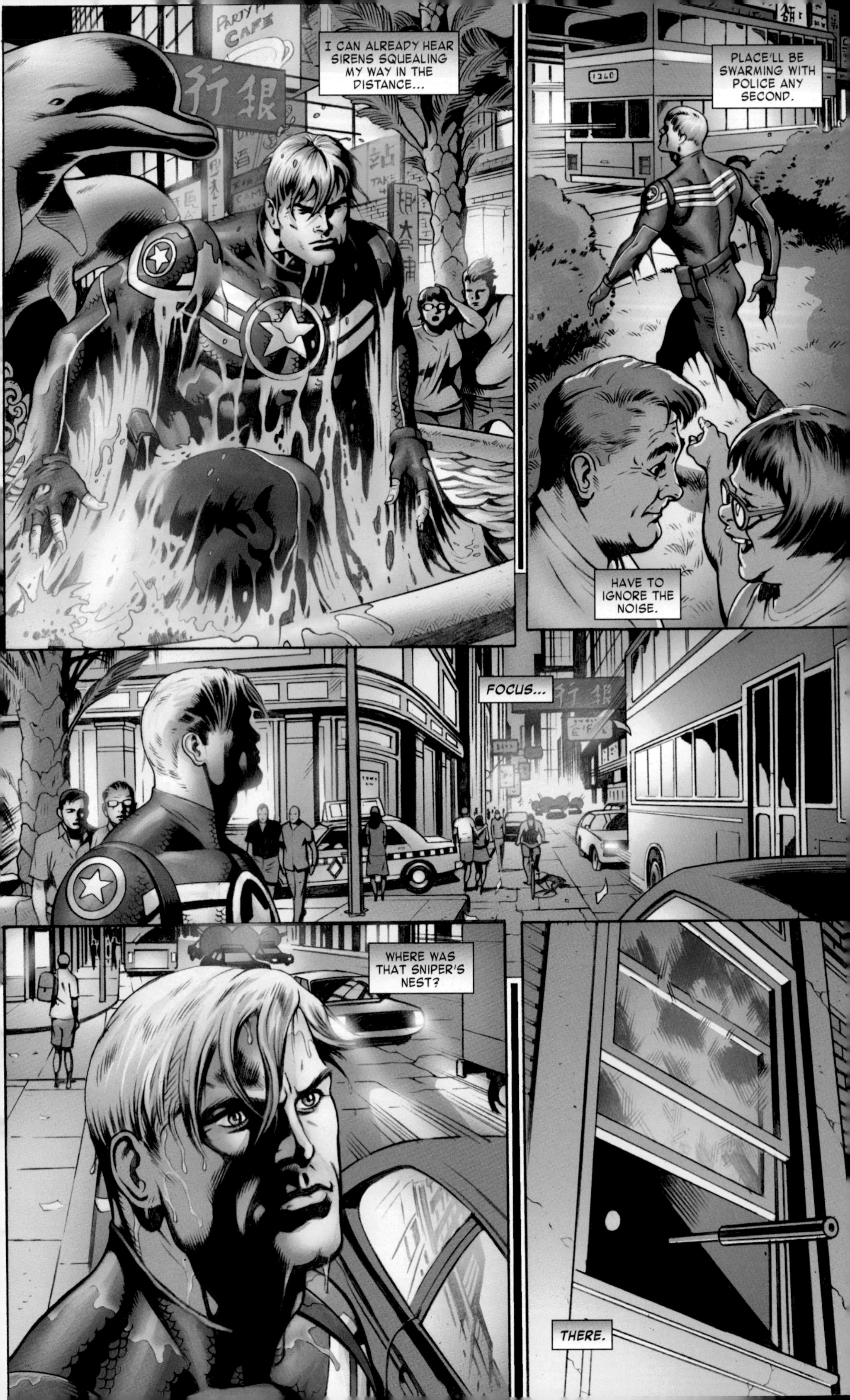

I CAN ALREADY HEAR SIRENS SQUEALING MY WAY IN THE DISTANCE...
PLACE'LL BE SWARMING WITH POLICE ANY SECOND.
HAVE TO IGNORE THE NOISE.
FOCUS...
WHERE WAS THAT SNIPER'S NEST?
THERE.

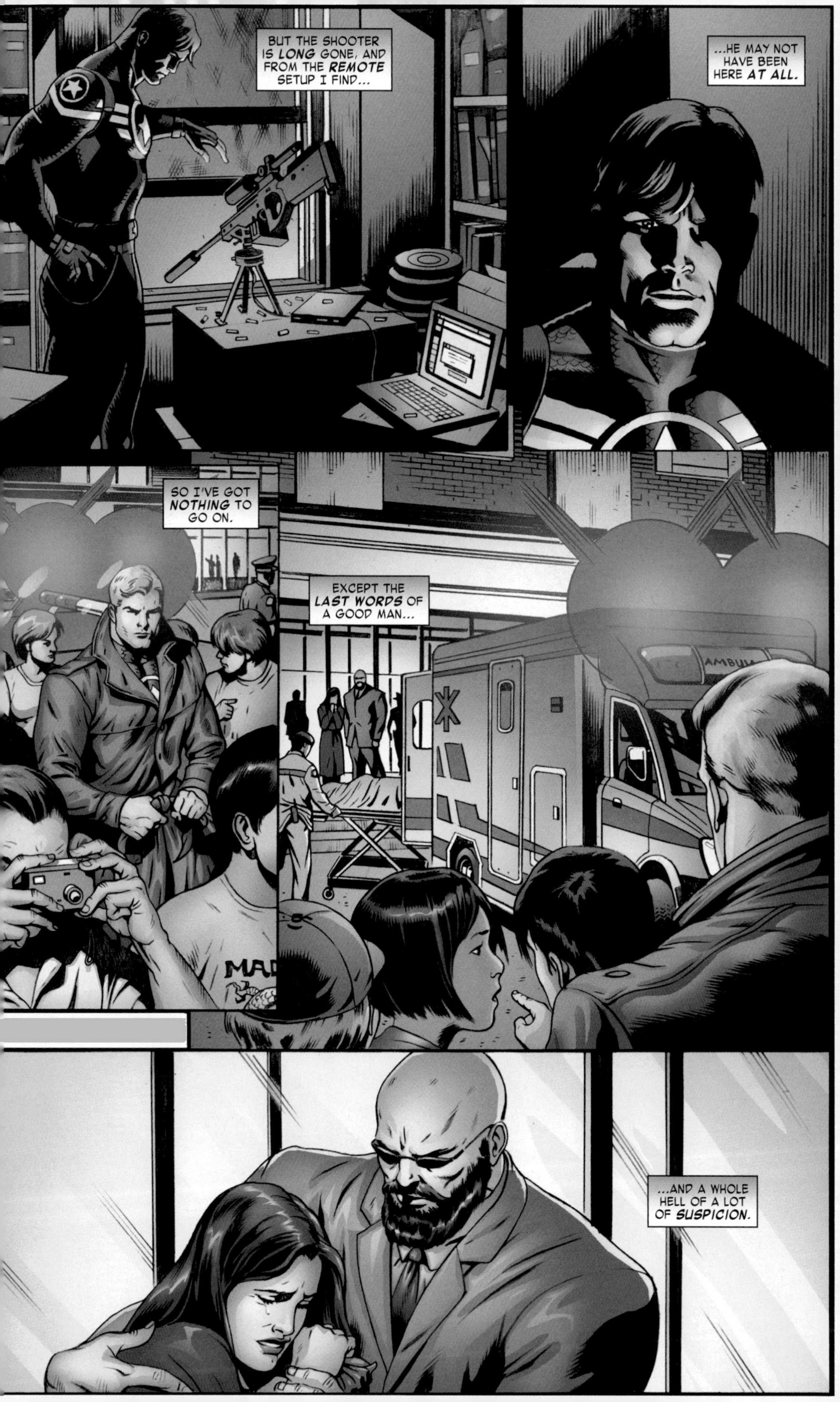

BUT THE SHOOTER IS LONG GONE, AND FROM THE REMOTE SETUP I FIND...
...HE MAY NOT HAVE BEEN HERE AT ALL.
SO I'VE GOT NOTHING TO GO ON.
EXCEPT THE LAST WORDS OF A GOOD MAN...
...AND A WHOLE HELL OF A LOT OF SUSPICION.

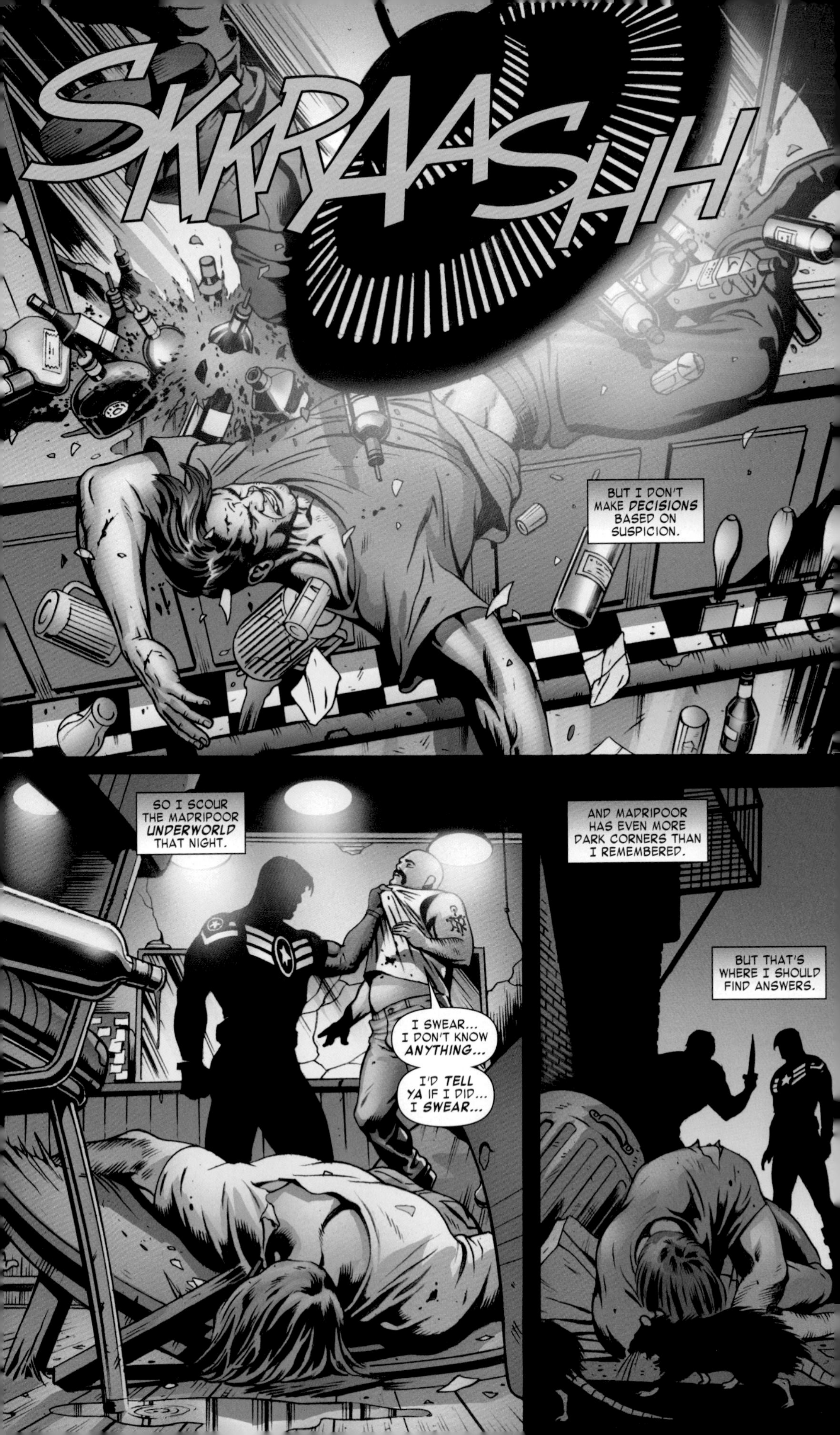
SKKRAASHH
BUT I DON'T MAKE *DECISIONS* BASED ON SUSPICION.
SO I SCOUR THE MADRIPOOR *UNDERWORLD* THAT NIGHT.
I SWEAR... I DON'T KNOW *ANYTHING*...
I'D *TELL YA* IF I DID... I *SWEAR*...
AND MADRIPOOR HAS EVEN MORE DARK CORNERS THAN I REMEMBERED.
BUT THAT'S WHERE I SHOULD FIND ANSWERS.

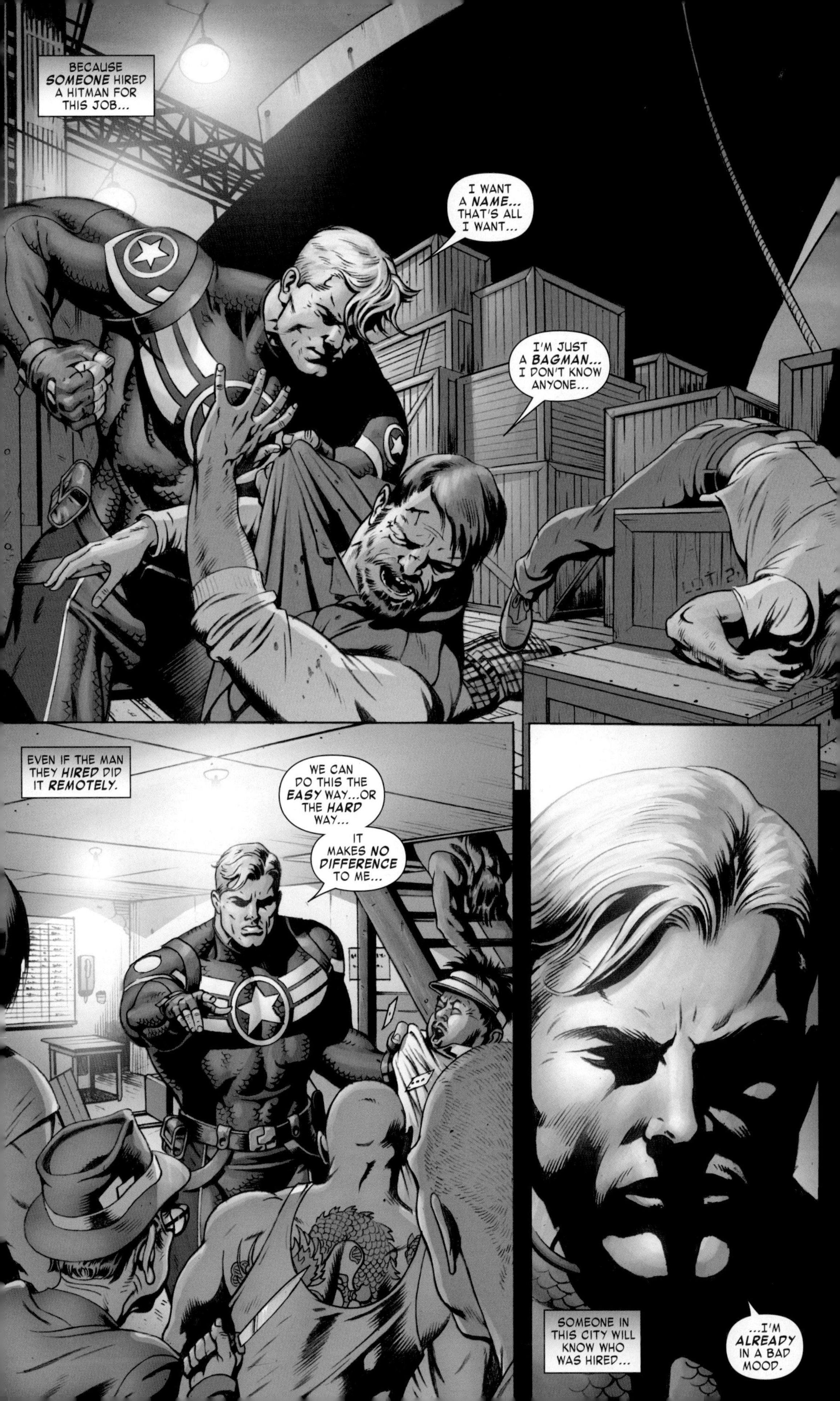
BECAUSE SOMEONE HIRED A HITMAN FOR THIS JOB...
I WANT A NAME... THAT'S ALL I WANT...
I'M JUST A BAGMAN... I DON'T KNOW ANYONE...
EVEN IF THE MAN THEY HIRED DID IT REMOTELY.
WE CAN DO THIS THE EASY WAY...OR THE HARD WAY...
IT MAKES NO DIFFERENCE TO ME...
SOMEONE IN THIS CITY WILL KNOW WHO WAS HIRED...
...I'M ALREADY IN A BAD MOOD.

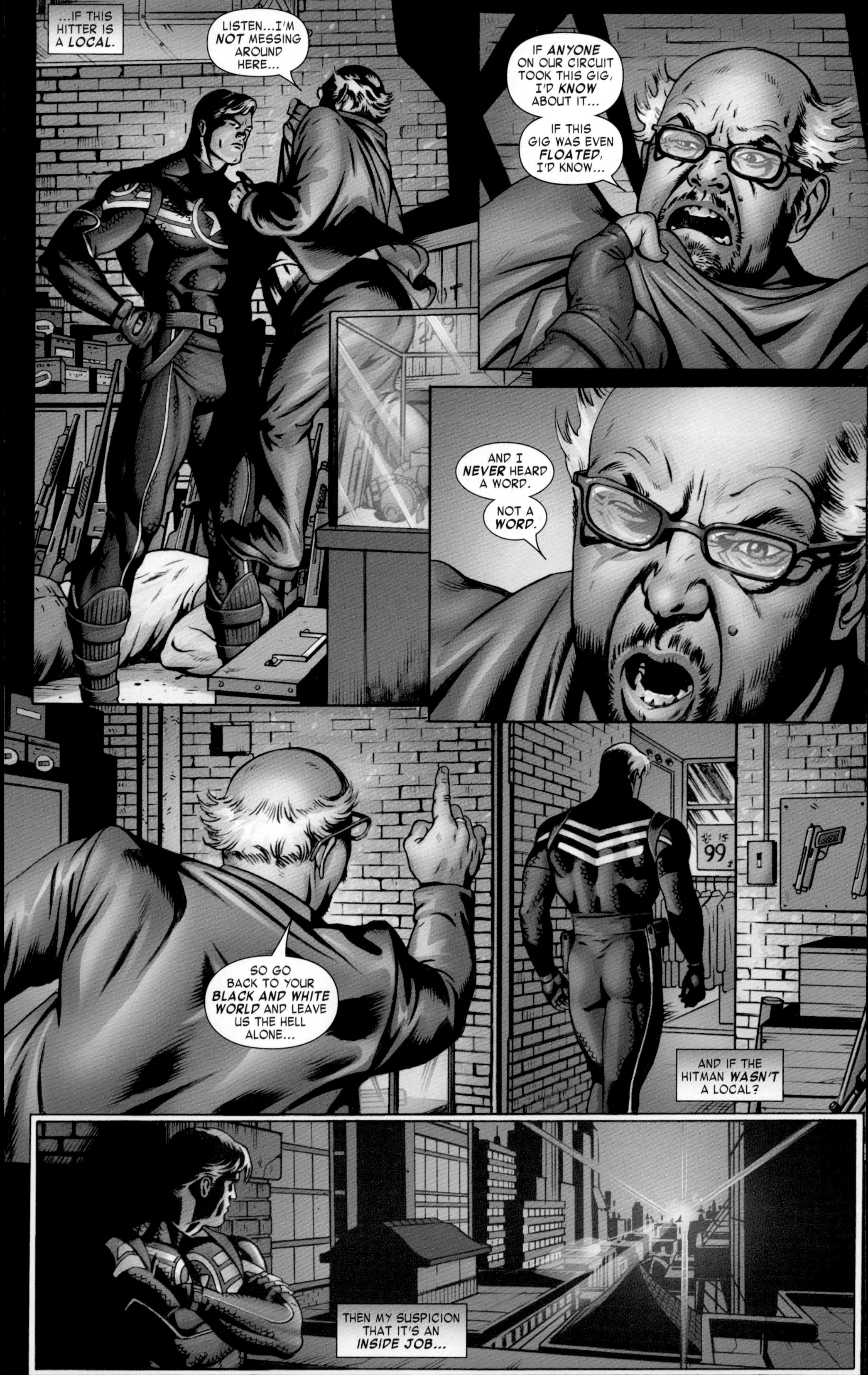

...IF THIS HITTER IS A *LOCAL.*
LISTEN...I'M **NOT** MESSING AROUND HERE...
IF ***ANYONE*** ON OUR CIRCUIT TOOK THIS GIG, I'D ***KNOW*** ABOUT IT...
IF THIS GIG WAS EVEN ***FLOATED***, I'D KNOW...
AND I ***NEVER*** HEARD A WORD.
NOT A ***WORD.***
SO GO BACK TO YOUR ***BLACK AND WHITE WORLD*** AND LEAVE US THE HELL ALONE...
AND IF THE HITMAN ***WASN'T*** A LOCAL?
THEN MY SUSPICION THAT IT'S AN ***INSIDE JOB...***

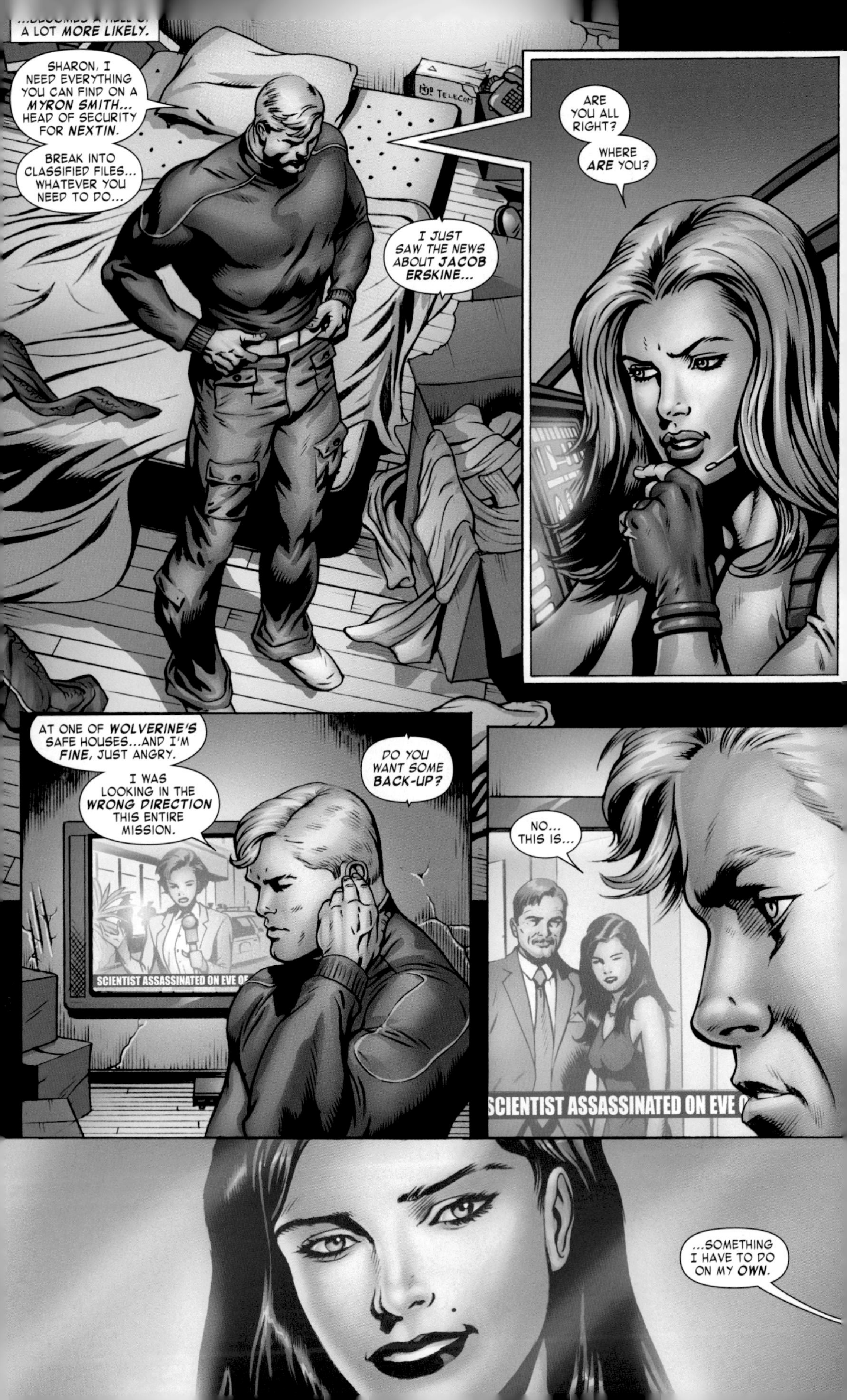
A LOT MORE LIKELY.
SHARON, I NEED EVERYTHING YOU CAN FIND ON A MYRON SMITH... HEAD OF SECURITY FOR NEXTIN.
BREAK INTO CLASSIFIED FILES... WHATEVER YOU NEED TO DO...
TELECOM
ARE YOU ALL RIGHT?
WHERE ARE YOU?
I JUST SAW THE NEWS ABOUT JACOB ERSKINE...
AT ONE OF WOLVERINE'S SAFE HOUSES...AND I'M FINE, JUST ANGRY.
I WAS LOOKING IN THE WRONG DIRECTION THIS ENTIRE MISSION.
DO YOU WANT SOME BACK-UP?
SCIENTIST ASSASSINATED ON EVE
NO... THIS IS...
SCIENTIST ASSASSINATED ON EVE
...SOMETHING I HAVE TO DO ON MY OWN.

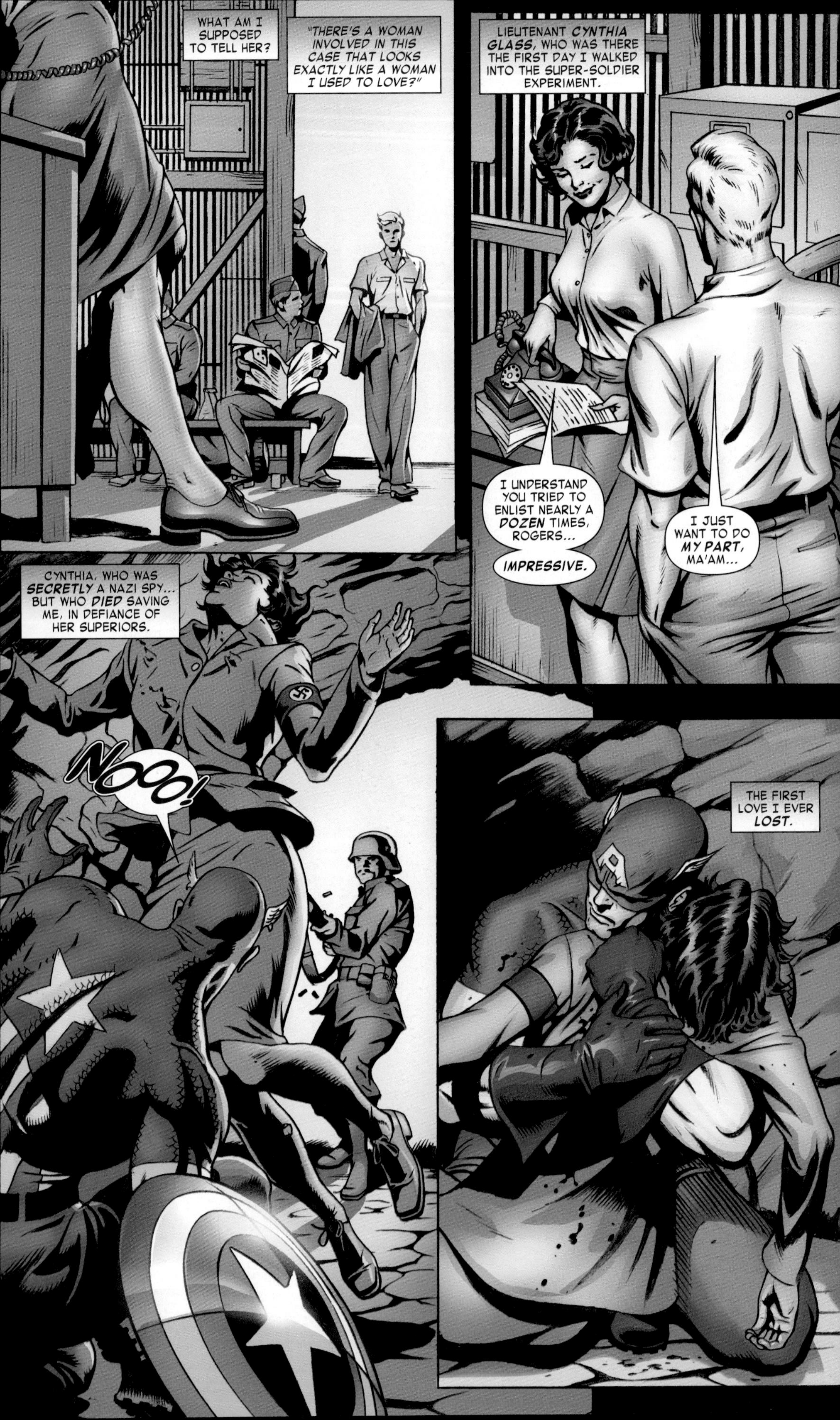
WHAT AM I SUPPOSED TO TELL HER?
"THERE'S A WOMAN INVOLVED IN THIS CASE THAT LOOKS EXACTLY LIKE A WOMAN I USED TO LOVE?"
LIEUTENANT CYNTHIA GLASS, WHO WAS THERE THE FIRST DAY I WALKED INTO THE SUPER-SOLDIER EXPERIMENT.
I UNDERSTAND YOU TRIED TO ENLIST NEARLY A DOZEN TIMES, ROGERS...
IMPRESSIVE.
I JUST WANT TO DO MY PART, MA'AM...
CYNTHIA, WHO WAS SECRETLY A NAZI SPY... BUT WHO DIED SAVING ME, IN DEFIANCE OF HER SUPERIORS.
NOOO!
THE FIRST LOVE I EVER LOST.

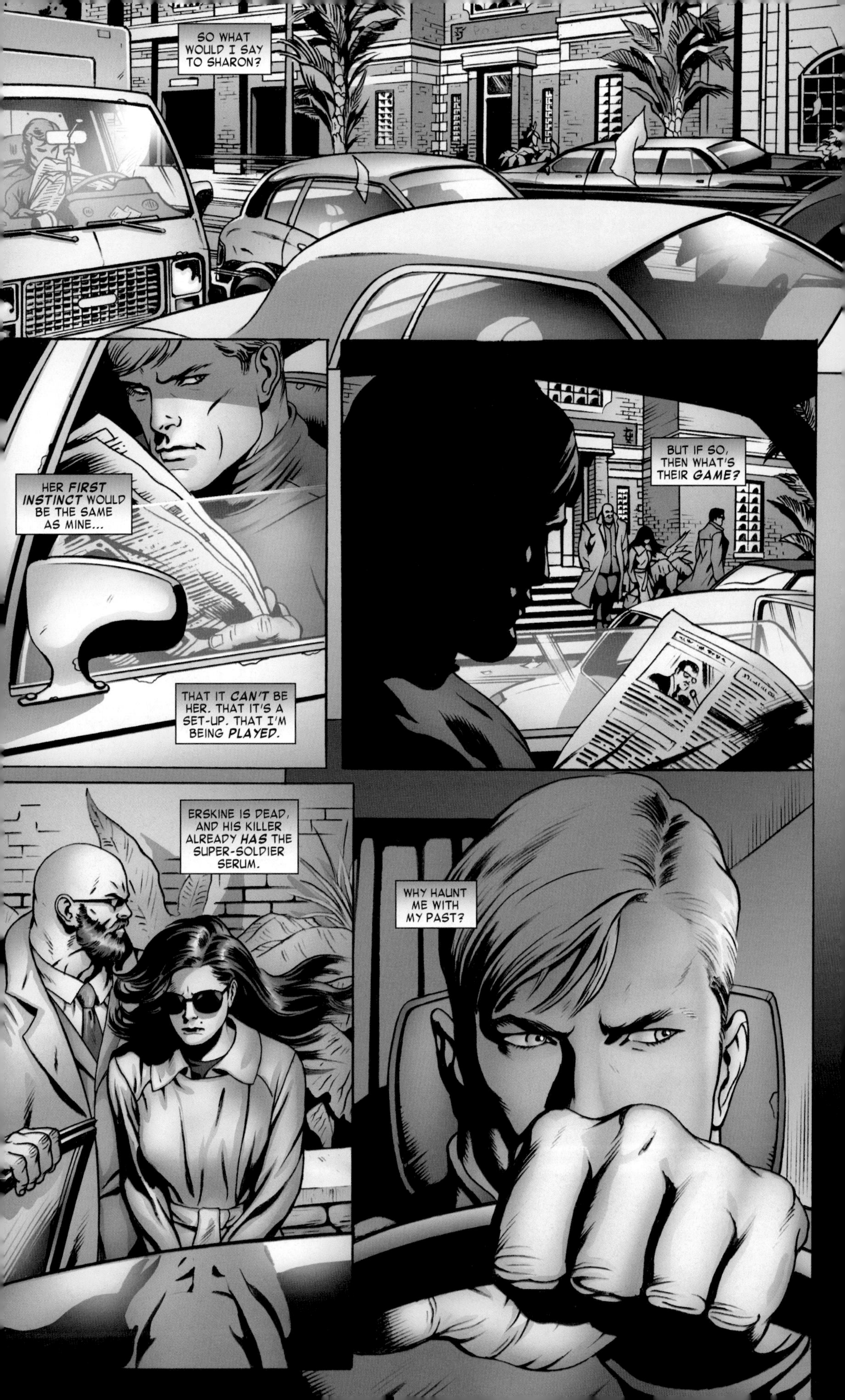
SO WHAT WOULD I SAY TO SHARON?
HER FIRST INSTINCT WOULD BE THE SAME AS MINE...
THAT IT CAN'T BE HER. THAT IT'S A SET-UP. THAT I'M BEING PLAYED.
BUT IF SO, THEN WHAT'S THEIR GAME?
ERSKINE IS DEAD, AND HIS KILLER ALREADY HAS THE SUPER-SOLDIER SERUM.
WHY HAUNT ME WITH MY PAST?

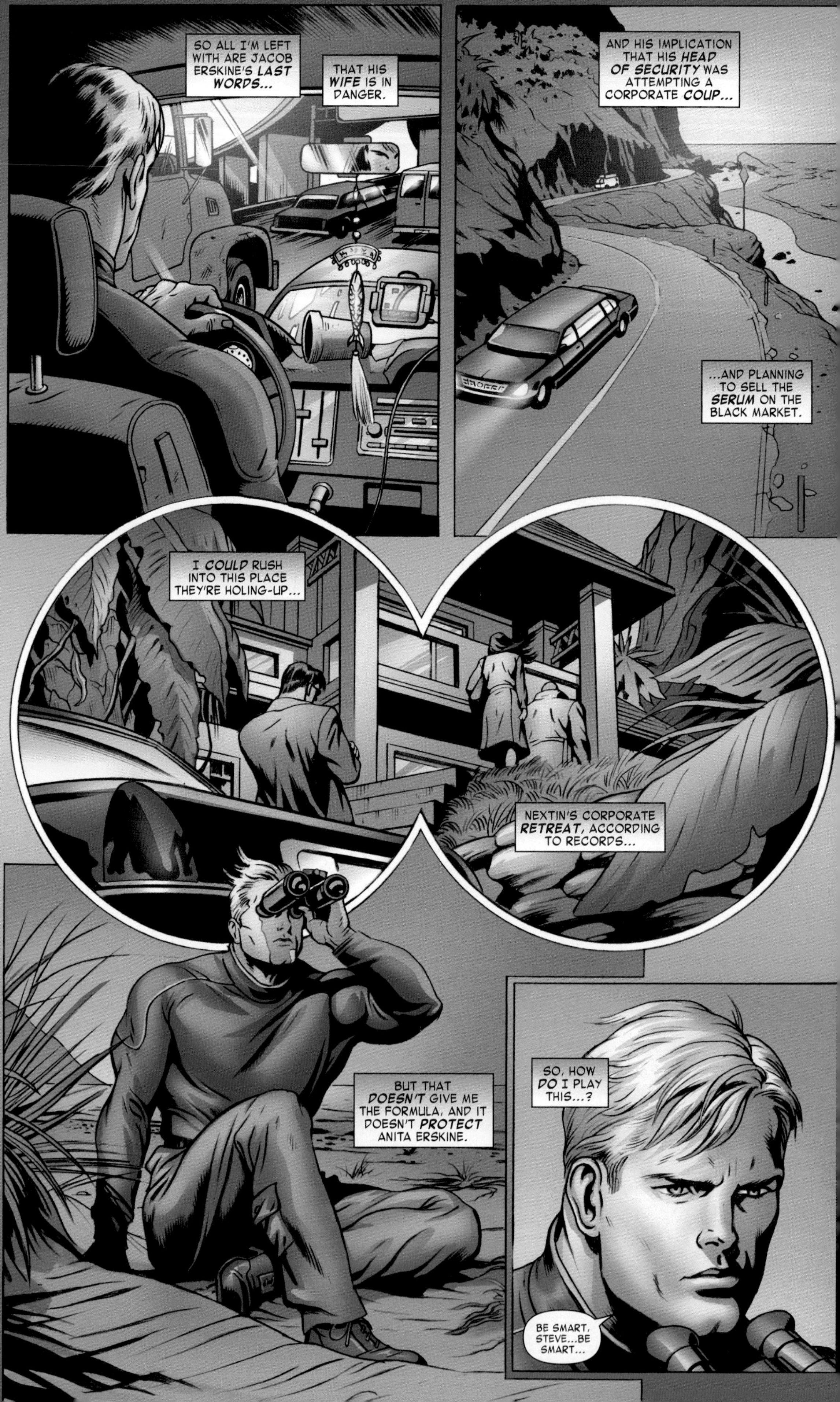
SO ALL I'M LEFT WITH ARE JACOB ERSKINE'S *LAST WORDS...*
THAT HIS *WIFE* IS IN DANGER.
AND HIS IMPLICATION THAT HIS *HEAD OF SECURITY* WAS ATTEMPTING A CORPORATE *COUP...*
...AND PLANNING TO SELL THE *SERUM* ON THE BLACK MARKET.
NEXTIN'S CORPORATE *RETREAT*, ACCORDING TO RECORDS...
I *COULD* RUSH INTO THIS PLACE THEY'RE HOLING-UP...
BUT THAT *DOESN'T* GIVE ME THE FORMULA, AND IT DOESN'T *PROTECT* ANITA ERSKINE.
SO, HOW *DO* I PLAY THIS...?
BE SMART, STEVE...BE SMART...

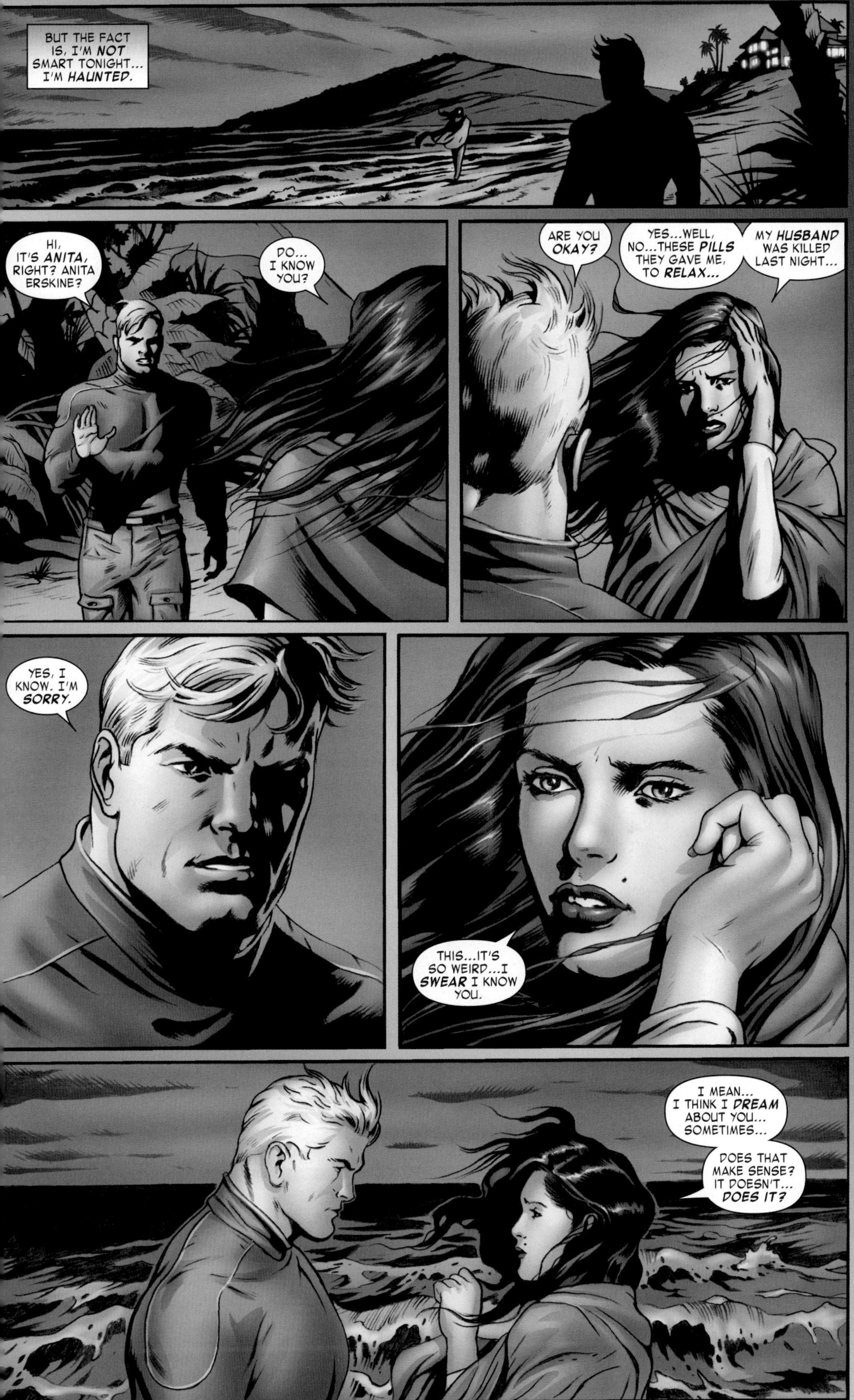
BUT THE FACT IS, I'M NOT SMART TONIGHT... I'M HAUNTED.
HI, IT'S ANITA, RIGHT? ANITA ERSKINE?
DO... I KNOW YOU?
ARE YOU OKAY?
YES...WELL, NO...THESE PILLS THEY GAVE ME, TO RELAX...
MY HUSBAND WAS KILLED LAST NIGHT...
YES, I KNOW. I'M SORRY.
THIS...IT'S SO WEIRD...I SWEAR I KNOW YOU.
I MEAN... I THINK I DREAM ABOUT YOU... SOMETIMES...
DOES THAT MAKE SENSE? IT DOESN'T... DOES IT?

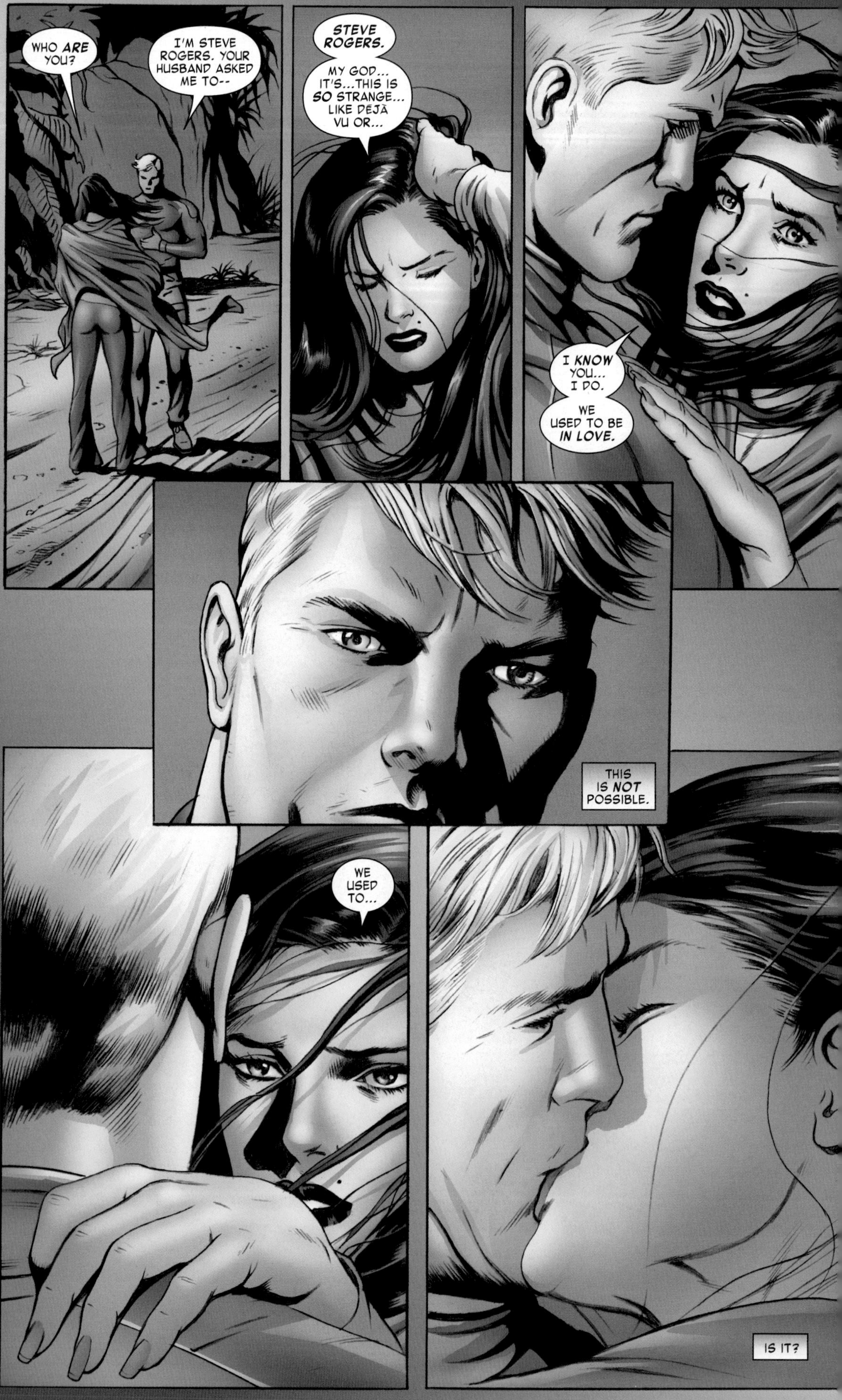
WHO ARE YOU?
I'M STEVE ROGERS. YOUR HUSBAND ASKED ME TO--
STEVE ROGERS.
MY GOD... IT'S...THIS IS SO STRANGE... LIKE DÉJÀ VU OR...
I KNOW YOU... I DO.
WE USED TO BE IN LOVE.
THIS IS NOT POSSIBLE.
WE USED TO...
IS IT?

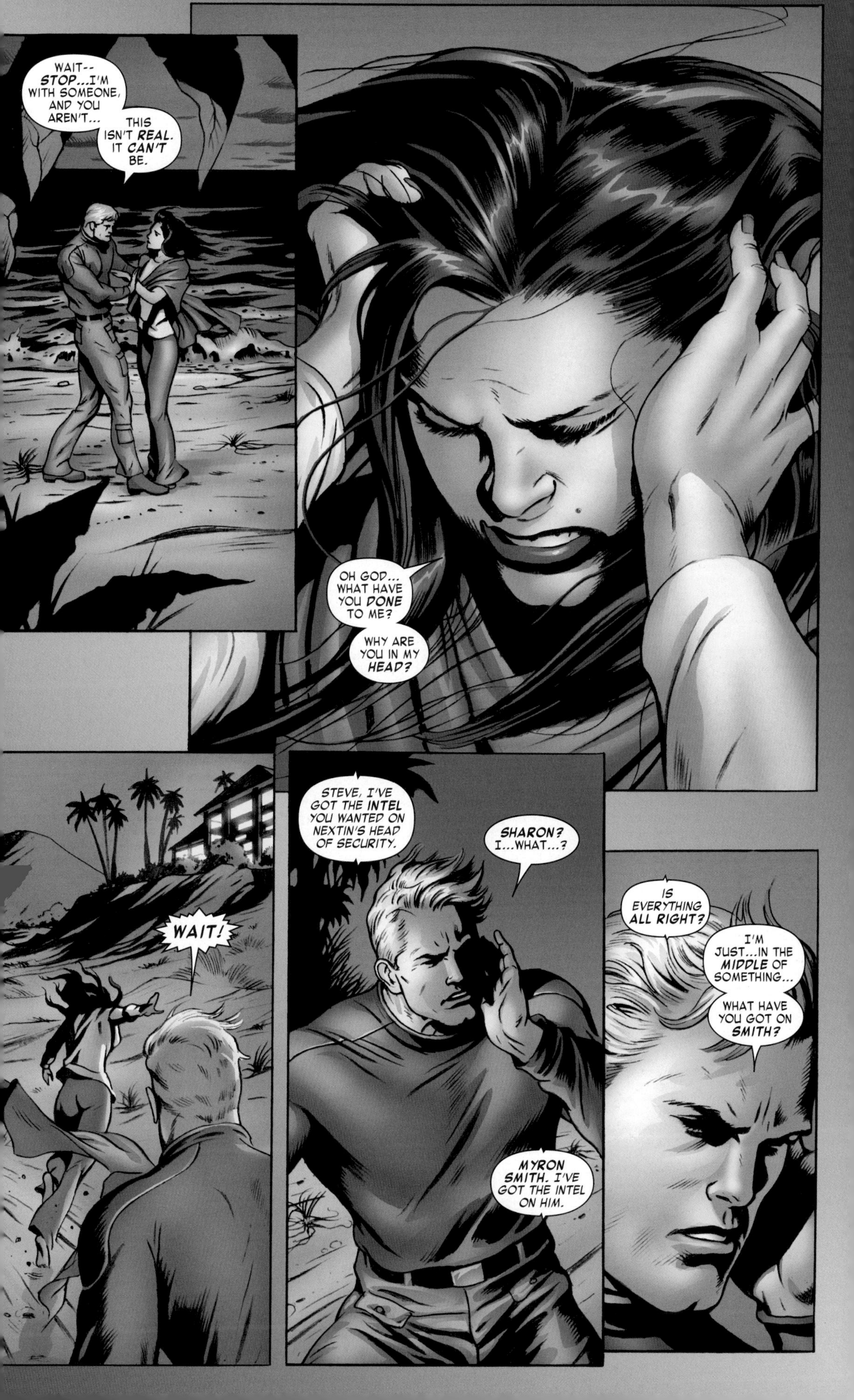
WAIT-- STOP...I'M WITH SOMEONE, AND YOU AREN'T...
THIS ISN'T REAL. IT CAN'T BE.
OH GOD... WHAT HAVE YOU DONE TO ME?
WHY ARE YOU IN MY HEAD?
WAIT!
STEVE, I'VE GOT THE INTEL YOU WANTED ON NEXTIN'S HEAD OF SECURITY.
SHARON? I...WHAT...?
IS EVERYTHING ALL RIGHT?
I'M JUST...IN THE MIDDLE OF SOMETHING...
WHAT HAVE YOU GOT ON SMITH?
MYRON SMITH. I'VE GOT THE INTEL ON HIM.

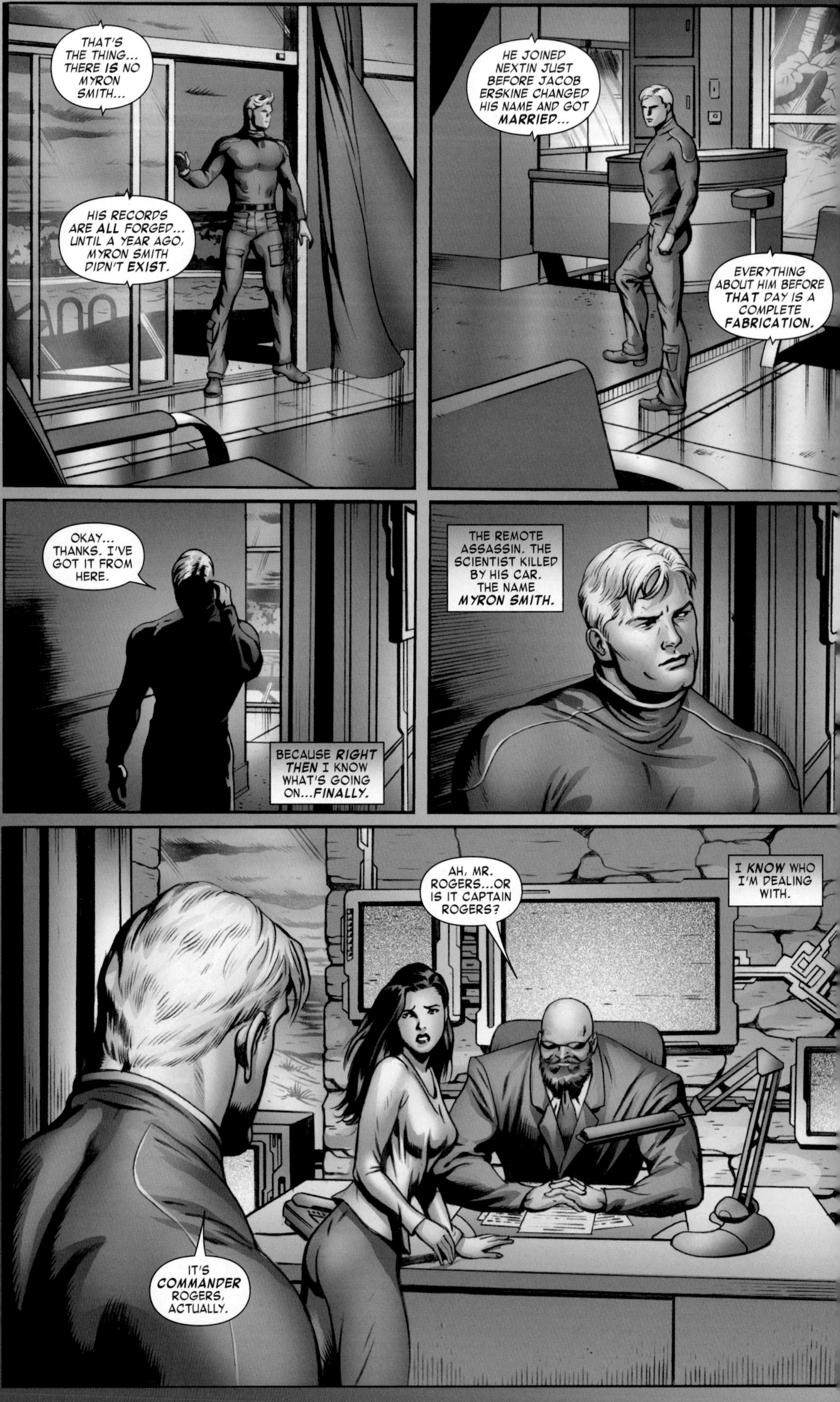
THAT'S THE THING... THERE IS NO MYRON SMITH...
HIS RECORDS ARE ALL FORGED... UNTIL A YEAR AGO, MYRON SMITH DIDN'T EXIST.
HE JOINED NEXTIN JUST BEFORE JACOB ERSKINE CHANGED HIS NAME AND GOT MARRIED...
EVERYTHING ABOUT HIM BEFORE THAT DAY IS A COMPLETE FABRICATION.
OKAY... THANKS. I'VE GOT IT FROM HERE.
BECAUSE RIGHT THEN I KNOW WHAT'S GOING ON...FINALLY.
THE REMOTE ASSASSIN. THE SCIENTIST KILLED BY HIS CAR. THE NAME MYRON SMITH.
I KNOW WHO I'M DEALING WITH.
AH, MR. ROGERS...OR IS IT CAPTAIN ROGERS?
IT'S COMMANDER ROGERS, ACTUALLY.

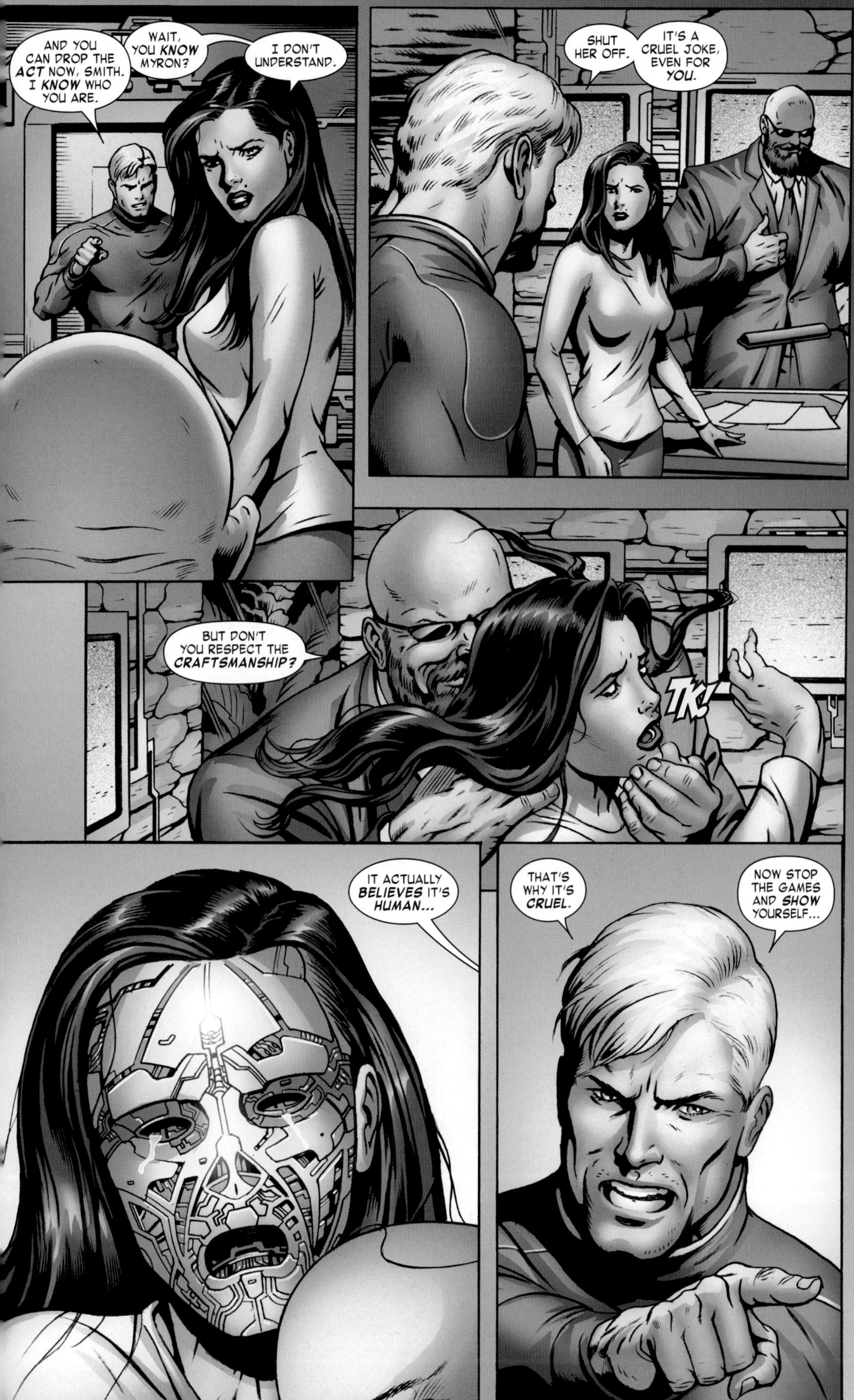
AND YOU CAN DROP THE ACT NOW, SMITH. I KNOW WHO YOU ARE.
WAIT, YOU KNOW MYRON?
I DON'T UNDERSTAND.
SHUT HER OFF.
IT'S A CRUEL JOKE, EVEN FOR YOU.
BUT DON'T YOU RESPECT THE CRAFTSMANSHIP?
TK!
IT ACTUALLY BELIEVES IT'S HUMAN...
THAT'S WHY IT'S CRUEL.
NOW STOP THE GAMES AND SHOW YOURSELF...

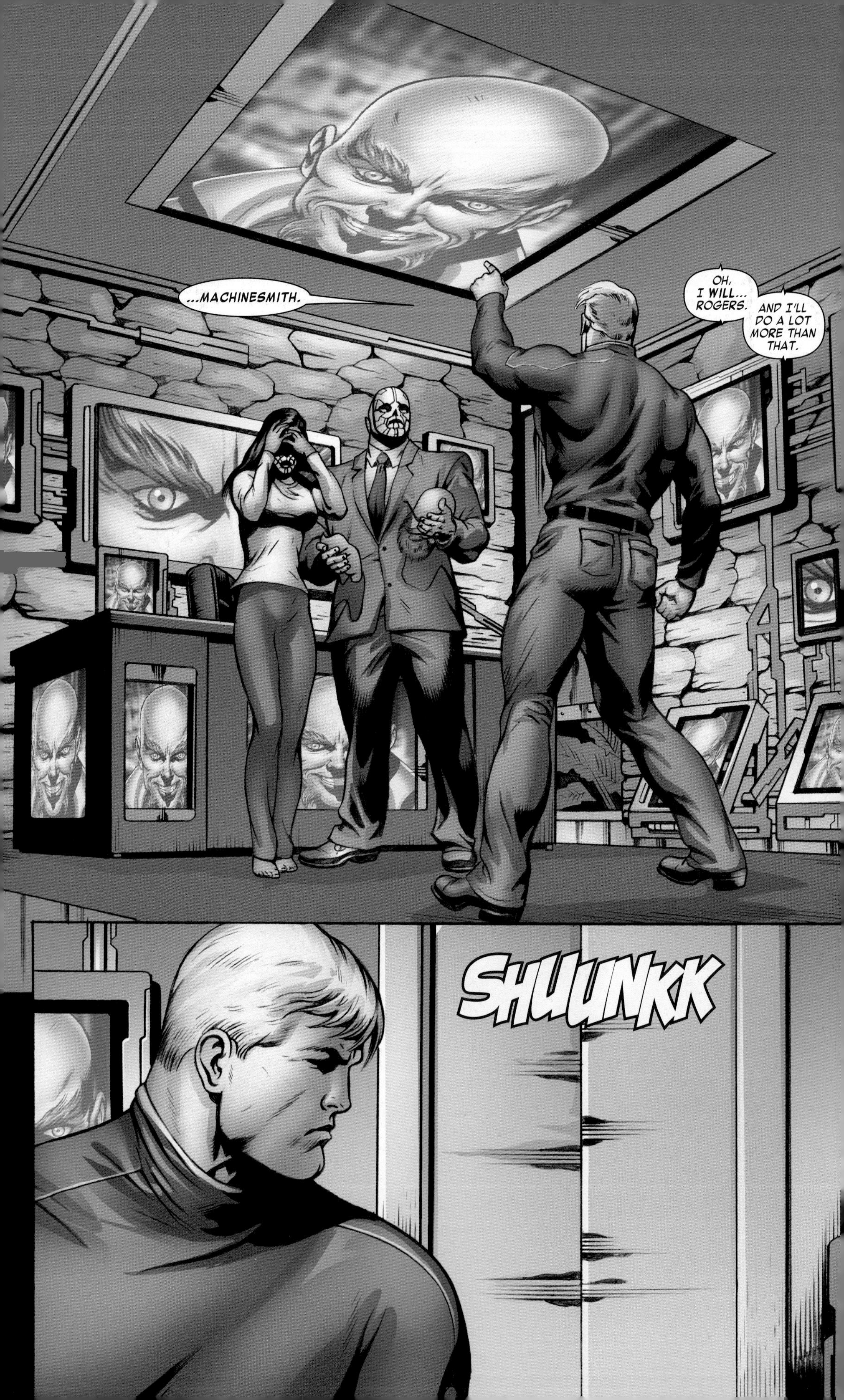
...MACHINESMITH.
OH, I WILL... ROGERS.
AND I'LL DO A LOT MORE THAN THAT.
SHUUNKK

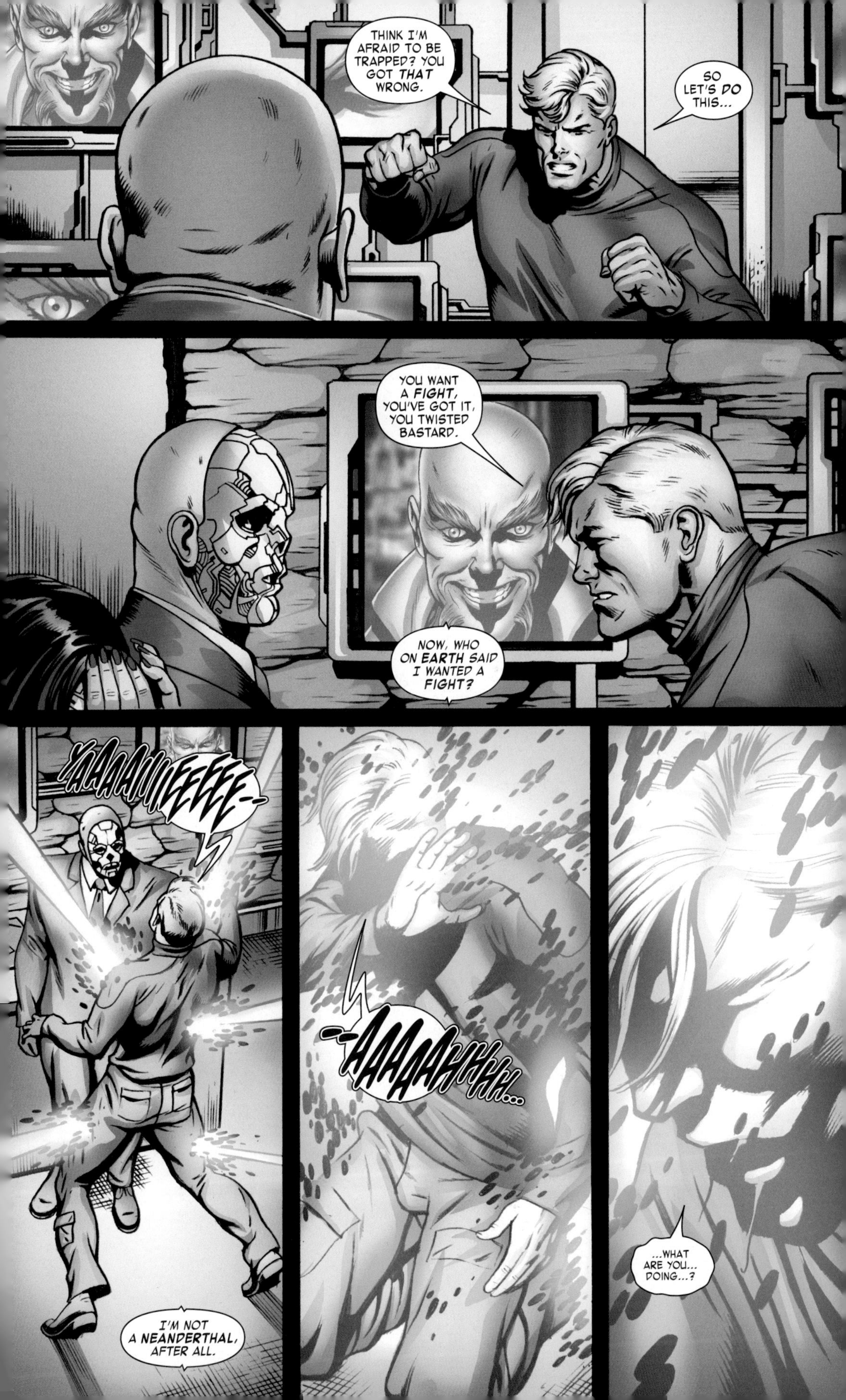

THINK I'M AFRAID TO BE TRAPPED? YOU GOT *THAT* WRONG.
SO LET'S *DO* THIS...
YOU WANT A *FIGHT*, YOU'VE GOT IT, YOU TWISTED BASTARD.
NOW, WHO ON **EARTH** SAID I WANTED A *FIGHT*?
YAAAAIIIEEEEE--
I'M NOT A **NEANDERTHAL**, AFTER ALL.
--AAAAAHHHH...
...WHAT ARE YOU... DOING...?

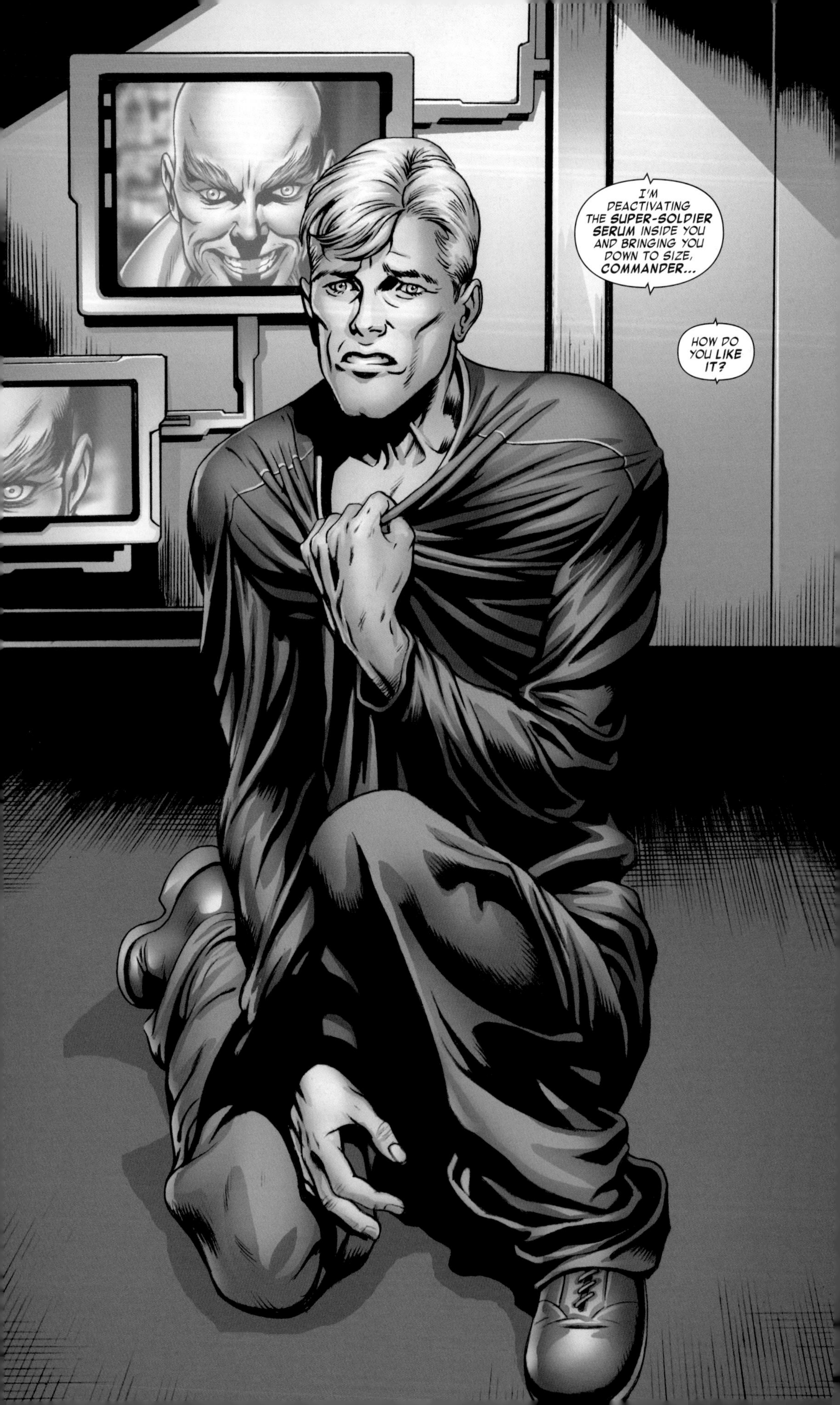
I'M DEACTIVATING THE SUPER-SOLDIER SERUM INSIDE YOU AND BRINGING YOU DOWN TO SIZE, COMMANDER...
HOW DO YOU LIKE IT?

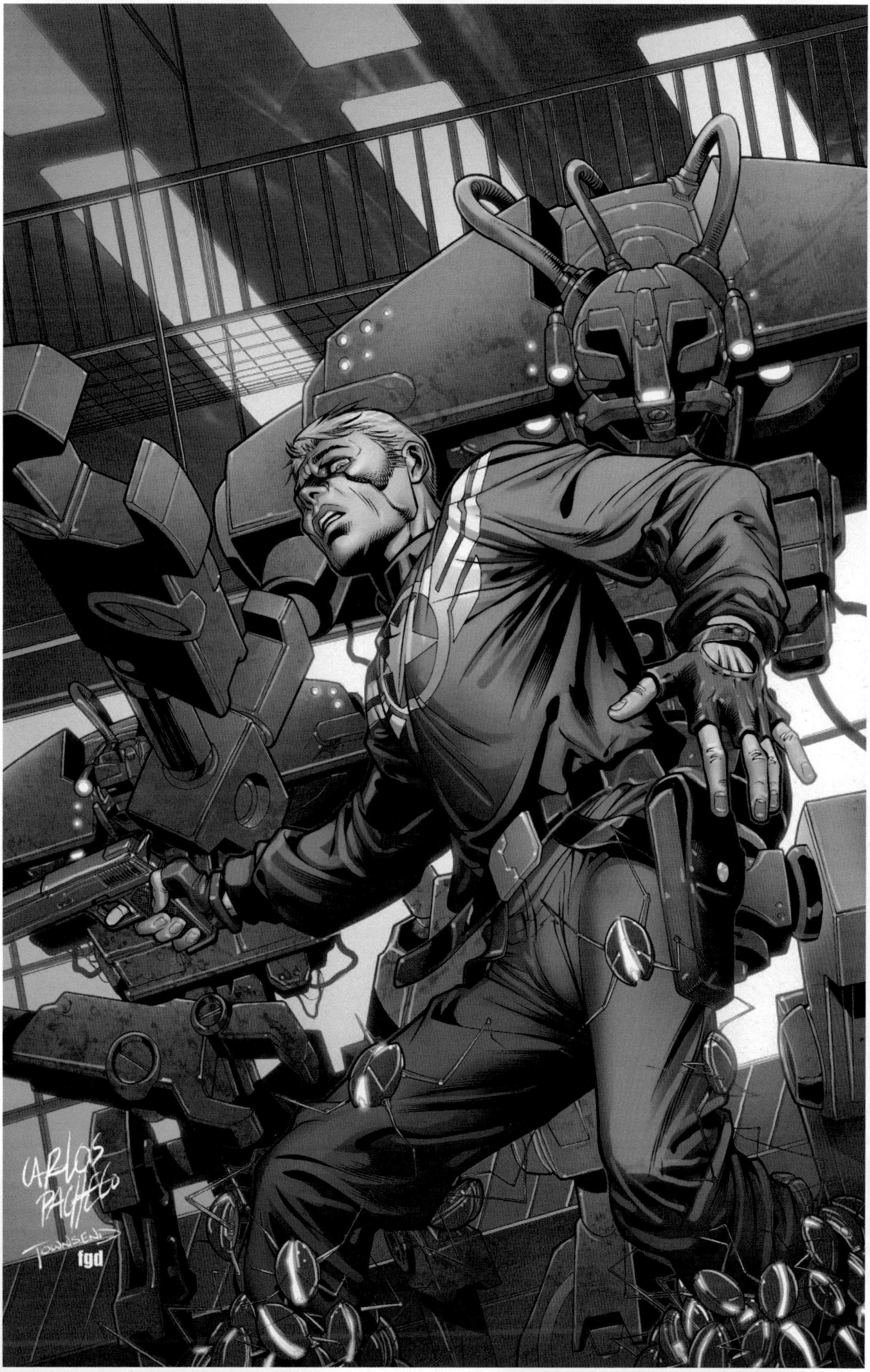
CARLOS PACHECO
TOWNSEND
fgd

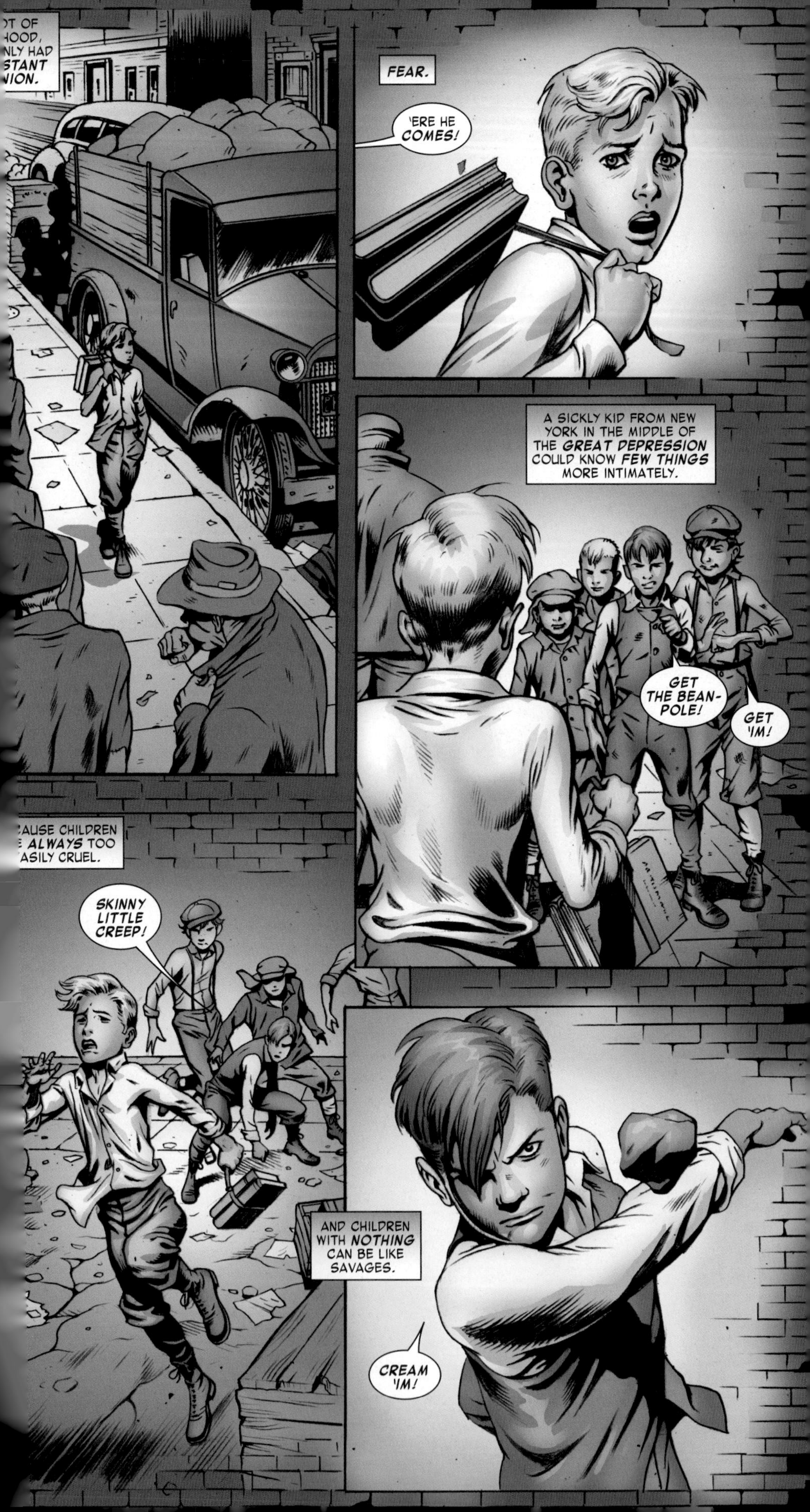

OT OF HOOD, NLY HAD STANT NION.
FEAR.
'ERE HE COMES!
A SICKLY KID FROM NEW YORK IN THE MIDDLE OF THE GREAT DEPRESSION COULD KNOW FEW THINGS MORE INTIMATELY.
GET THE BEAN-POLE!
GET 'IM!
CAUSE CHILDREN E ALWAYS TOO ASILY CRUEL.
SKINNY LITTLE CREEP!
AND CHILDREN WITH NOTHING CAN BE LIKE SAVAGES.
CREAM 'IM!

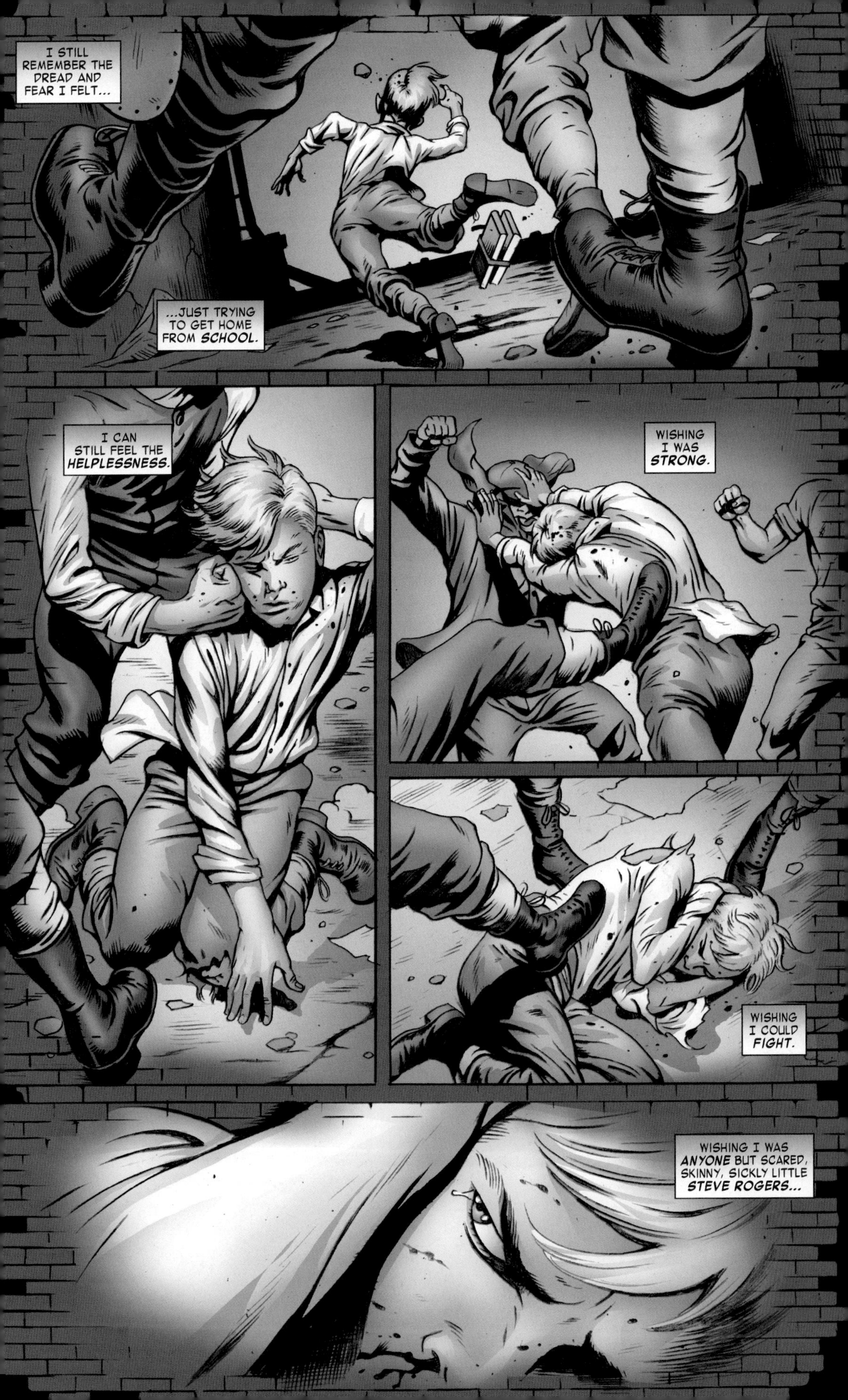
I STILL REMEMBER THE DREAD AND FEAR I FELT...
...JUST TRYING TO GET HOME FROM SCHOOL.
I CAN STILL FEEL THE HELPLESSNESS.
WISHING I WAS STRONG.
WISHING I COULD FIGHT.
WISHING I WAS ANYONE BUT SCARED, SKINNY, SICKLY LITTLE STEVE ROGERS...

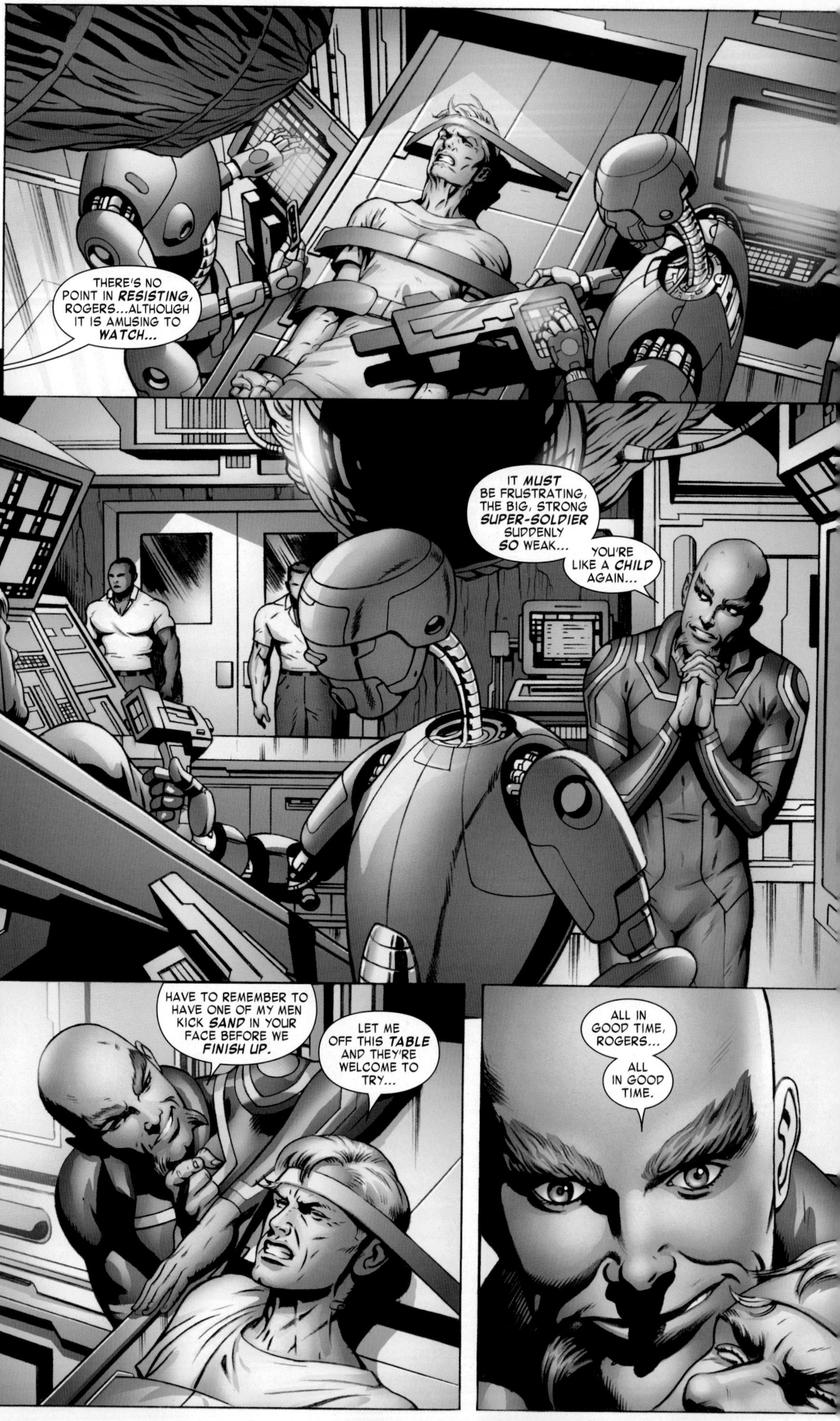
THERE'S NO POINT IN RESISTING, ROGERS...ALTHOUGH IT IS AMUSING TO WATCH...
IT MUST BE FRUSTRATING, THE BIG, STRONG SUPER-SOLDIER SUDDENLY SO WEAK...
YOU'RE LIKE A CHILD AGAIN...
HAVE TO REMEMBER TO HAVE ONE OF MY MEN KICK SAND IN YOUR FACE BEFORE WE FINISH UP.
LET ME OFF THIS TABLE AND THEY'RE WELCOME TO TRY...
ALL IN GOOD TIME, ROGERS...
ALL IN GOOD TIME.

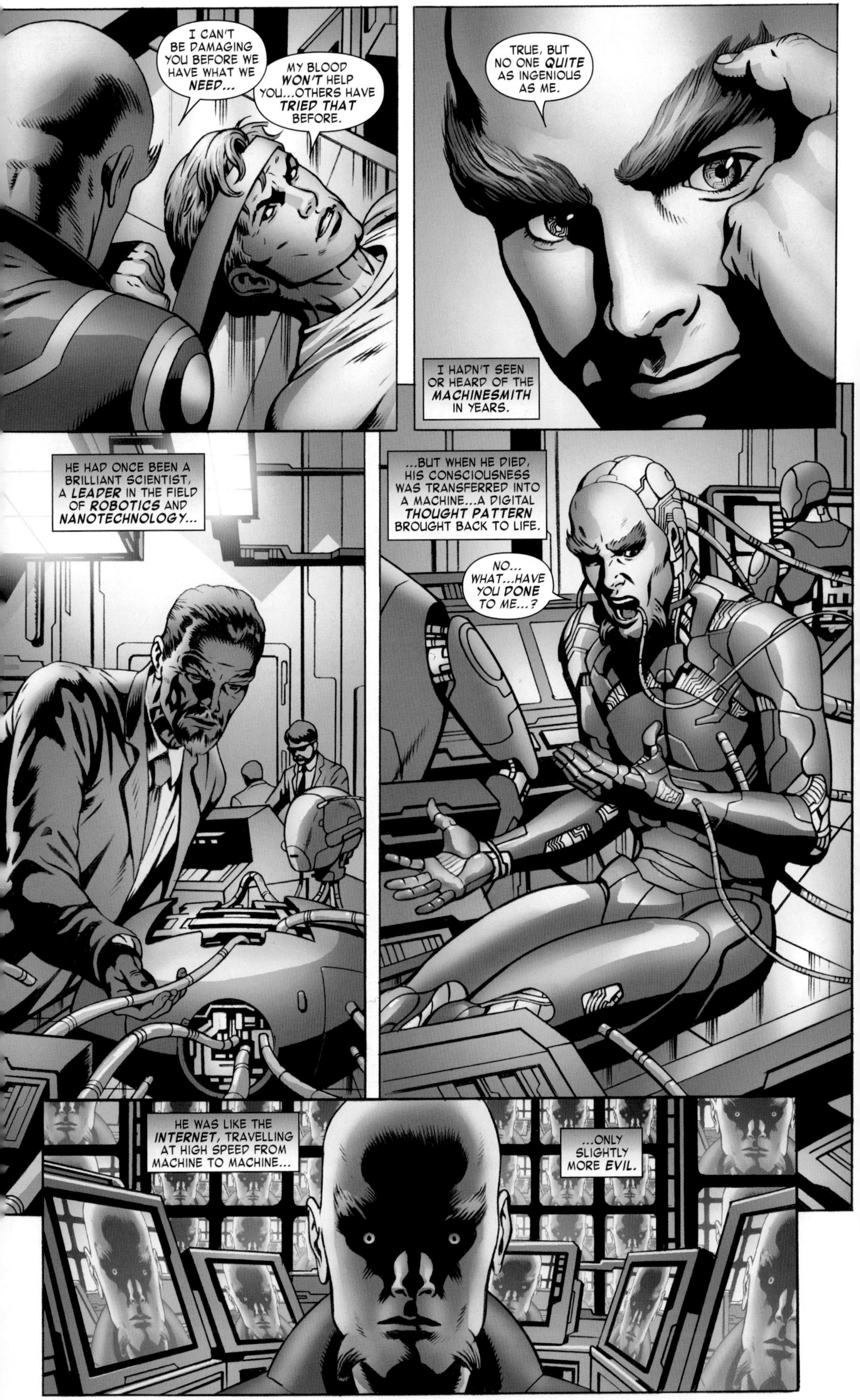

I CAN'T BE DAMAGING YOU BEFORE WE HAVE WHAT WE NEED...
MY BLOOD WON'T HELP YOU...OTHERS HAVE TRIED THAT BEFORE.
TRUE, BUT NO ONE QUITE AS INGENIOUS AS ME.
I HADN'T SEEN OR HEARD OF THE MACHINESMITH IN YEARS.
HE HAD ONCE BEEN A BRILLIANT SCIENTIST, A LEADER IN THE FIELD OF ROBOTICS AND NANOTECHNOLOGY...
...BUT WHEN HE DIED, HIS CONSCIOUSNESS WAS TRANSFERRED INTO A MACHINE...A DIGITAL THOUGHT PATTERN BROUGHT BACK TO LIFE.
NO... WHAT...HAVE YOU DONE TO ME...?
HE WAS LIKE THE INTERNET, TRAVELLING AT HIGH SPEED FROM MACHINE TO MACHINE...
...ONLY SLIGHTLY MORE EVIL.

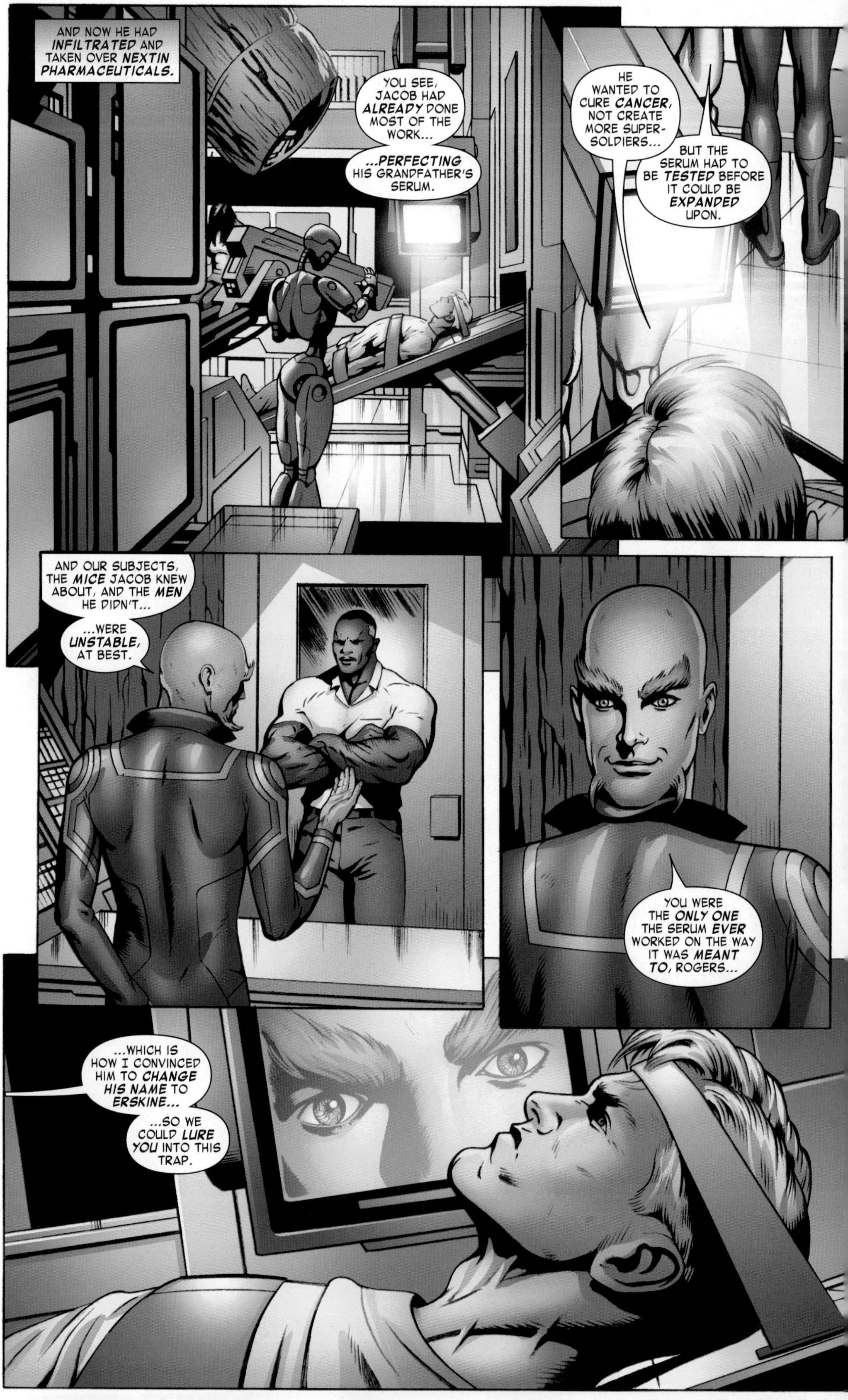
AND NOW HE HAD INFILTRATED AND TAKEN OVER NEXTIN PHARMACEUTICALS.
YOU SEE, JACOB HAD ALREADY DONE MOST OF THE WORK...
...PERFECTING HIS GRANDFATHER'S SERUM.
HE WANTED TO CURE CANCER, NOT CREATE MORE SUPER-SOLDIERS...
BUT THE SERUM HAD TO BE TESTED BEFORE IT COULD BE EXPANDED UPON.
AND OUR SUBJECTS, THE MICE JACOB KNEW ABOUT, AND THE MEN HE DIDN'T...
...WERE UNSTABLE, AT BEST.
YOU WERE THE ONLY ONE THE SERUM EVER WORKED ON THE WAY IT WAS MEANT TO, ROGERS...
...WHICH IS HOW I CONVINCED HIM TO CHANGE HIS NAME TO ERSKINE...
...SO WE COULD LURE YOU INTO THIS TRAP.

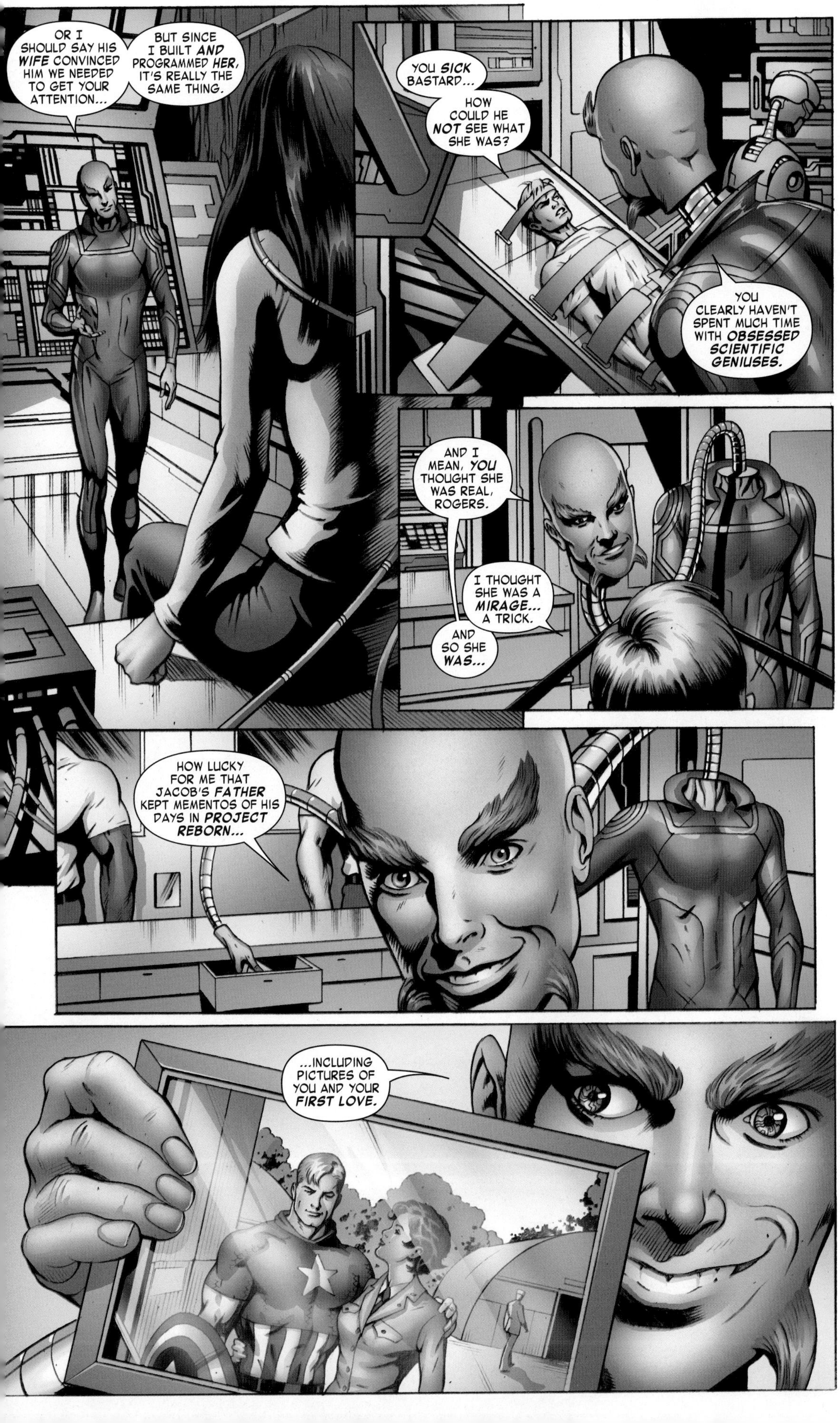
OR I SHOULD SAY HIS WIFE CONVINCED HIM WE NEEDED TO GET YOUR ATTENTION...
BUT SINCE I BUILT AND PROGRAMMED HER, IT'S REALLY THE SAME THING.
YOU SICK BASTARD...
HOW COULD HE NOT SEE WHAT SHE WAS?
YOU CLEARLY HAVEN'T SPENT MUCH TIME WITH OBSESSED SCIENTIFIC GENIUSES.
AND I MEAN, YOU THOUGHT SHE WAS REAL, ROGERS.
I THOUGHT SHE WAS A MIRAGE... A TRICK.
AND SO SHE WAS...
HOW LUCKY FOR ME THAT JACOB'S FATHER KEPT MEMENTOS OF HIS DAYS IN PROJECT REBORN...
...INCLUDING PICTURES OF YOU AND YOUR FIRST LOVE.

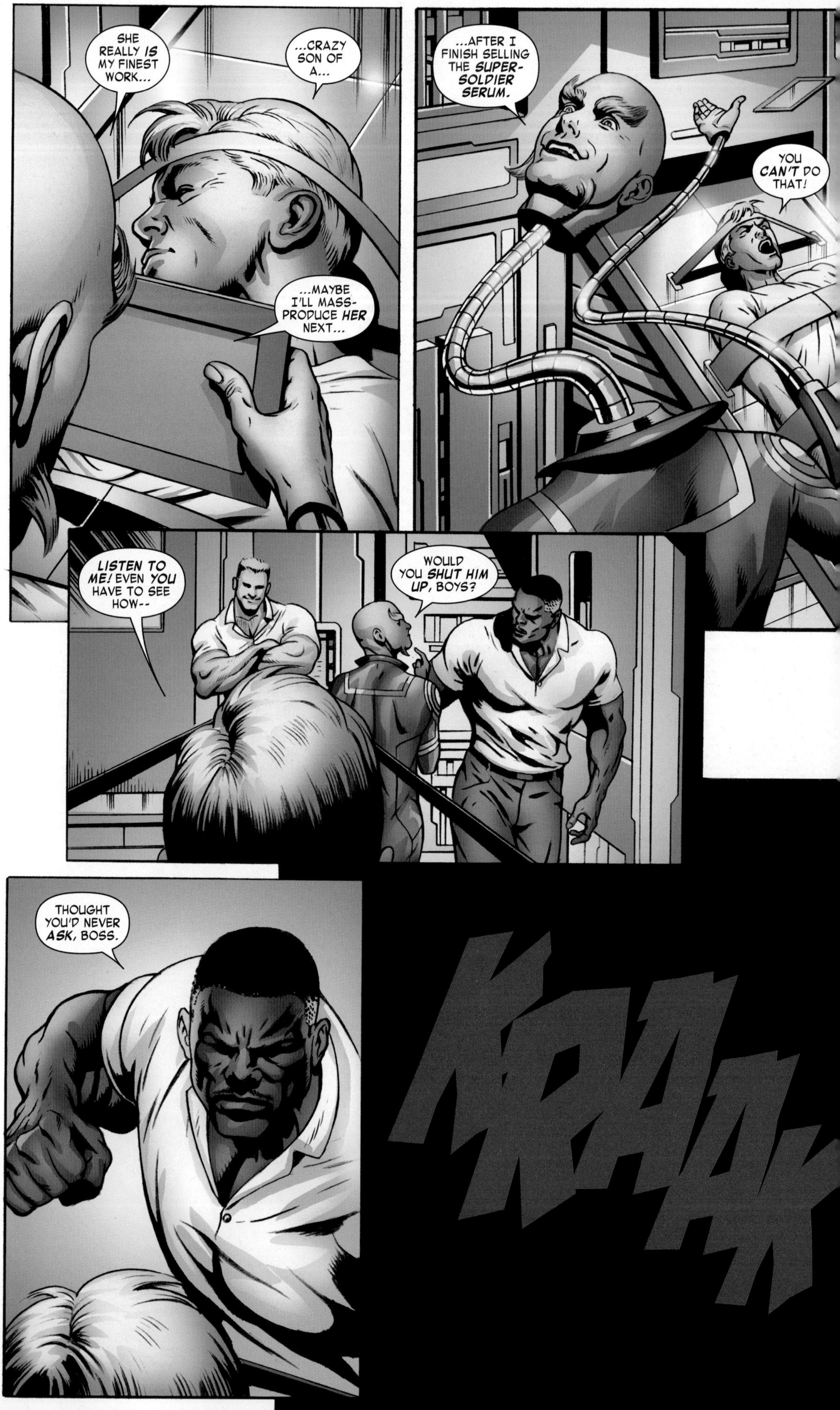

SHE REALLY IS MY FINEST WORK...
...CRAZY SON OF A...
...MAYBE I'LL MASS-PRODUCE HER NEXT...
...AFTER I FINISH SELLING THE SUPER-SOLDIER SERUM.
YOU CAN'T DO THAT!
LISTEN TO ME! EVEN YOU HAVE TO SEE HOW--
WOULD YOU SHUT HIM UP, BOYS?
THOUGHT YOU'D NEVER ASK, BOSS.
KRAAK

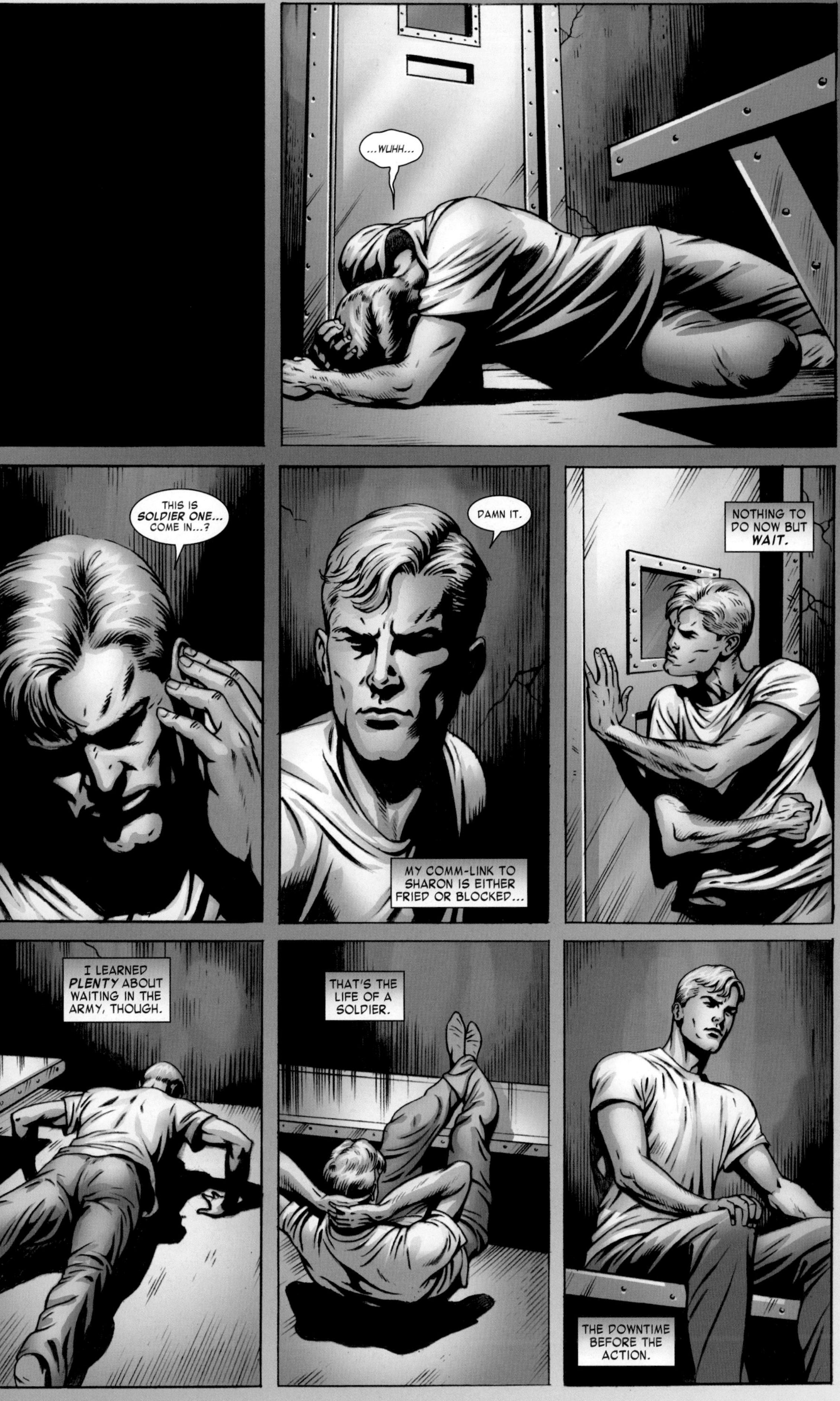
...WUHH...
THIS IS SOLDIER ONE... COME IN...?
DAMN IT.
MY COMM-LINK TO SHARON IS EITHER FRIED OR BLOCKED...
NOTHING TO DO NOW BUT WAIT.
I LEARNED PLENTY ABOUT WAITING IN THE ARMY, THOUGH.
THAT'S THE LIFE OF A SOLDIER.
THE DOWNTIME BEFORE THE ACTION.

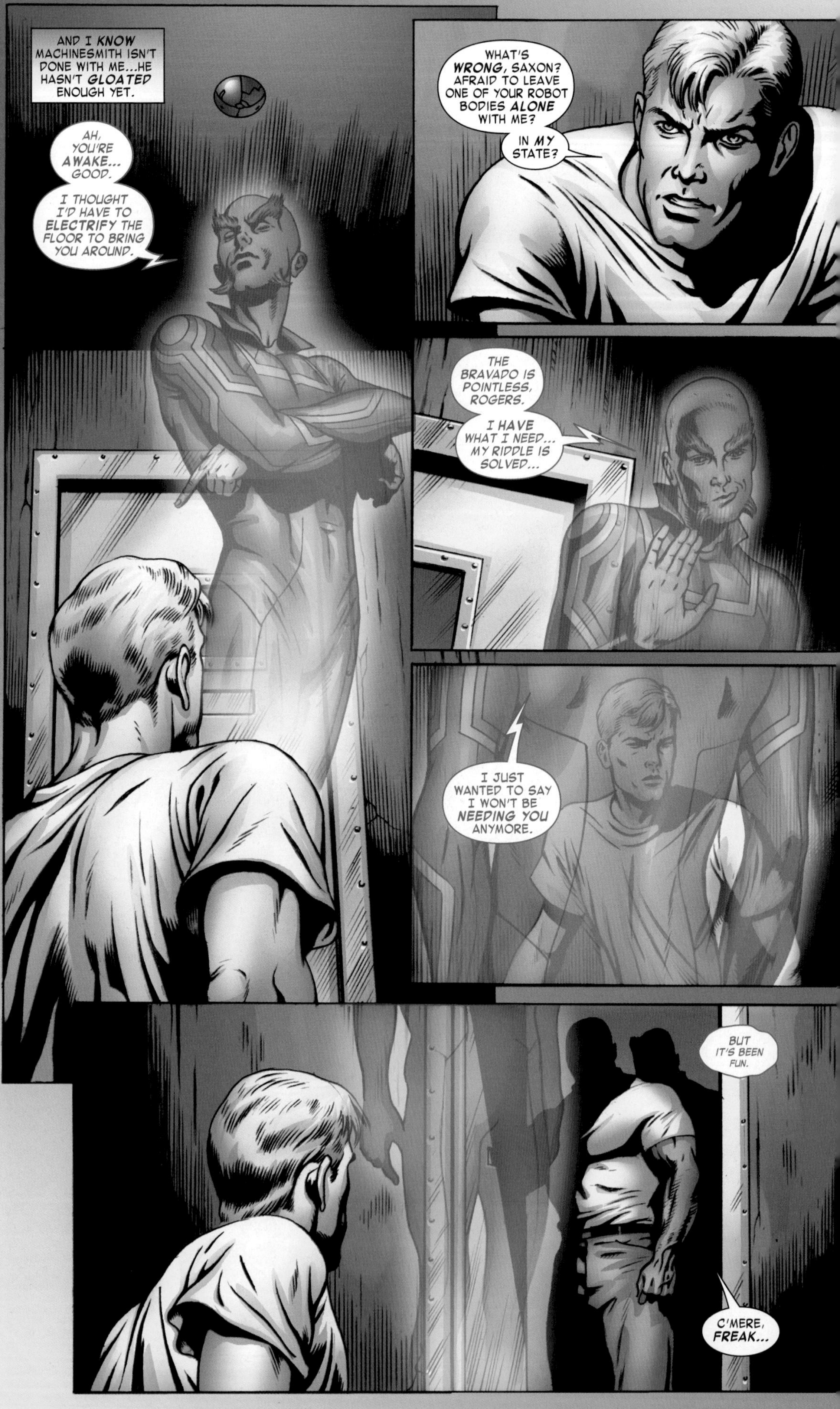
AND I KNOW MACHINESMITH ISN'T DONE WITH ME...HE HASN'T GLOATED ENOUGH YET.
AH, YOU'RE AWAKE... GOOD.
I THOUGHT I'D HAVE TO ELECTRIFY THE FLOOR TO BRING YOU AROUND.
WHAT'S WRONG, SAXON? AFRAID TO LEAVE ONE OF YOUR ROBOT BODIES ALONE WITH ME?
IN MY STATE?
THE BRAVADO IS POINTLESS, ROGERS.
I HAVE WHAT I NEED... MY RIDDLE IS SOLVED...
I JUST WANTED TO SAY I WON'T BE NEEDING YOU ANYMORE.
BUT IT'S BEEN FUN.
C'MERE, FREAK...

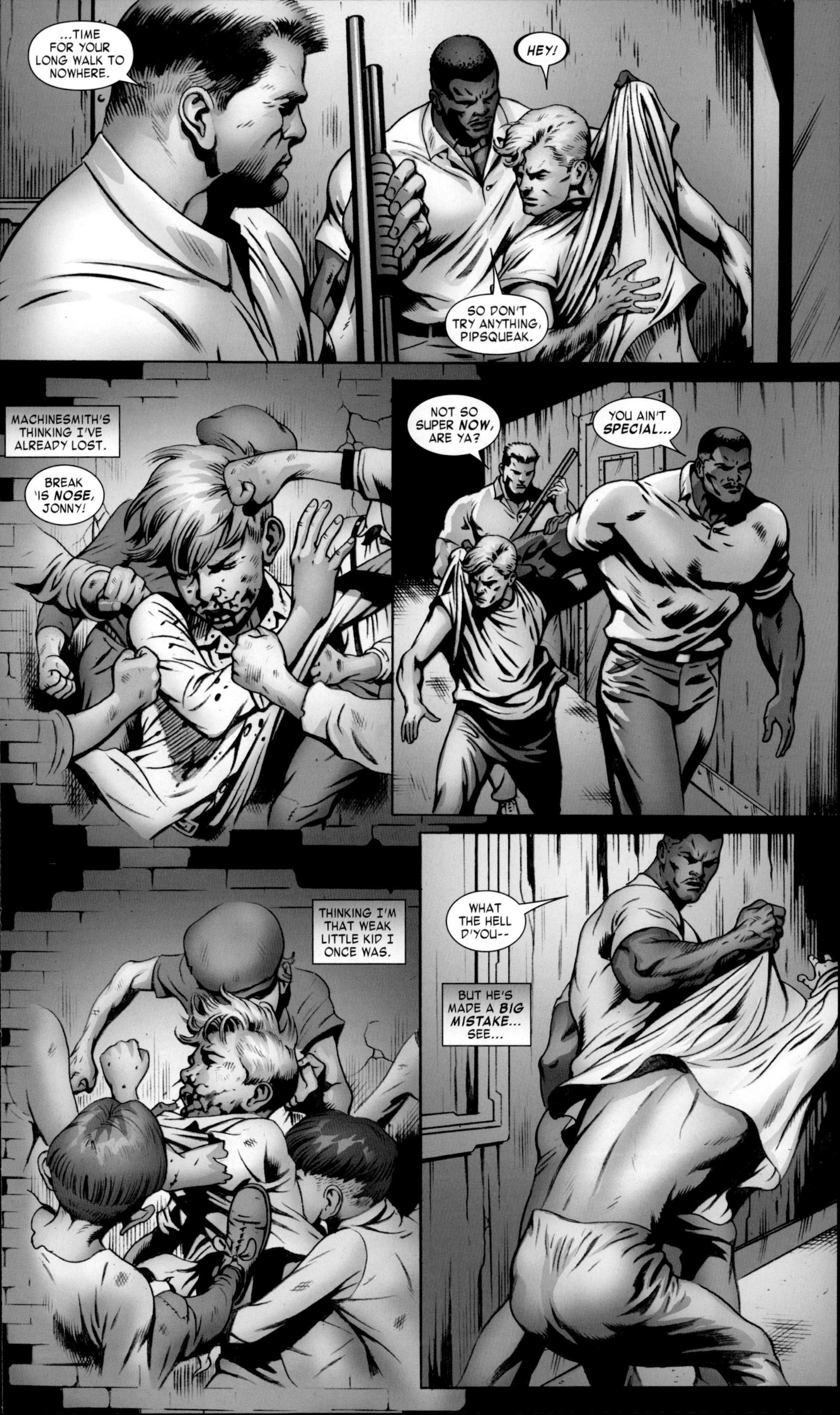
...TIME FOR YOUR LONG WALK TO NOWHERE.
HEY!
SO DON'T TRY ANYTHING, PIPSQUEAK.
MACHINESMITH'S THINKING I'VE ALREADY LOST.
BREAK 'IS NOSE, JONNY!
NOT SO SUPER NOW, ARE YA?
YOU AIN'T SPECIAL...
THINKING I'M THAT WEAK LITTLE KID I ONCE WAS.
WHAT THE HELL D'YOU--
BUT HE'S MADE A BIG MISTAKE... SEE...

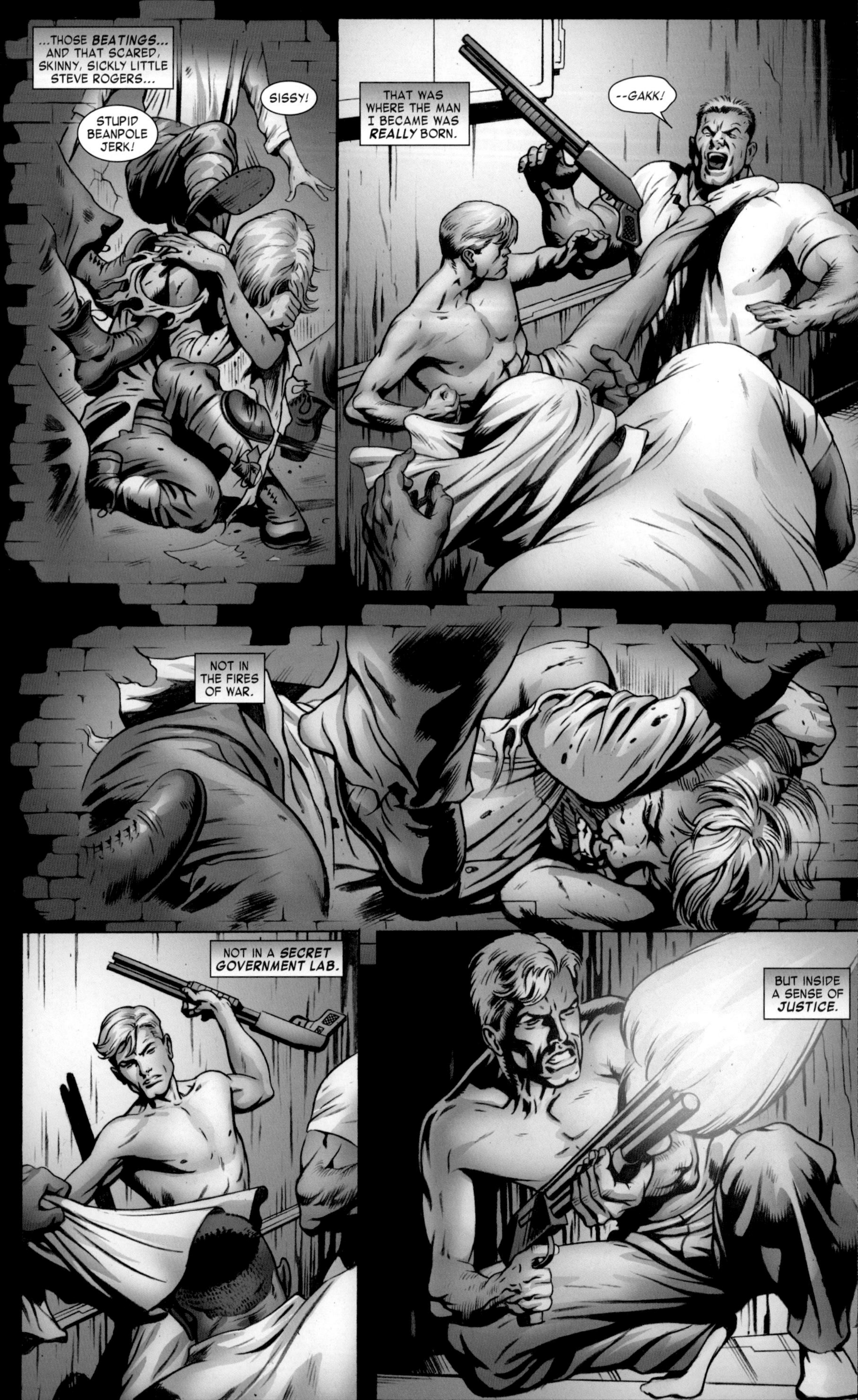
...THOSE BEATINGS... AND THAT SCARED, SKINNY, SICKLY LITTLE STEVE ROGERS...
SISSY!
STUPID BEANPOLE JERK!
THAT WAS WHERE THE MAN I BECAME WAS REALLY BORN.
--GAKK!
NOT IN THE FIRES OF WAR.
NOT IN A SECRET GOVERNMENT LAB.
BUT INSIDE A SENSE OF JUSTICE.

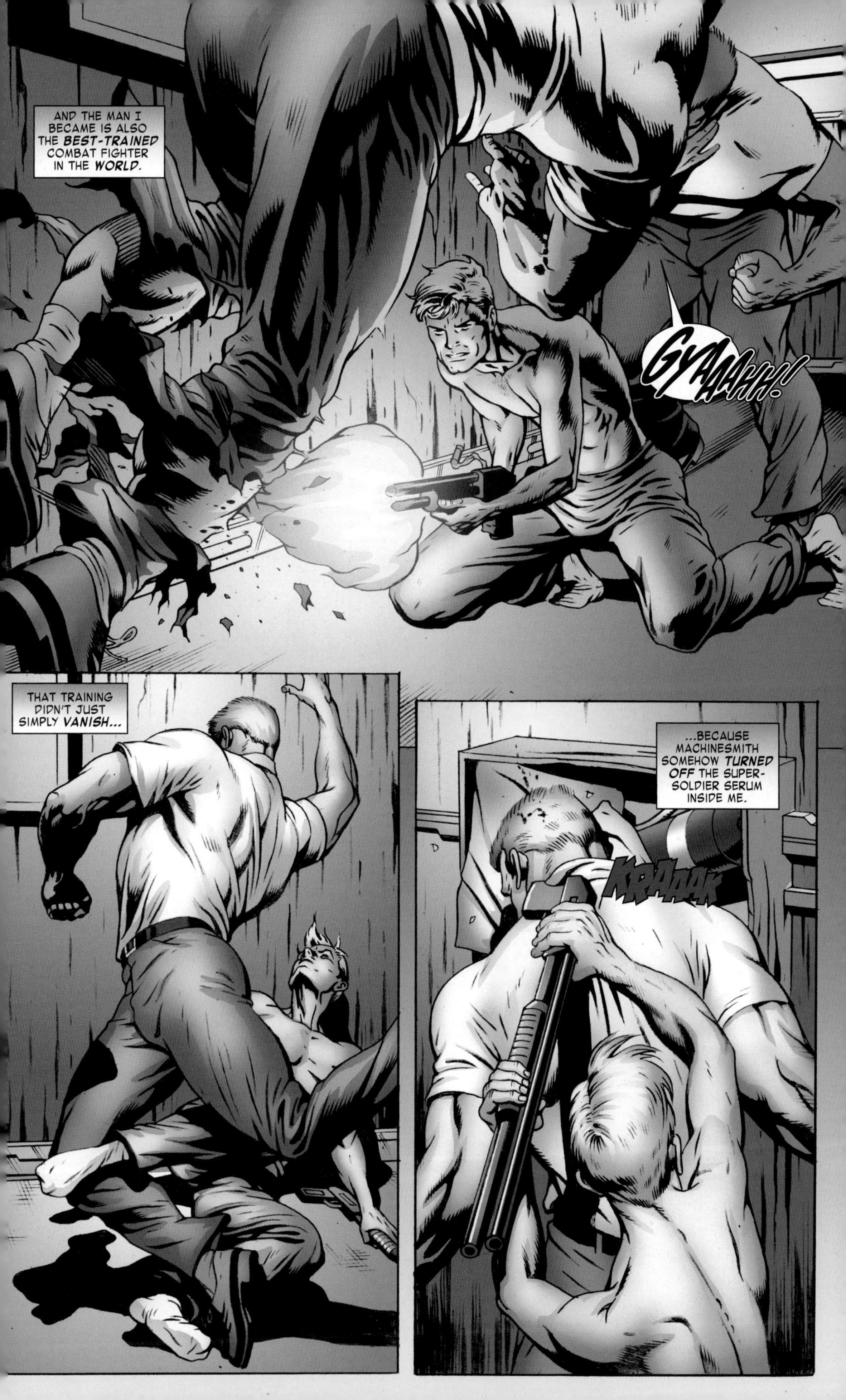
AND THE MAN I BECAME IS ALSO THE BEST-TRAINED COMBAT FIGHTER IN THE WORLD.
GYAAAAHH!
THAT TRAINING DIDN'T JUST SIMPLY VANISH...
...BECAUSE MACHINESMITH SOMEHOW TURNED OFF THE SUPER-SOLDIER SERUM INSIDE ME.
KRAAAK

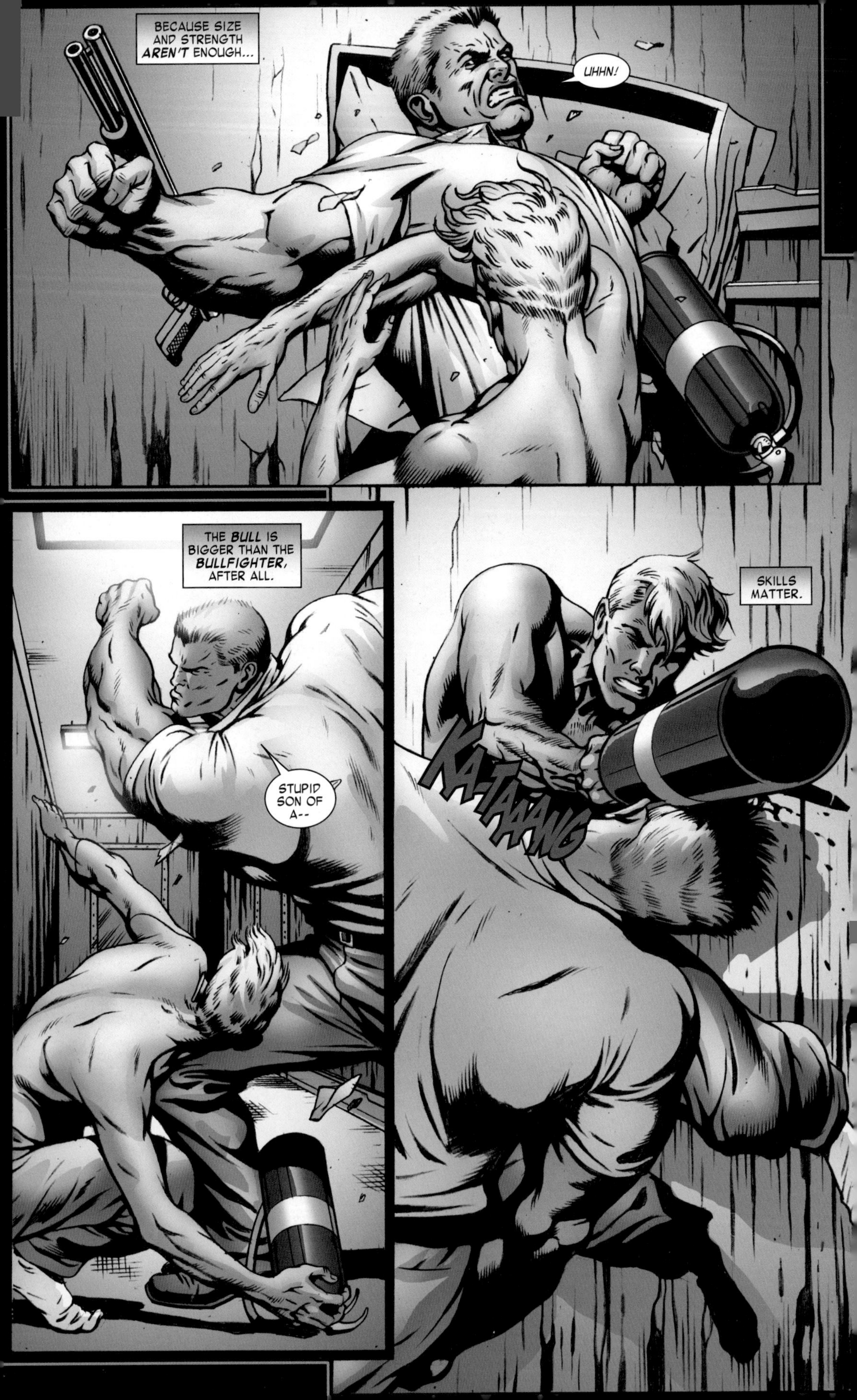
BECAUSE SIZE AND STRENGTH AREN'T ENOUGH...
UHHN!
THE BULL IS BIGGER THAN THE BULLFIGHTER, AFTER ALL.
STUPID SON OF A--
SKILLS MATTER.
KA-TAAANG

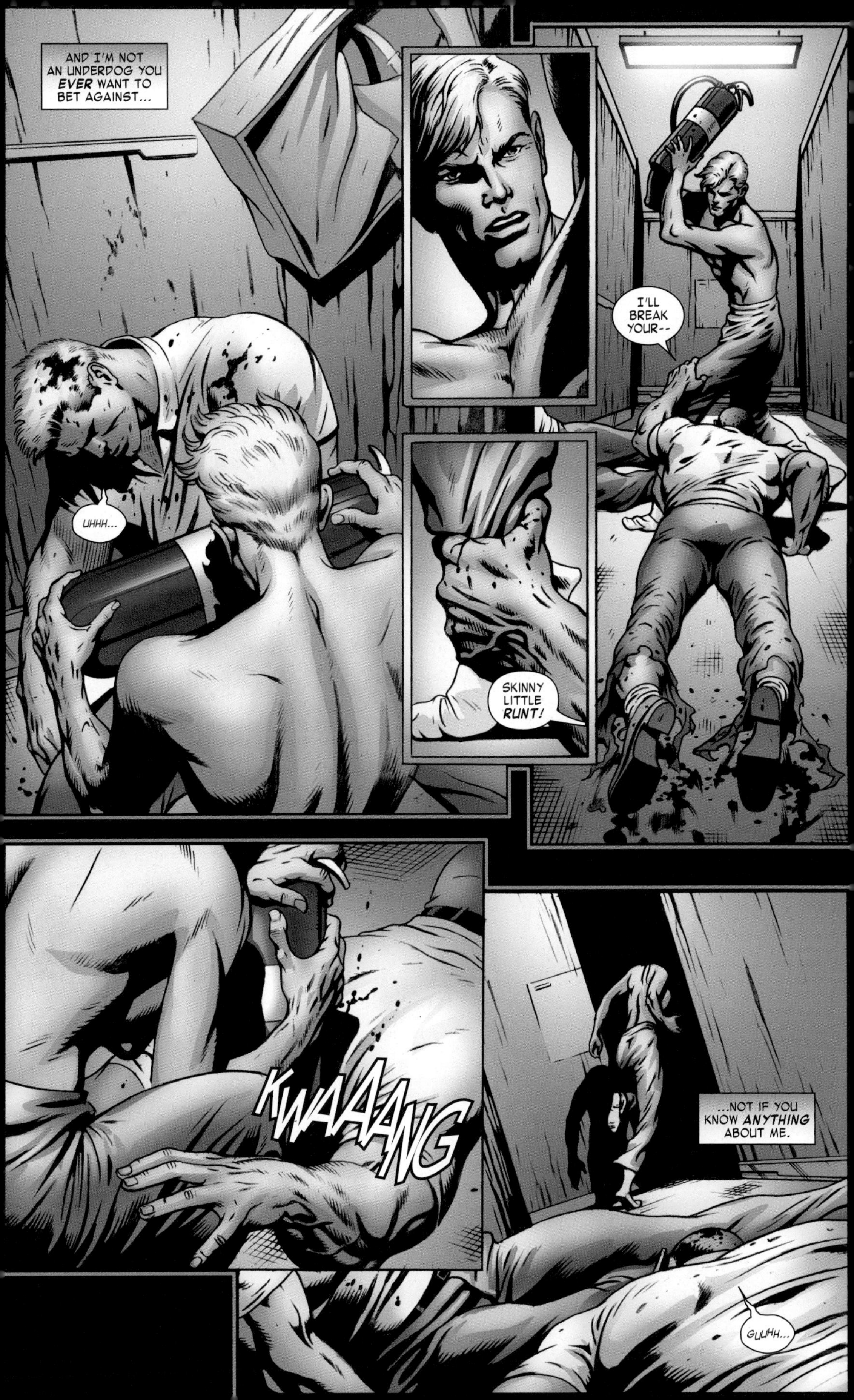
AND I'M NOT AN UNDERDOG YOU EVER WANT TO BET AGAINST...
UHHH...
I'LL BREAK YOUR--
SKINNY LITTLE RUNT!
KWAAAANG
...NOT IF YOU KNOW ANYTHING ABOUT ME.
GUUHH...

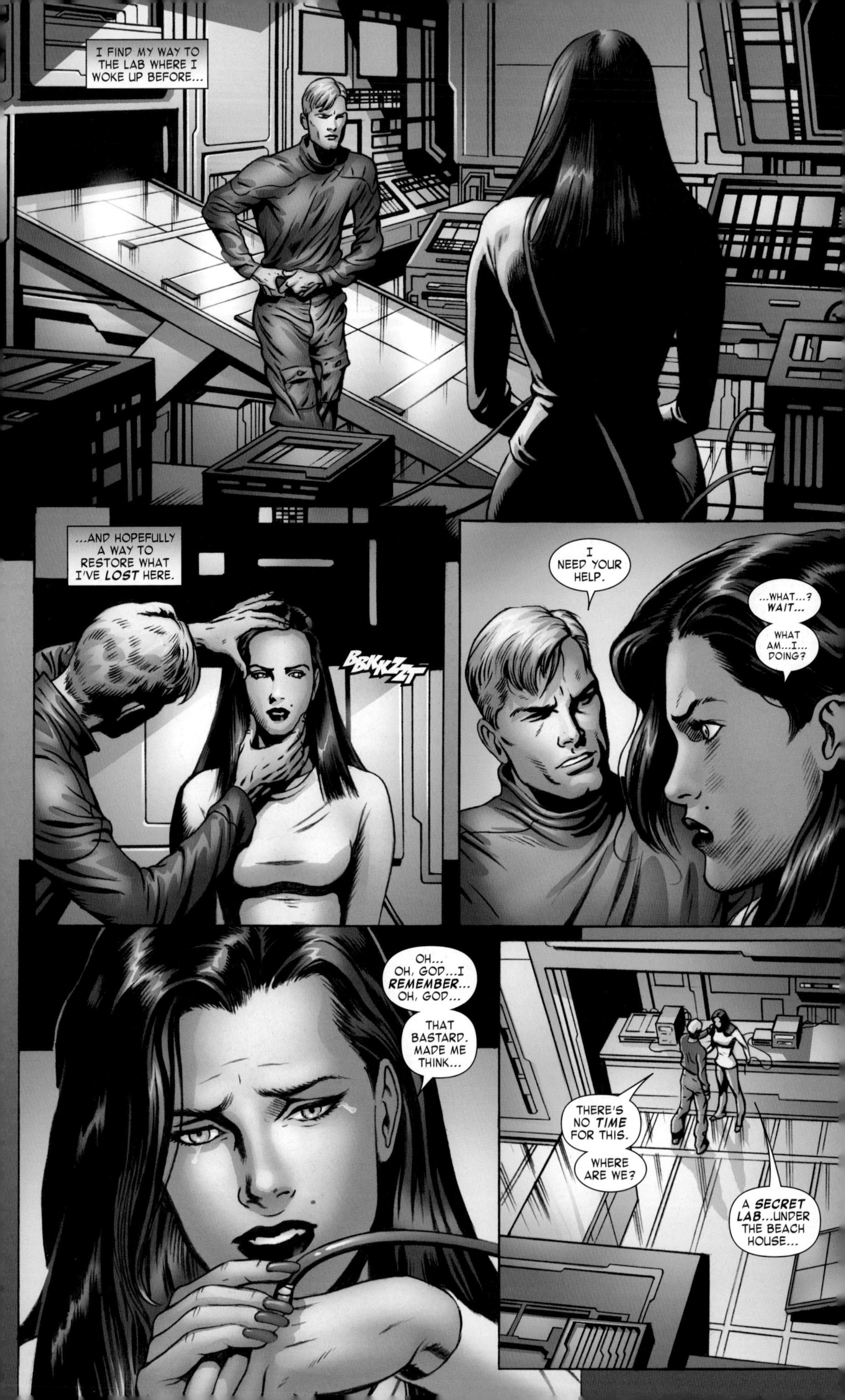
I FIND MY WAY TO THE LAB WHERE I WOKE UP BEFORE...
...AND HOPEFULLY A WAY TO RESTORE WHAT I'VE LOST HERE.
BBKKZZT
I NEED YOUR HELP.
...WHAT...? WAIT...
WHAT AM...I... DOING?
OH... OH, GOD...I REMEMBER... OH, GOD...
THAT BASTARD. MADE ME THINK...
THERE'S NO TIME FOR THIS.
WHERE ARE WE?
A SECRET LAB...UNDER THE BEACH HOUSE...

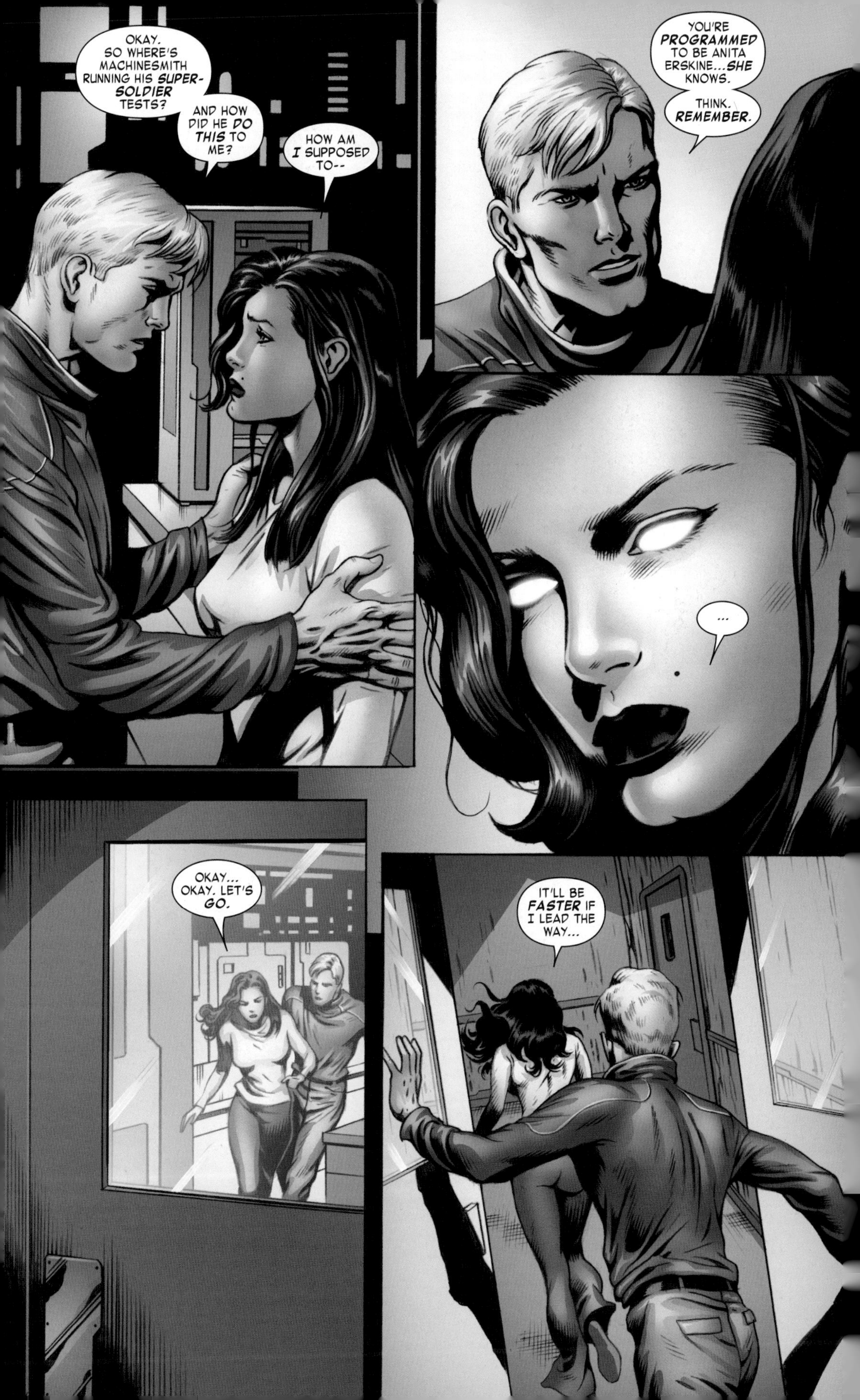
OKAY. SO WHERE'S MACHINESMITH RUNNING HIS SUPER-SOLDIER TESTS?
AND HOW DID HE DO THIS TO ME?
HOW AM I SUPPOSED TO--
YOU'RE PROGRAMMED TO BE ANITA ERSKINE...SHE KNOWS.
THINK. REMEMBER.
...
OKAY... OKAY. LET'S GO.
IT'LL BE FASTER IF I LEAD THE WAY...

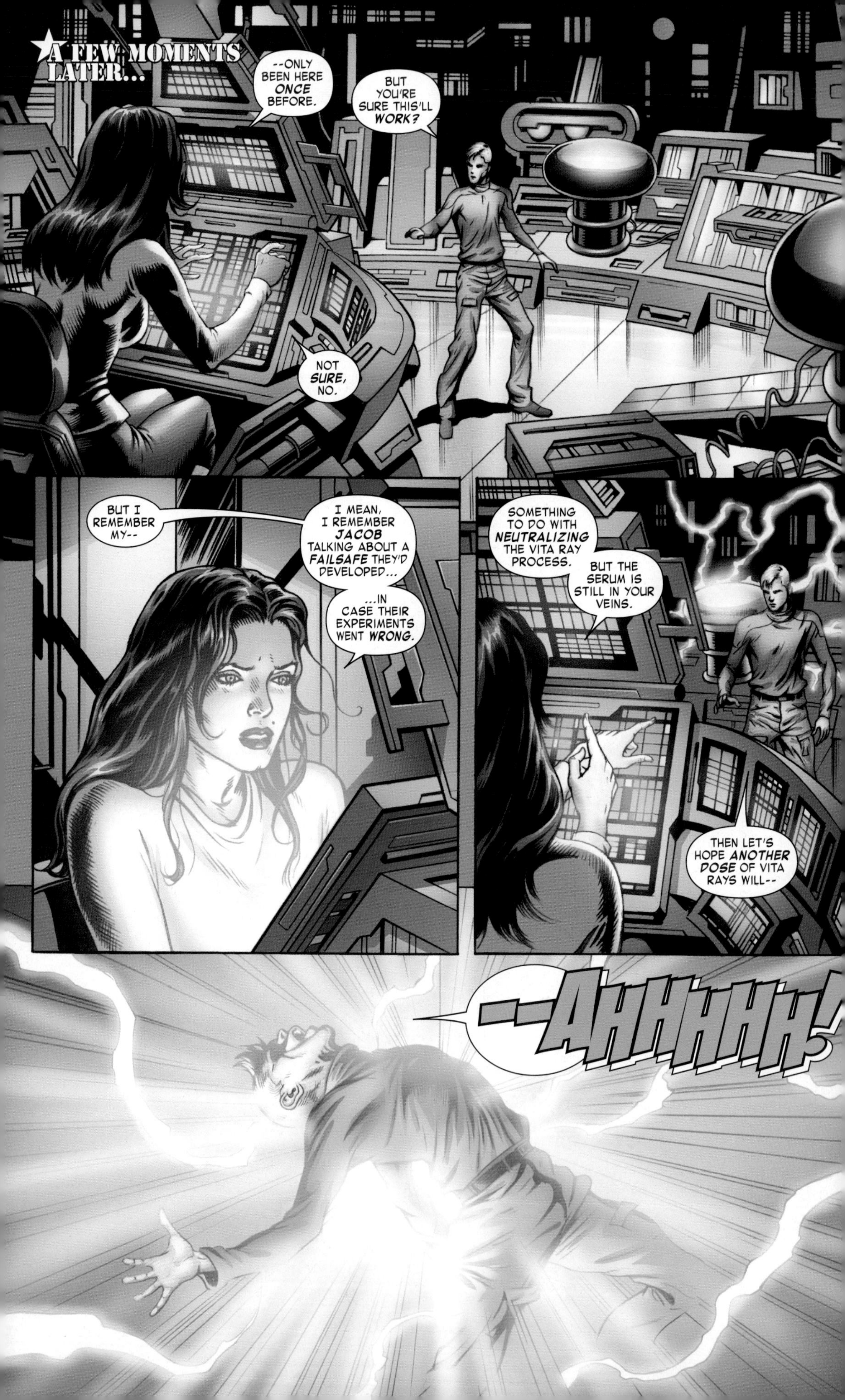
A FEW MOMENTS LATER...
--ONLY BEEN HERE ONCE BEFORE.
BUT YOU'RE SURE THIS'LL WORK?
NOT SURE, NO.
BUT I REMEMBER MY--
I MEAN, I REMEMBER JACOB TALKING ABOUT A FAILSAFE THEY'D DEVELOPED...
...IN CASE THEIR EXPERIMENTS WENT WRONG.
SOMETHING TO DO WITH NEUTRALIZING THE VITA RAY PROCESS.
BUT THE SERUM IS STILL IN YOUR VEINS.
THEN LET'S HOPE ANOTHER DOSE OF VITA RAYS WILL--
--AHHHHH!

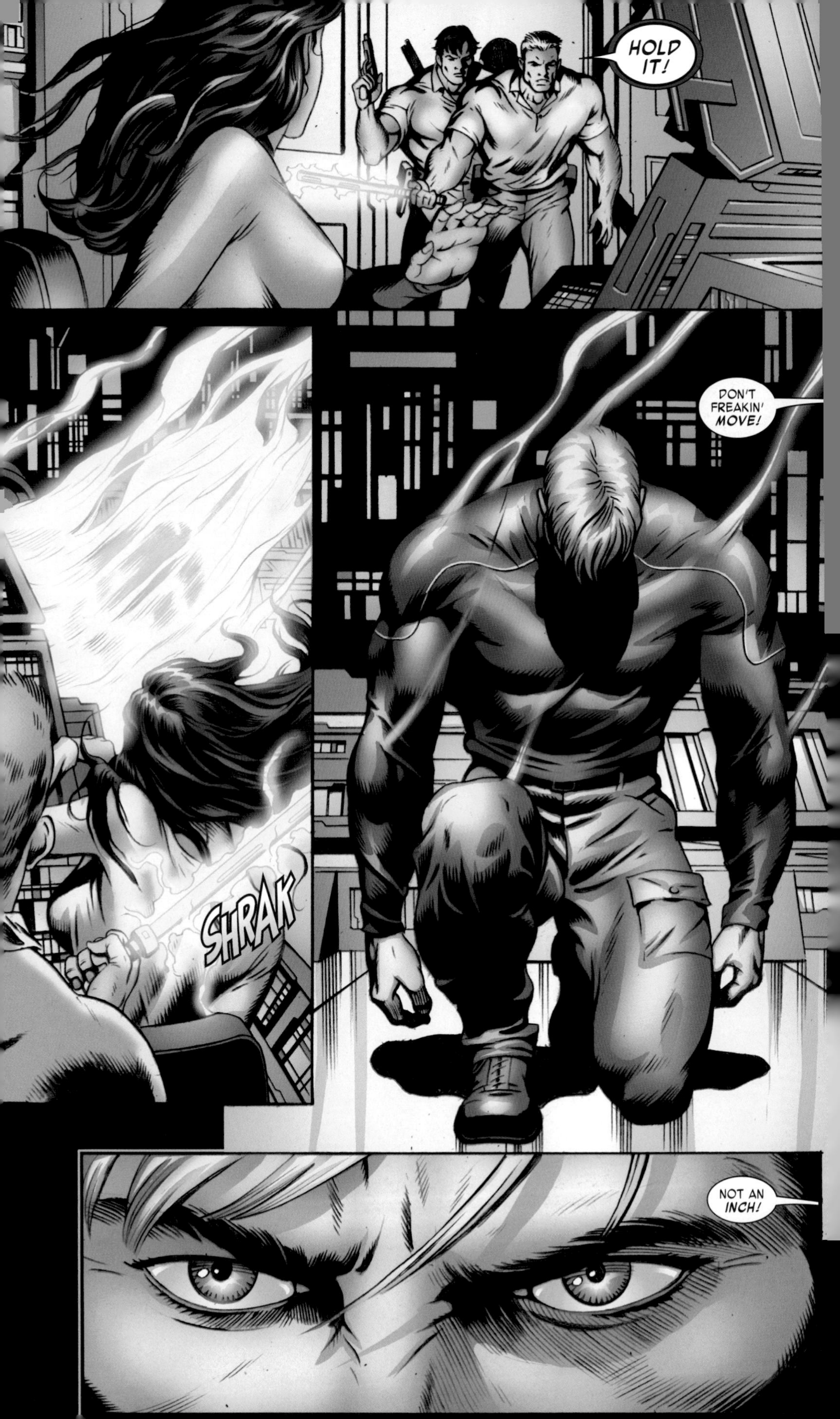
HOLD IT!
DON'T FREAKIN' MOVE!
SHRAK
NOT AN INCH!

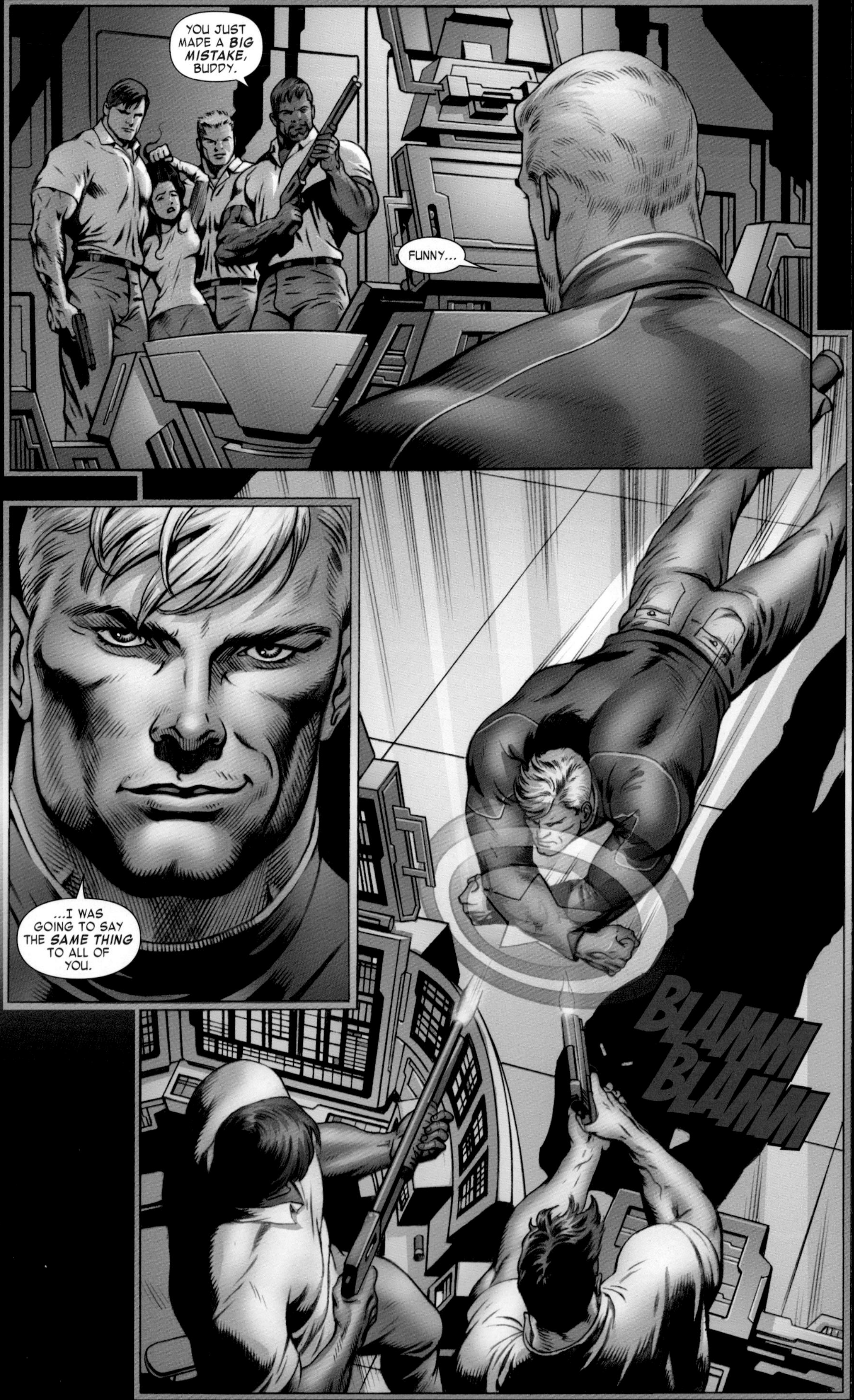
YOU JUST MADE A BIG MISTAKE, BUDDY.
FUNNY...
...I WAS GOING TO SAY THE SAME THING TO ALL OF YOU.
BLAMM
BLAMM

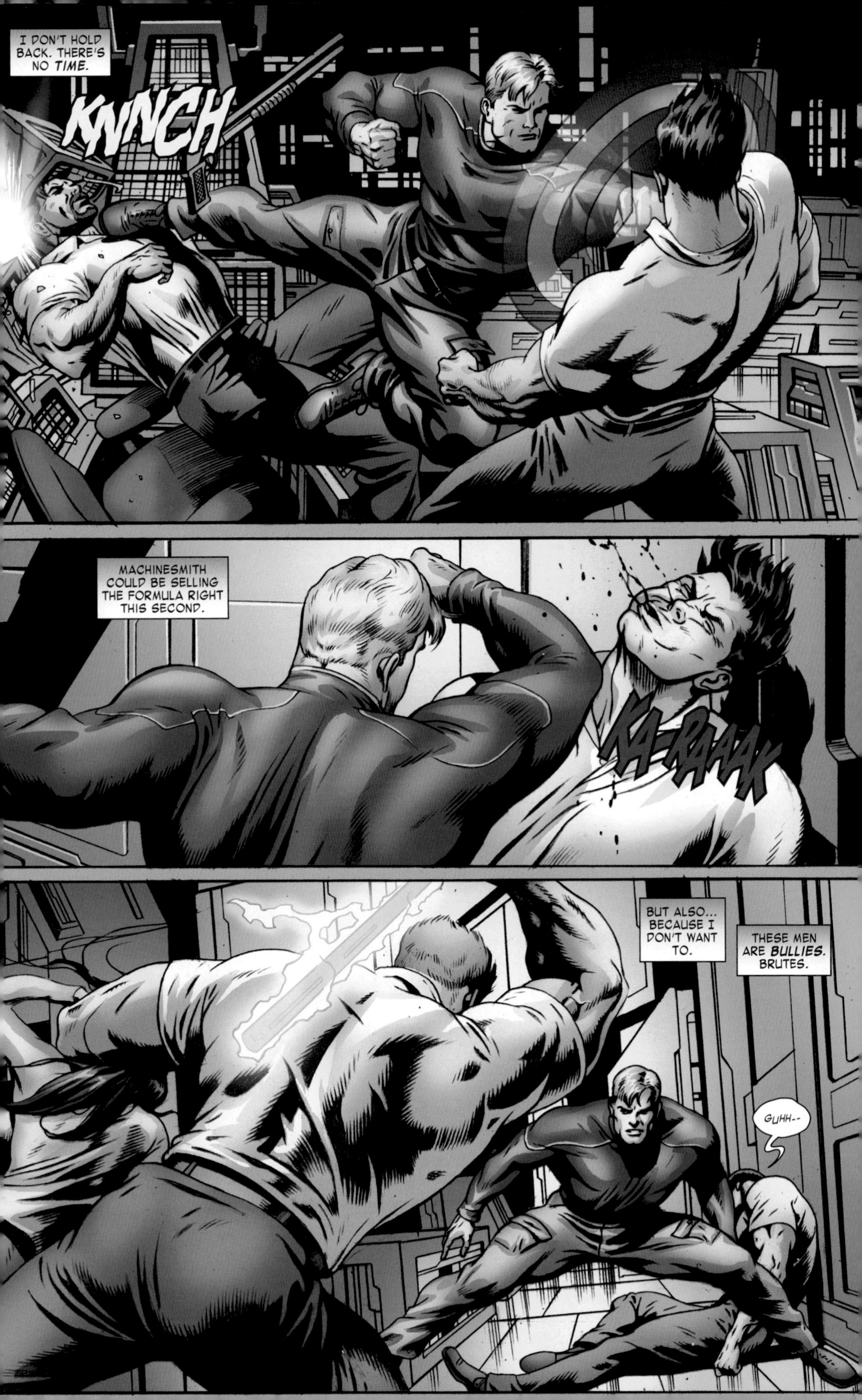
I DON'T HOLD BACK. THERE'S NO TIME.
KNNCH
MACHINESMITH COULD BE SELLING THE FORMULA RIGHT THIS SECOND.
KA-RAAAK
BUT ALSO... BECAUSE I DON'T WANT TO.
THESE MEN ARE BULLIES. BRUTES.
GUHH--

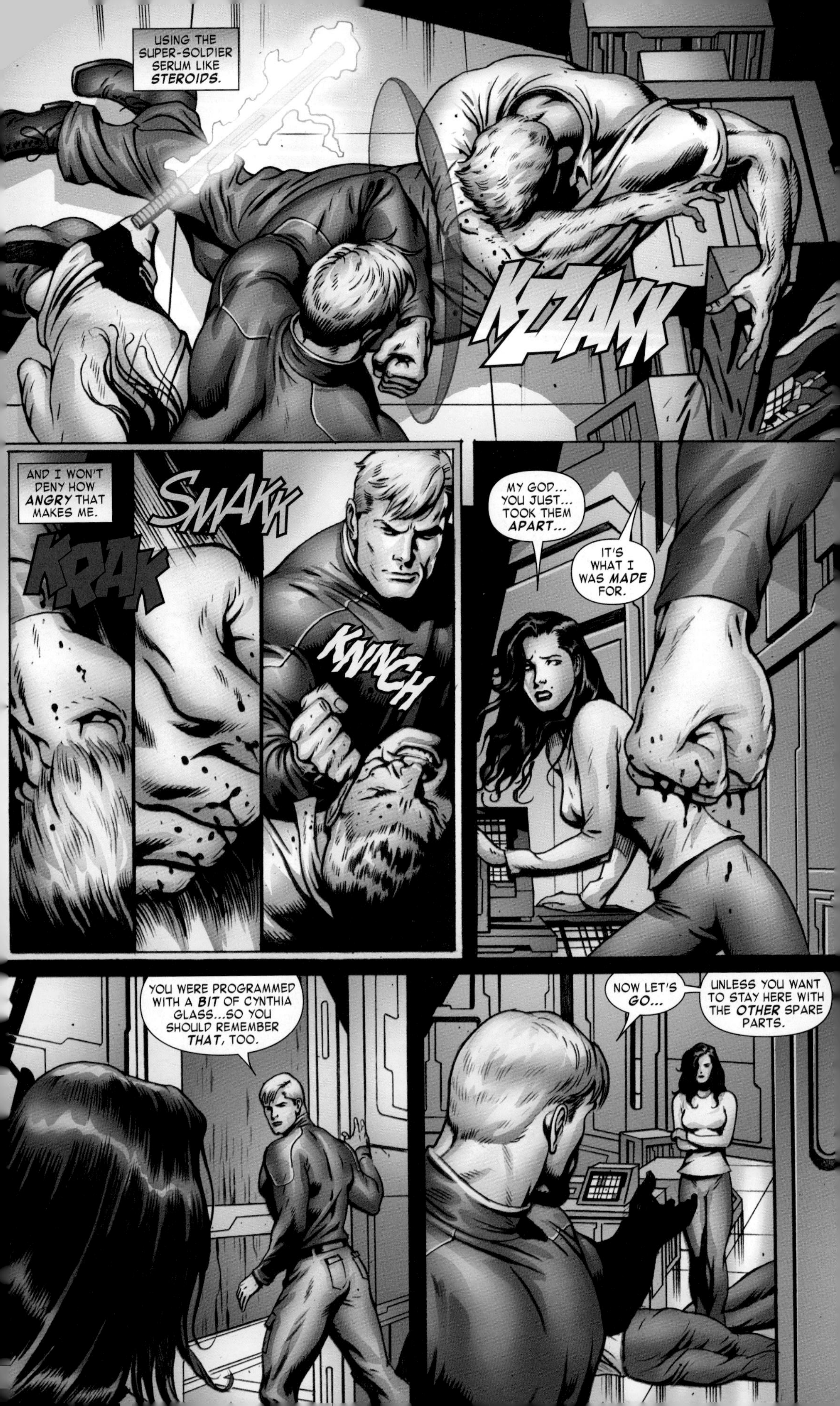
USING THE SUPER-SOLDIER SERUM LIKE STEROIDS.
KZZAKK
AND I WON'T DENY HOW ANGRY THAT MAKES ME.
SMAKK
KRAK
KNNCH
MY GOD... YOU JUST... TOOK THEM APART...
IT'S WHAT I WAS MADE FOR.
YOU WERE PROGRAMMED WITH A BIT OF CYNTHIA GLASS...SO YOU SHOULD REMEMBER THAT, TOO.
NOW LET'S GO...
UNLESS YOU WANT TO STAY HERE WITH THE OTHER SPARE PARTS.

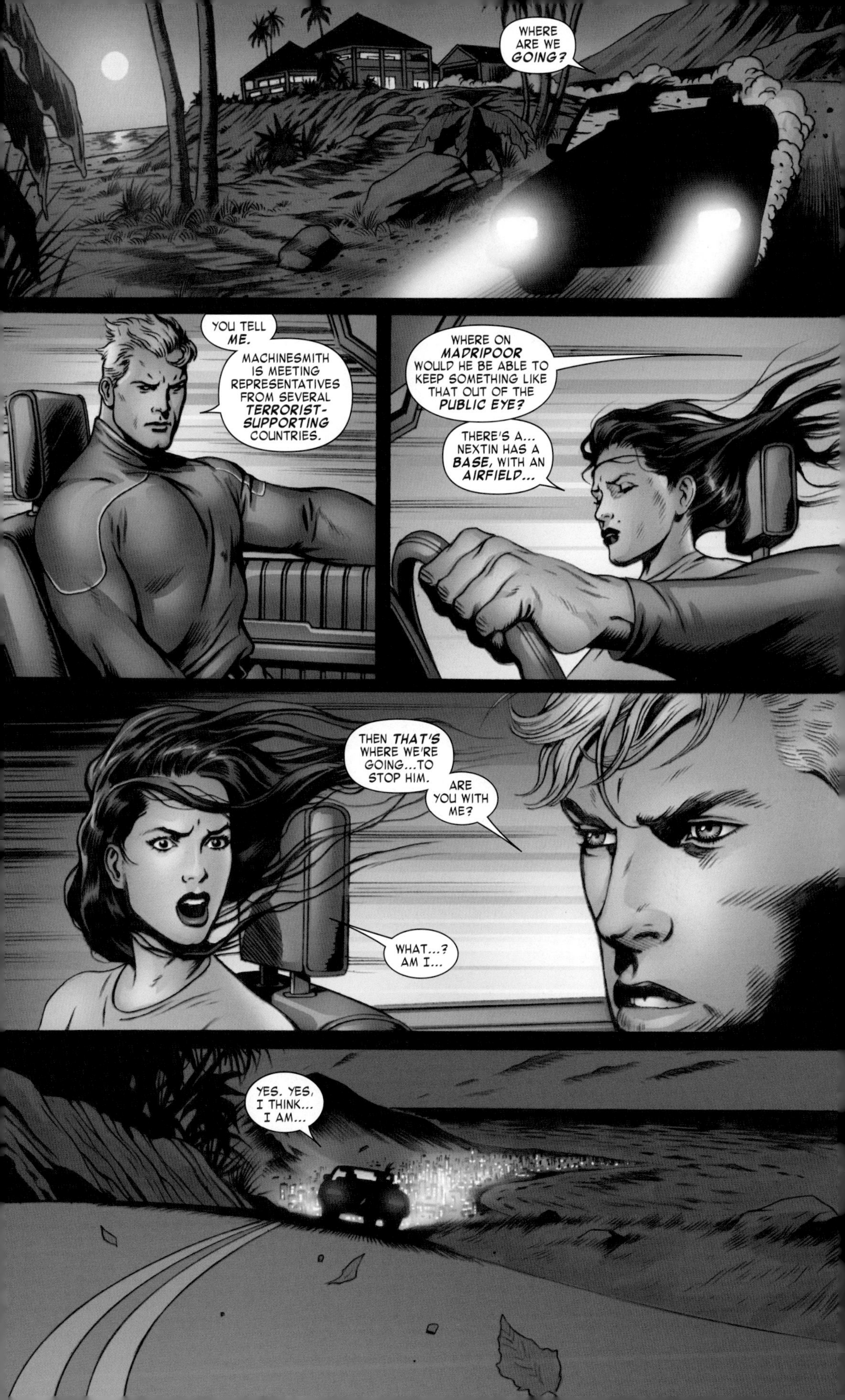
WHERE ARE WE GOING?
YOU TELL ME.
MACHINESMITH IS MEETING REPRESENTATIVES FROM SEVERAL TERRORIST-SUPPORTING COUNTRIES.
WHERE ON MADRIPOOR WOULD HE BE ABLE TO KEEP SOMETHING LIKE THAT OUT OF THE PUBLIC EYE?
THERE'S A... NEXTIN HAS A BASE, WITH AN AIRFIELD...
THEN THAT'S WHERE WE'RE GOING...TO STOP HIM.
ARE YOU WITH ME?
WHAT...? AM I...
YES. YES, I THINK... I AM...

4

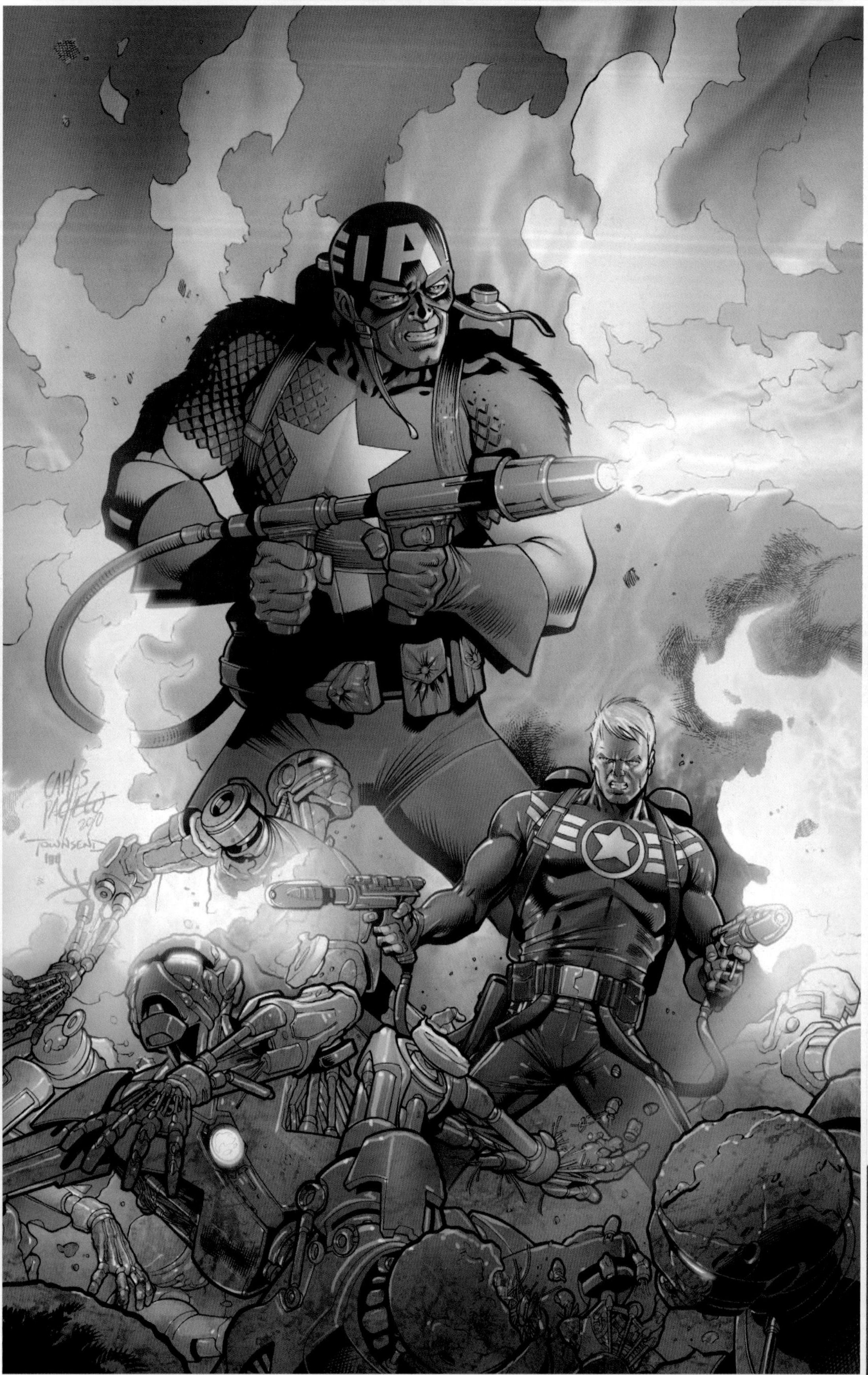
TOWNSEND

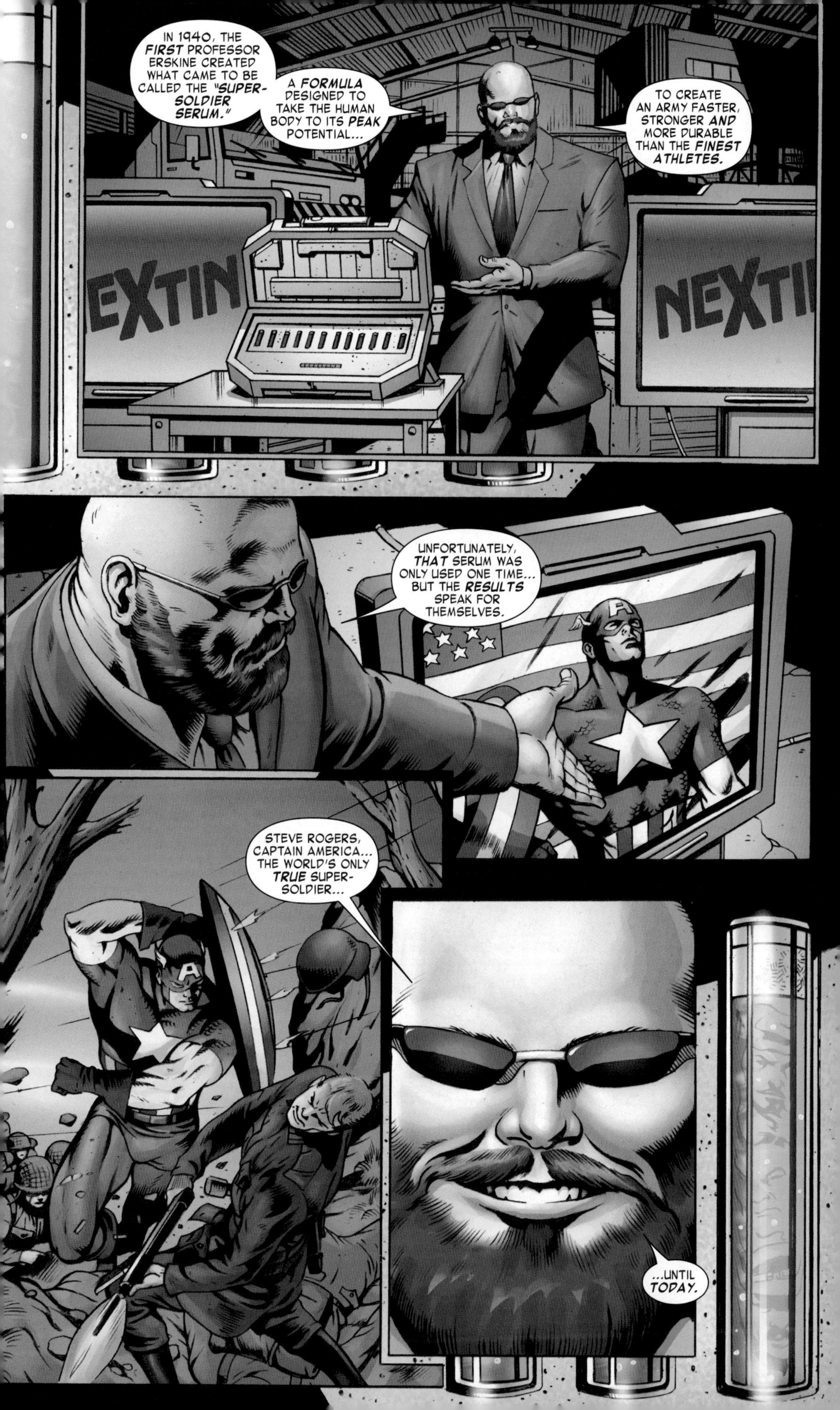
IN 1940, THE FIRST PROFESSOR ERSKINE CREATED WHAT CAME TO BE CALLED THE "SUPER-SOLDIER SERUM."
A FORMULA DESIGNED TO TAKE THE HUMAN BODY TO ITS PEAK POTENTIAL...
TO CREATE AN ARMY FASTER, STRONGER AND MORE DURABLE THAN THE FINEST ATHLETES.
NEXTIN
NEXTI
UNFORTUNATELY, THAT SERUM WAS ONLY USED ONE TIME... BUT THE RESULTS SPEAK FOR THEMSELVES.
STEVE ROGERS, CAPTAIN AMERICA... THE WORLD'S ONLY TRUE SUPER-SOLDIER...
...UNTIL TODAY.

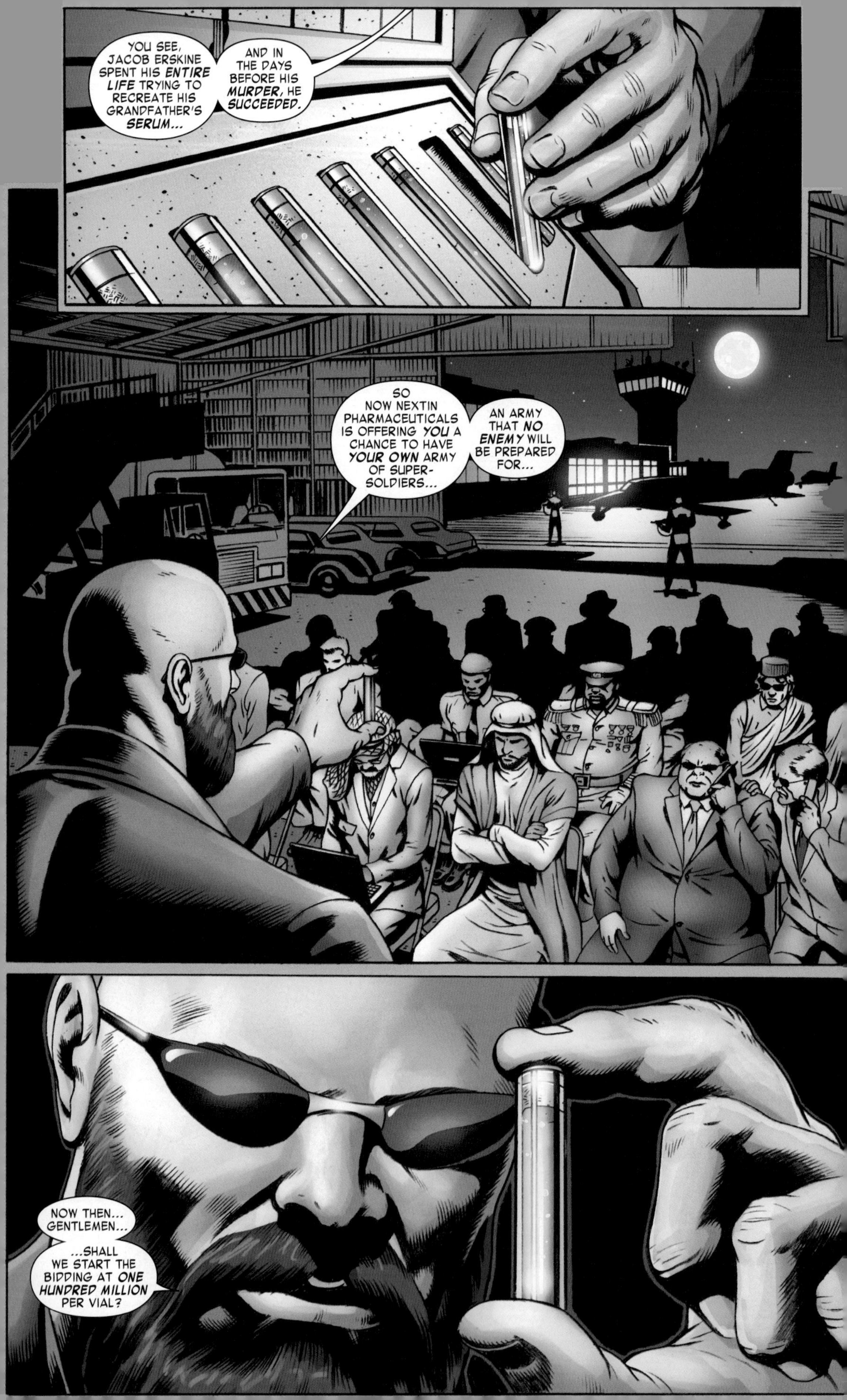
YOU SEE, JACOB ERSKINE SPENT HIS ENTIRE LIFE TRYING TO RECREATE HIS GRANDFATHER'S SERUM...
AND IN THE DAYS BEFORE HIS MURDER, HE SUCCEEDED.
SO NOW NEXTIN PHARMACEUTICALS IS OFFERING YOU A CHANCE TO HAVE YOUR OWN ARMY OF SUPER-SOLDIERS...
AN ARMY THAT NO ENEMY WILL BE PREPARED FOR...
NOW THEN... GENTLEMEN...
...SHALL WE START THE BIDDING AT ONE HUNDRED MILLION PER VIAL?

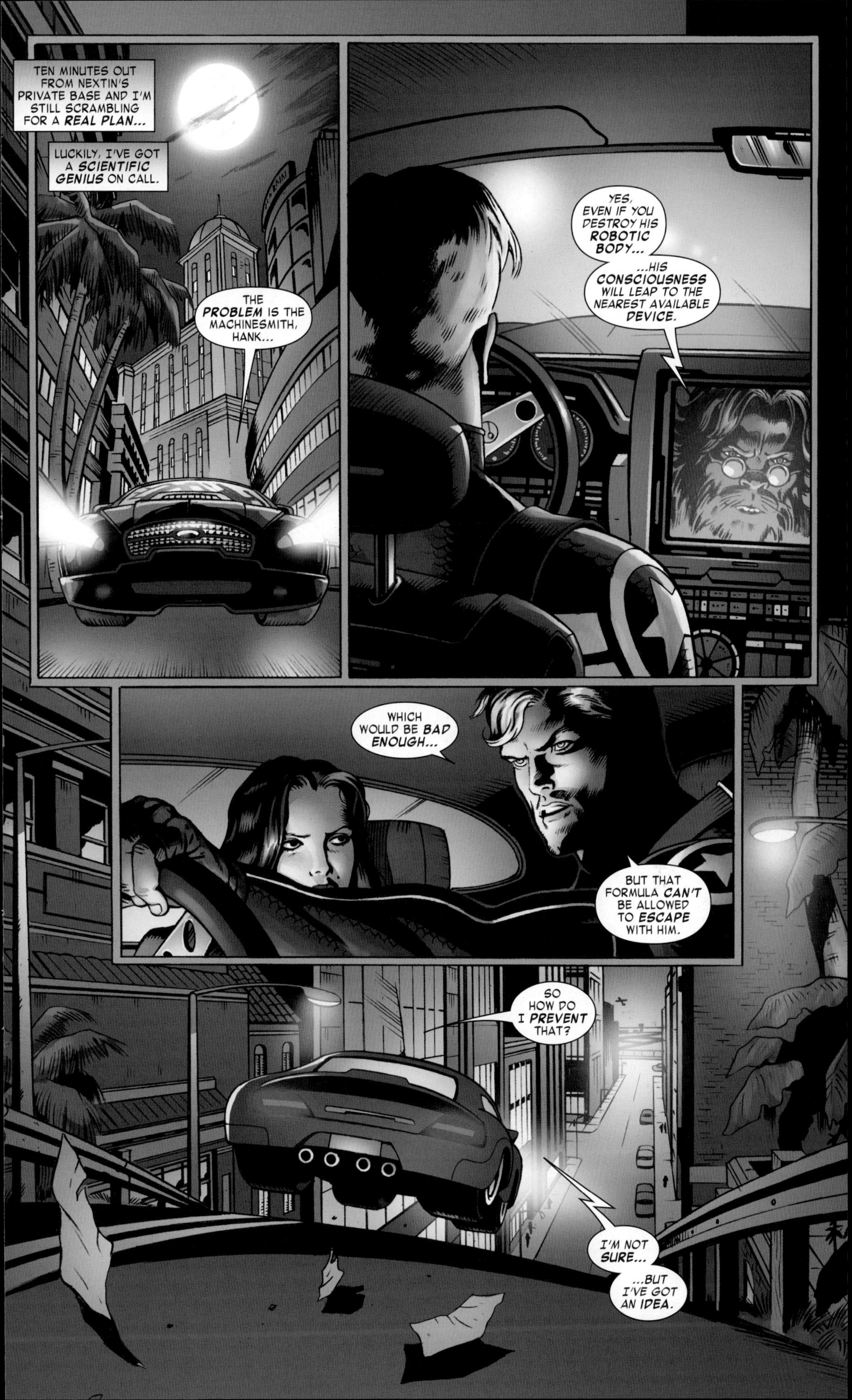
TEN MINUTES OUT FROM NEXTIN'S PRIVATE BASE AND I'M STILL SCRAMBLING FOR A REAL PLAN...
LUCKILY, I'VE GOT A SCIENTIFIC GENIUS ON CALL.
THE PROBLEM IS THE MACHINESMITH, HANK...
YES, EVEN IF YOU DESTROY HIS ROBOTIC BODY...
...HIS CONSCIOUSNESS WILL LEAP TO THE NEAREST AVAILABLE DEVICE.
WHICH WOULD BE BAD ENOUGH...
BUT THAT FORMULA CAN'T BE ALLOWED TO ESCAPE WITH HIM.
SO HOW DO I PREVENT THAT?
I'M NOT SURE...
...BUT I'VE GOT AN IDEA.

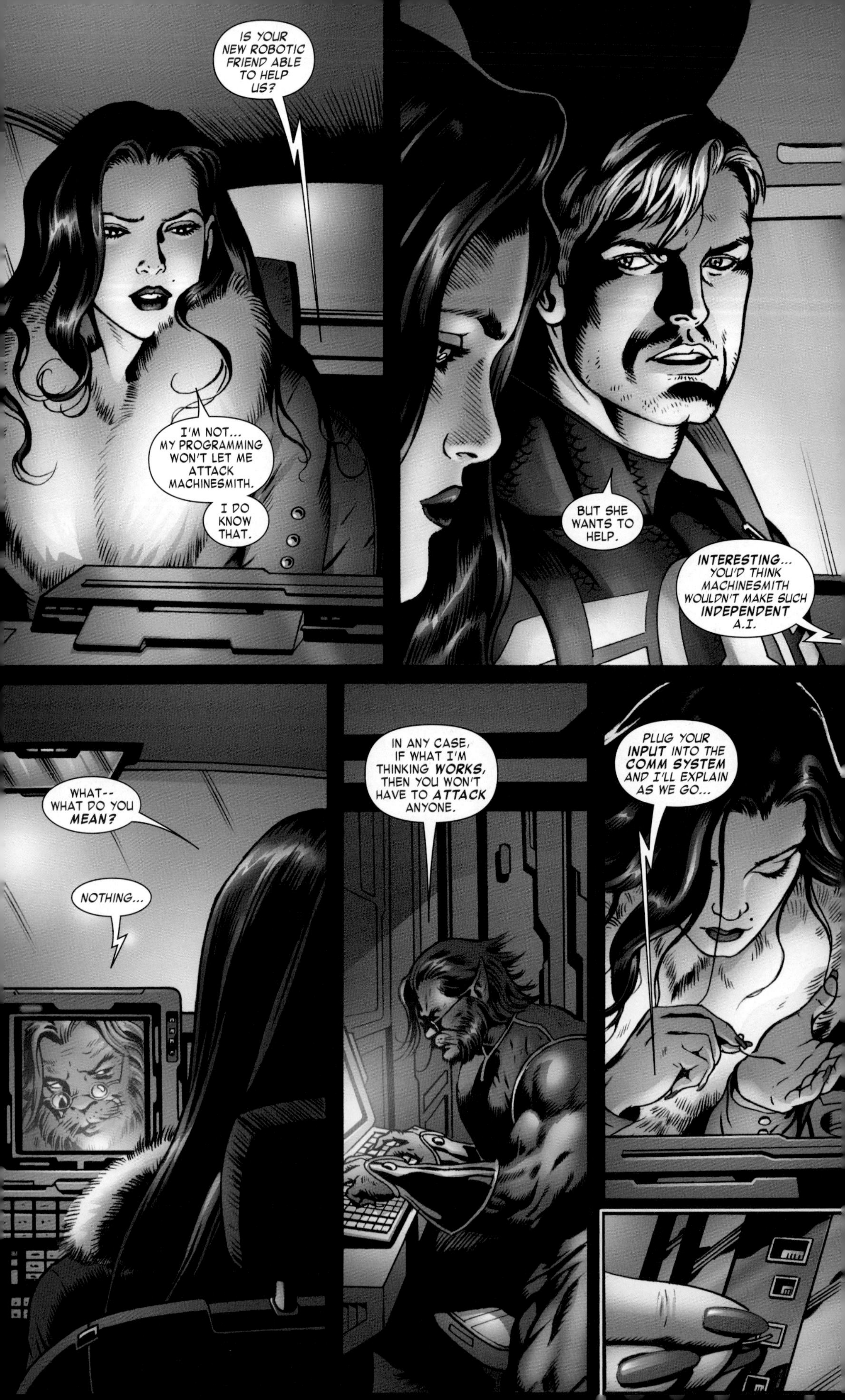
IS YOUR NEW ROBOTIC FRIEND ABLE TO HELP US?
I'M NOT... MY PROGRAMMING WON'T LET ME ATTACK MACHINESMITH.
I DO KNOW THAT.
BUT SHE WANTS TO HELP.
INTERESTING... YOU'D THINK MACHINESMITH WOULDN'T MAKE SUCH INDEPENDENT A.I.
WHAT-- WHAT DO YOU MEAN?
NOTHING...
IN ANY CASE, IF WHAT I'M THINKING WORKS, THEN YOU WON'T HAVE TO ATTACK ANYONE.
PLUG YOUR INPUT INTO THE COMM SYSTEM AND I'LL EXPLAIN AS WE GO...

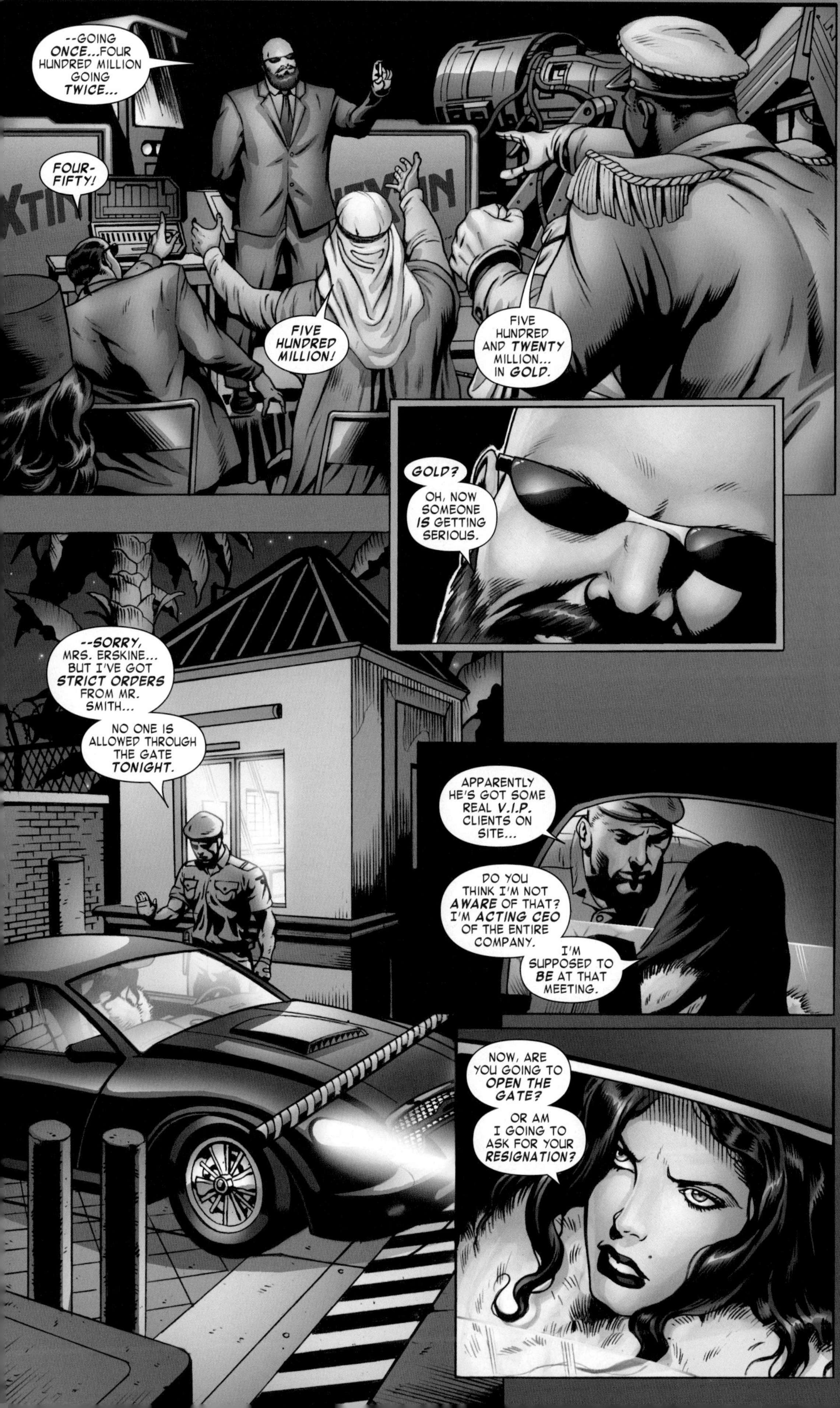
--GOING ONCE...FOUR HUNDRED MILLION GOING TWICE...
FOUR-FIFTY!
FIVE HUNDRED MILLION!
FIVE HUNDRED AND TWENTY MILLION... IN GOLD.
GOLD?
OH, NOW SOMEONE IS GETTING SERIOUS.
--SORRY, MRS. ERSKINE... BUT I'VE GOT STRICT ORDERS FROM MR. SMITH...
NO ONE IS ALLOWED THROUGH THE GATE TONIGHT.
APPARENTLY HE'S GOT SOME REAL V.I.P. CLIENTS ON SITE...
DO YOU THINK I'M NOT AWARE OF THAT? I'M ACTING CEO OF THE ENTIRE COMPANY.
I'M SUPPOSED TO BE AT THAT MEETING.
NOW, ARE YOU GOING TO OPEN THE GATE?
OR AM I GOING TO ASK FOR YOUR RESIGNATION?

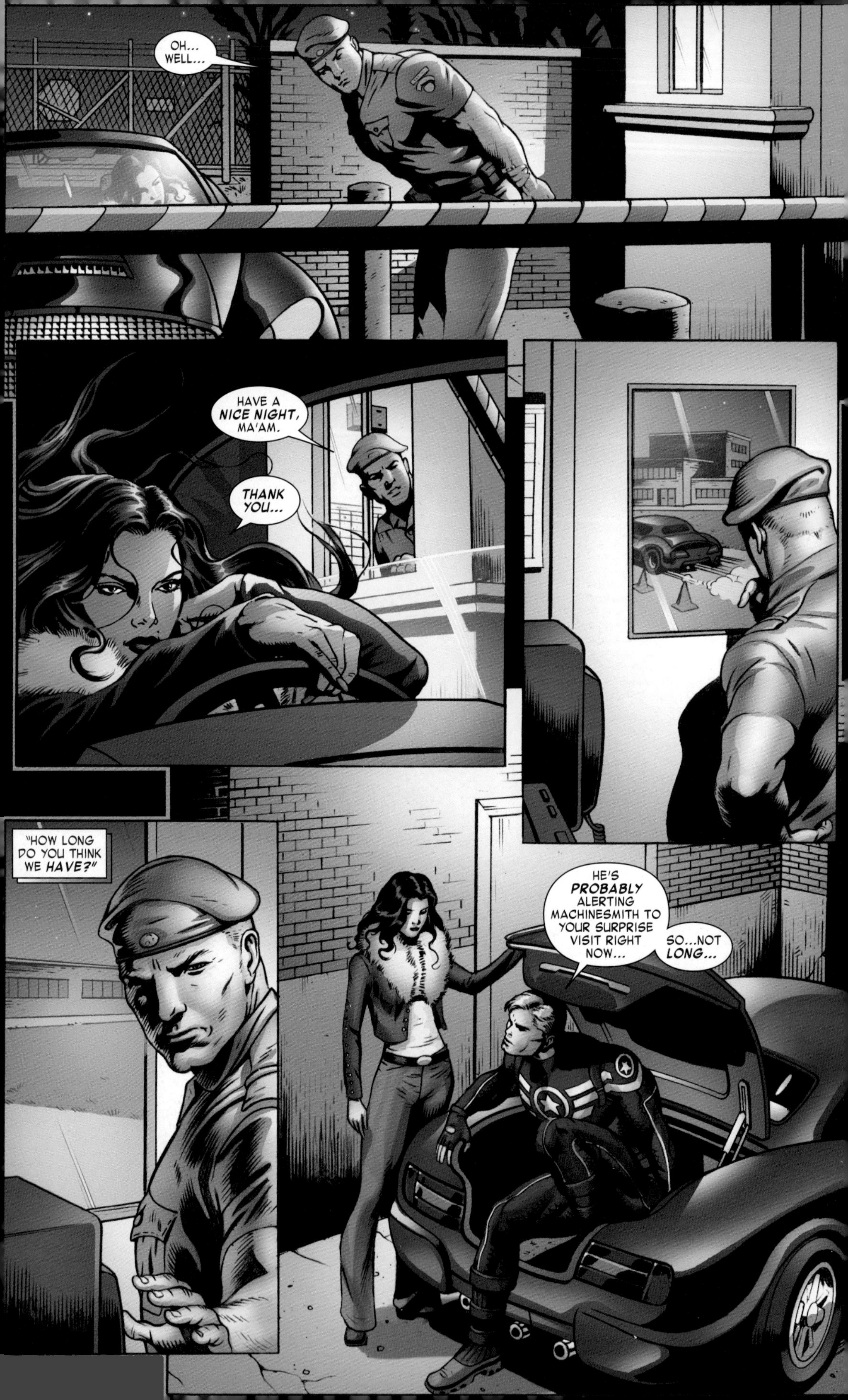
OH... WELL...
HAVE A NICE NIGHT, MA'AM.
THANK YOU...
"HOW LONG DO YOU THINK WE HAVE?"
HE'S PROBABLY ALERTING MACHINESMITH TO YOUR SURPRISE VISIT RIGHT NOW...
SO...NOT LONG...

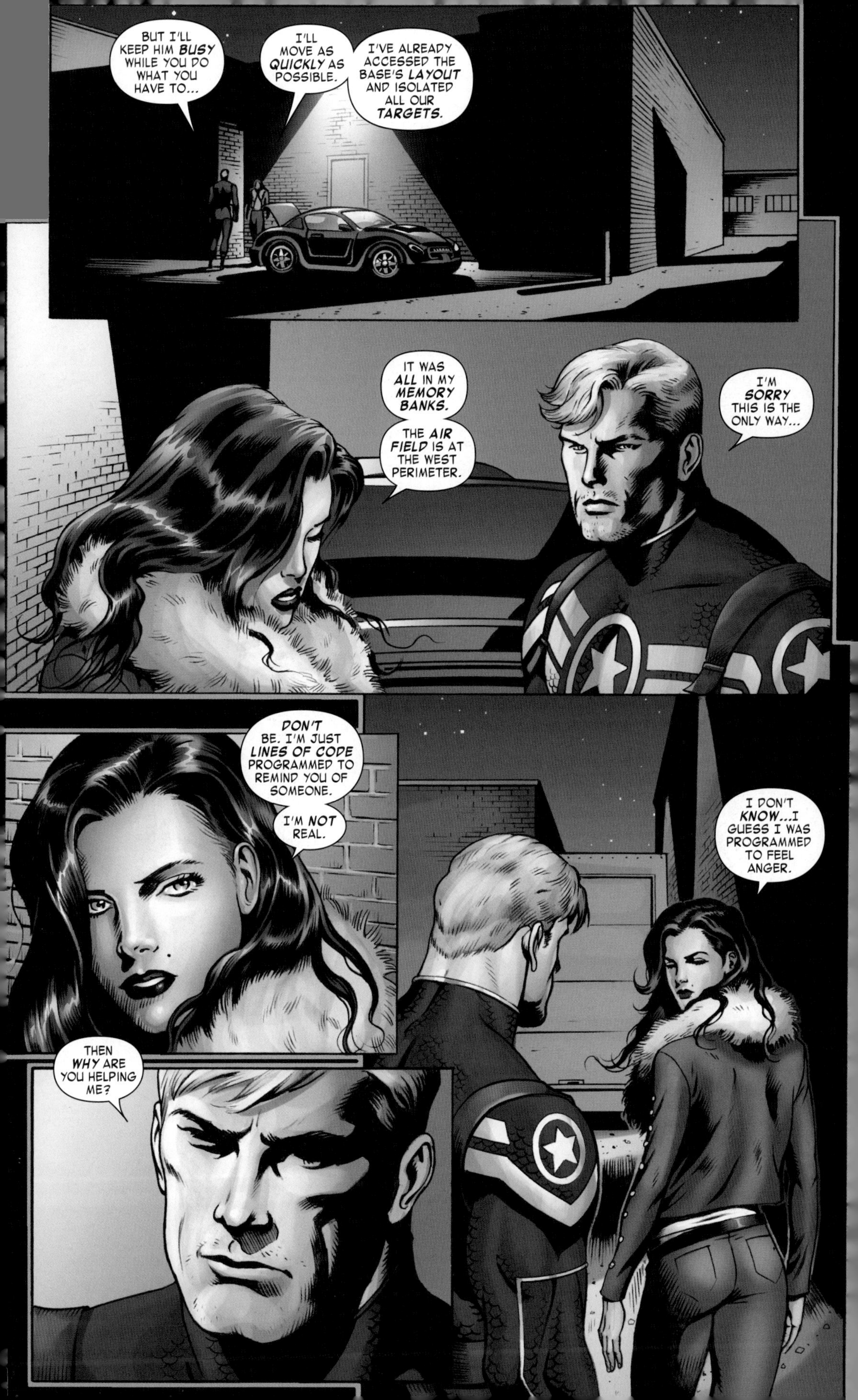
BUT I'LL KEEP HIM BUSY WHILE YOU DO WHAT YOU HAVE TO...
I'LL MOVE AS QUICKLY AS POSSIBLE.
I'VE ALREADY ACCESSED THE BASE'S LAYOUT AND ISOLATED ALL OUR TARGETS.
IT WAS ALL IN MY MEMORY BANKS.
THE AIR FIELD IS AT THE WEST PERIMETER.
I'M SORRY THIS IS THE ONLY WAY...
DON'T BE. I'M JUST LINES OF CODE PROGRAMMED TO REMIND YOU OF SOMEONE.
I'M NOT REAL.
THEN WHY ARE YOU HELPING ME?
I DON'T KNOW...I GUESS I WAS PROGRAMMED TO FEEL ANGER.

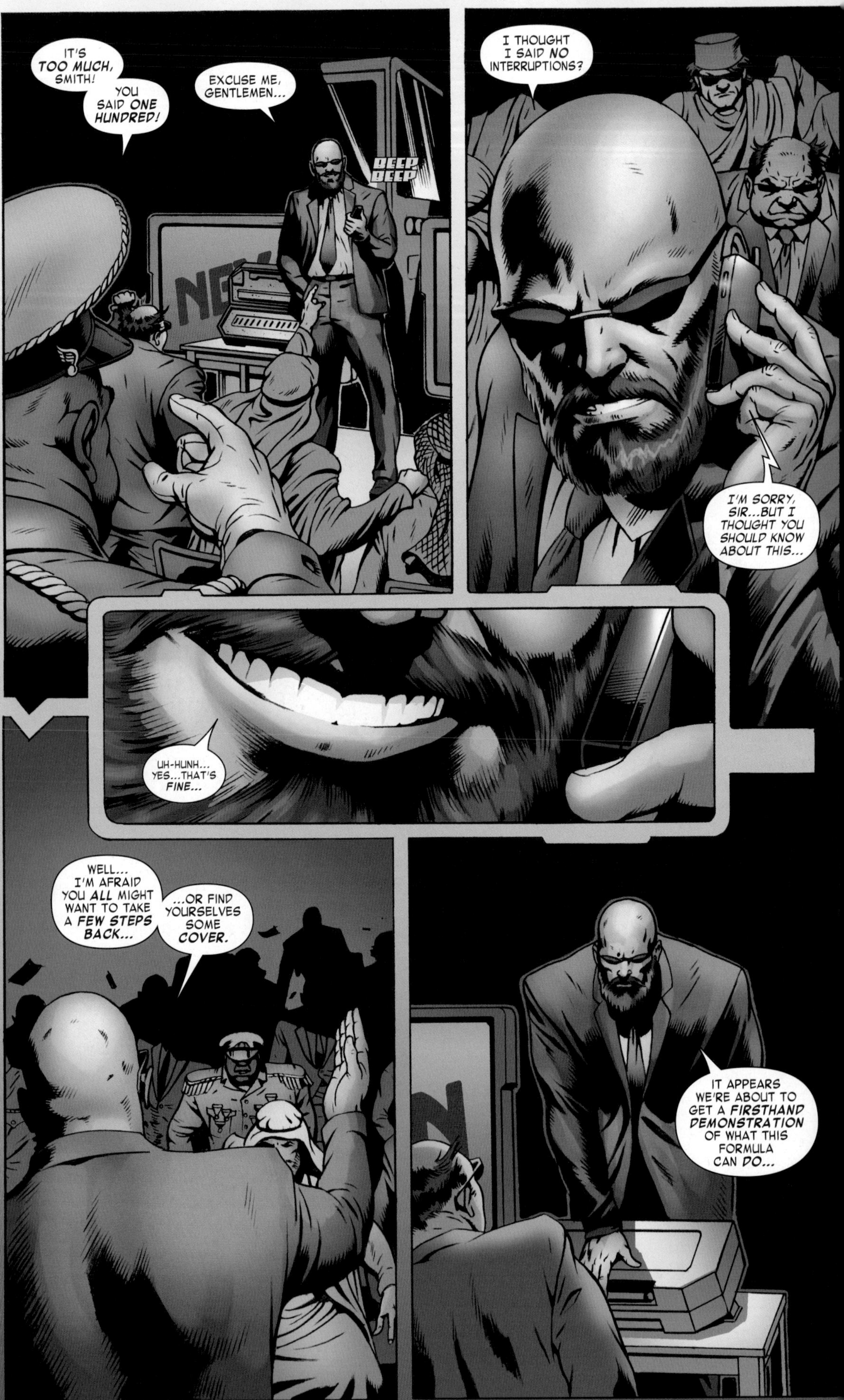

IT'S TOO MUCH, SMITH!
YOU SAID ONE HUNDRED!
EXCUSE ME, GENTLEMEN...
BEEP BEEP
I THOUGHT I SAID NO INTERRUPTIONS?
I'M SORRY, SIR...BUT I THOUGHT YOU SHOULD KNOW ABOUT THIS...
UH-HUNH... YES...THAT'S FINE...
WELL... I'M AFRAID YOU ALL MIGHT WANT TO TAKE A FEW STEPS BACK...
...OR FIND YOURSELVES SOME COVER.
IT APPEARS WE'RE ABOUT TO GET A FIRSTHAND DEMONSTRATION OF WHAT THIS FORMULA CAN DO...

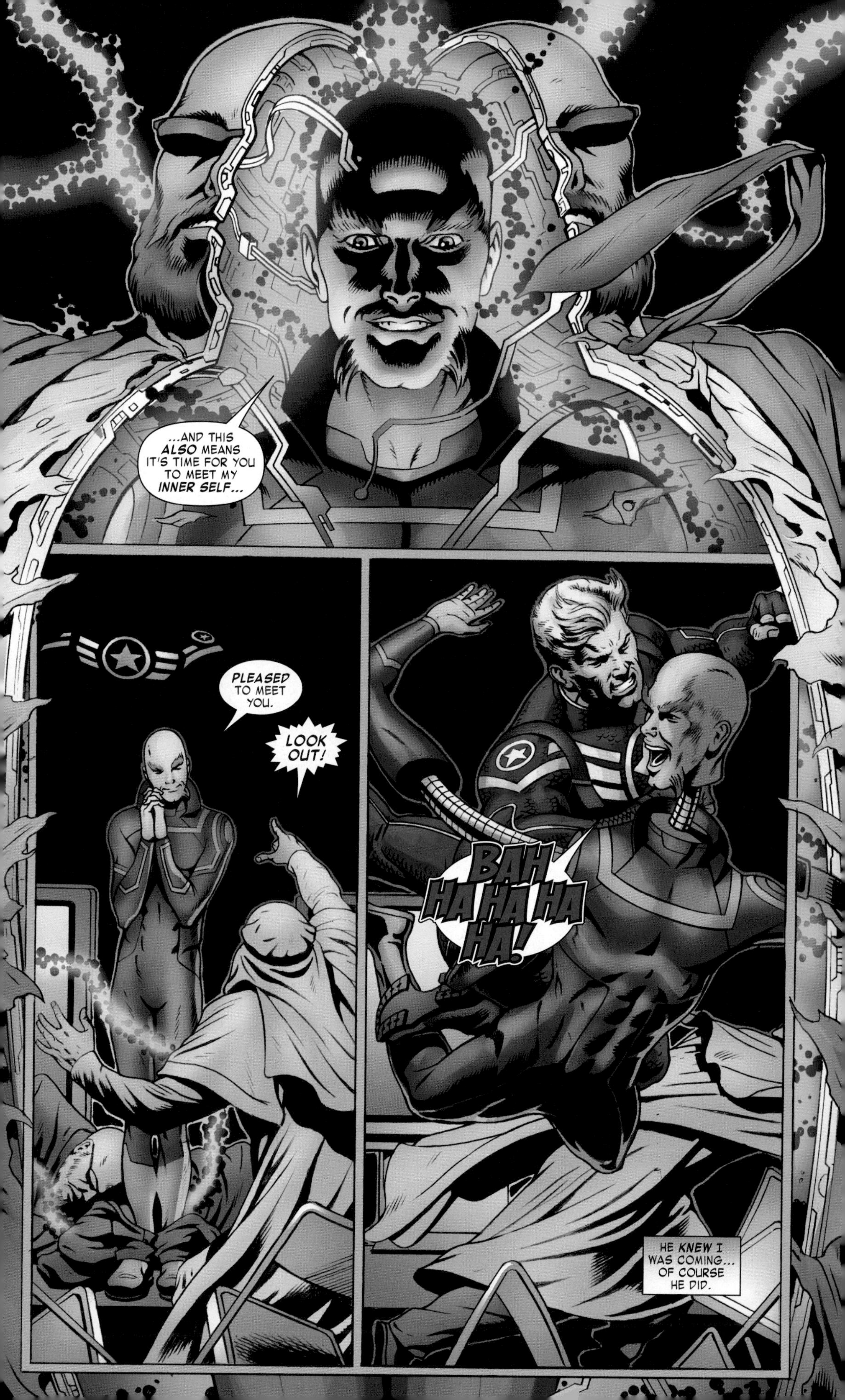
...AND THIS ALSO MEANS IT'S TIME FOR YOU TO MEET MY INNER SELF...
PLEASED TO MEET YOU.
LOOK OUT!
BAH HA HA HA HA!
HE KNEW I WAS COMING... OF COURSE HE DID.

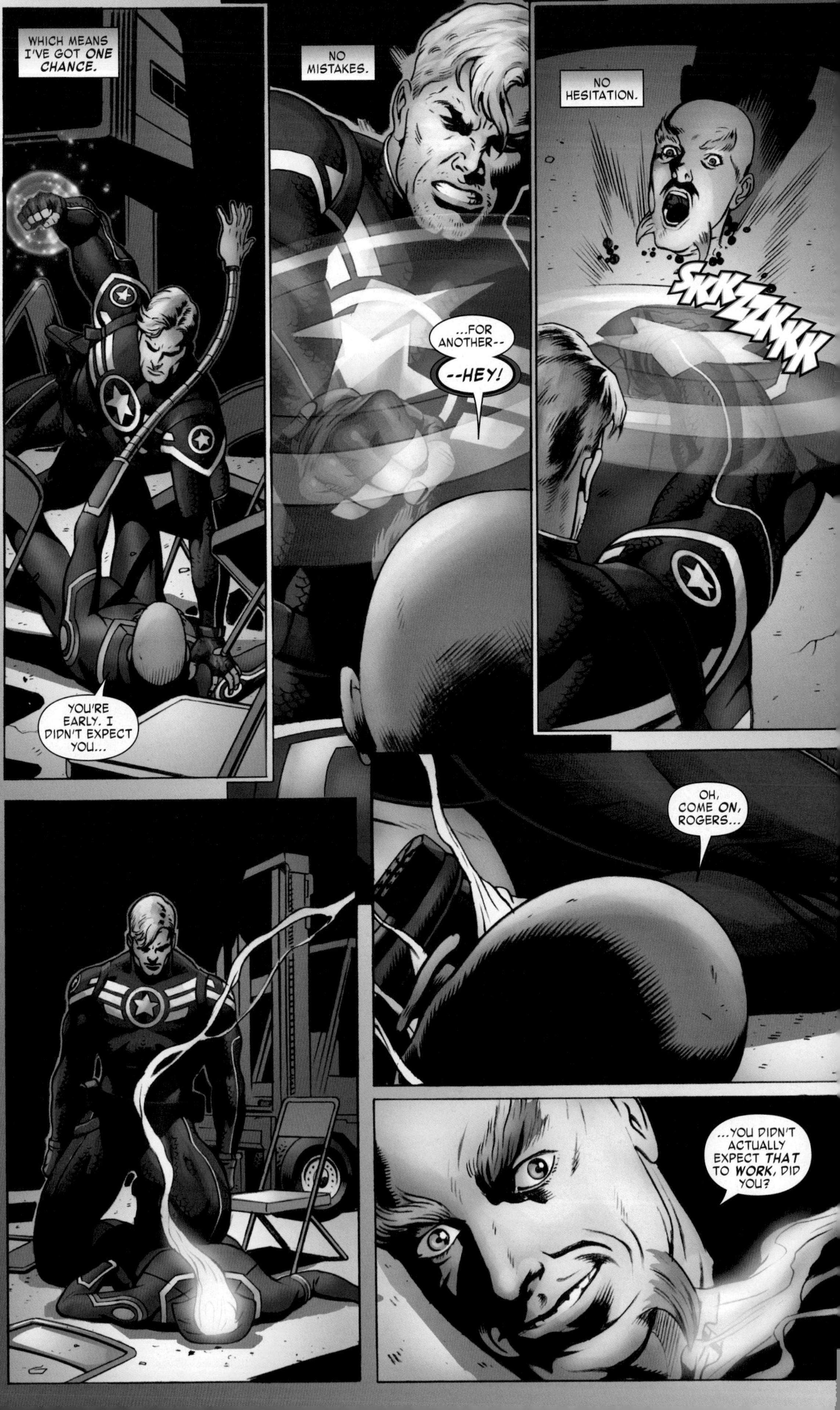
WHICH MEANS I'VE GOT ONE CHANCE.
YOU'RE EARLY. I DIDN'T EXPECT YOU...
NO MISTAKES.
...FOR ANOTHER--
--HEY!
NO HESITATION.
SKKZZNKKK
OH, COME ON, ROGERS...
...YOU DIDN'T ACTUALLY EXPECT THAT TO WORK, DID YOU?

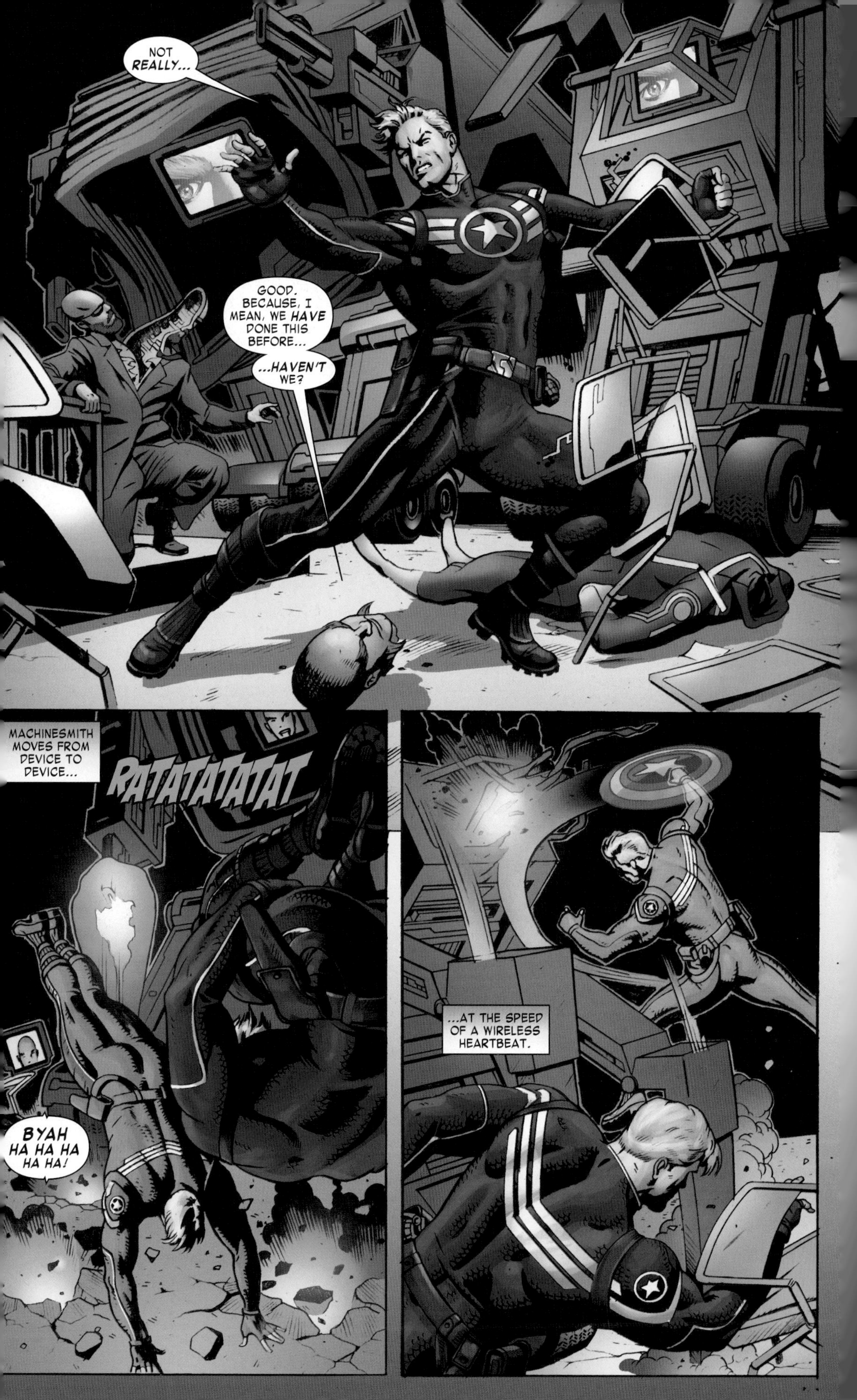
NOT REALLY...
GOOD. BECAUSE, I MEAN, WE HAVE DONE THIS BEFORE...
...HAVEN'T WE?
MACHINESMITH MOVES FROM DEVICE TO DEVICE...
RATATATATAT
BYAH HA HA HA HA HA!
...AT THE SPEED OF A WIRELESS HEARTBEAT.

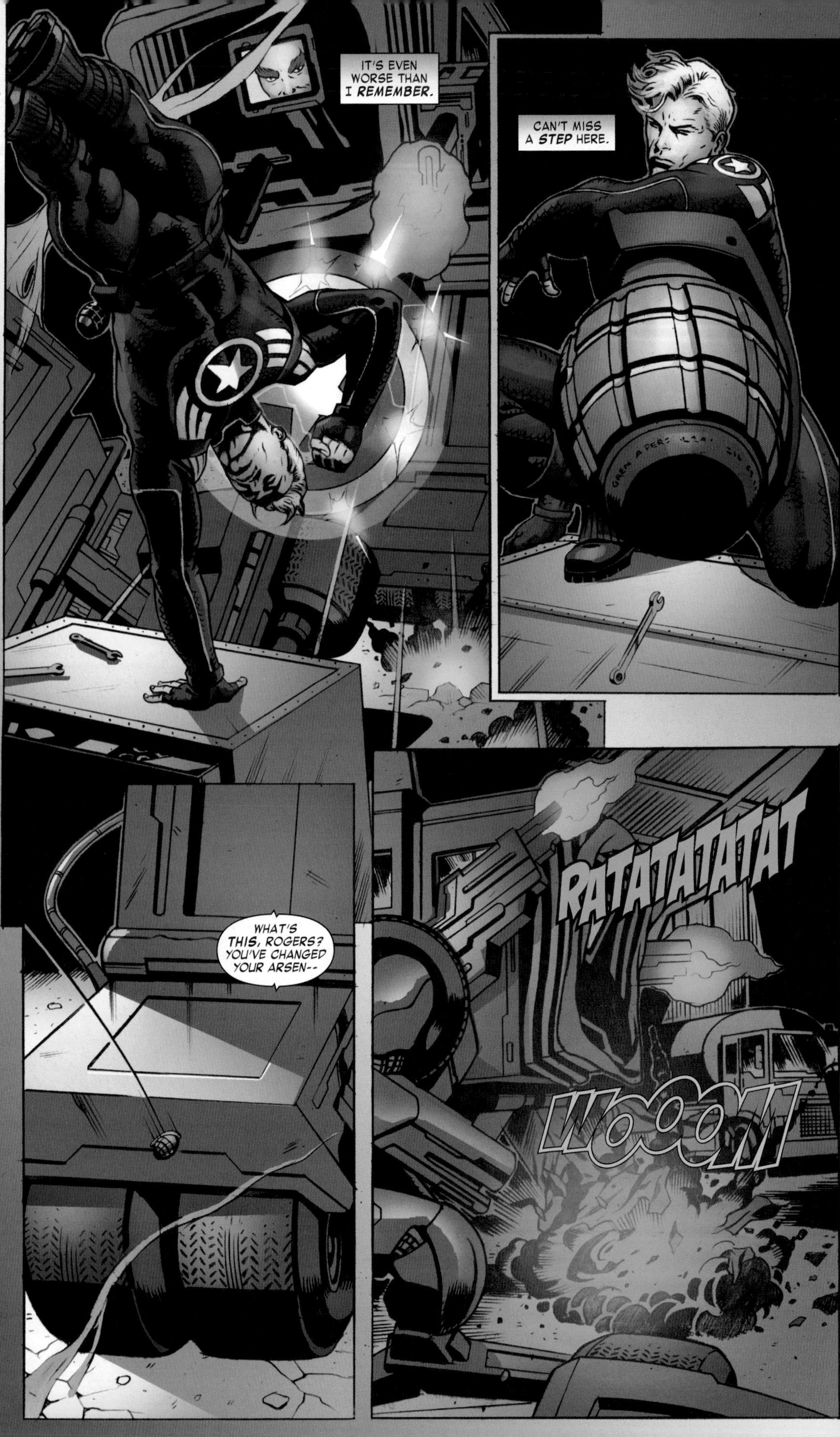
IT'S EVEN WORSE THAN I REMEMBER.
CAN'T MISS A STEP HERE.
WHAT'S THIS, ROGERS? YOU'VE CHANGED YOUR ARSEN--
RATATATATAT
WOOOM

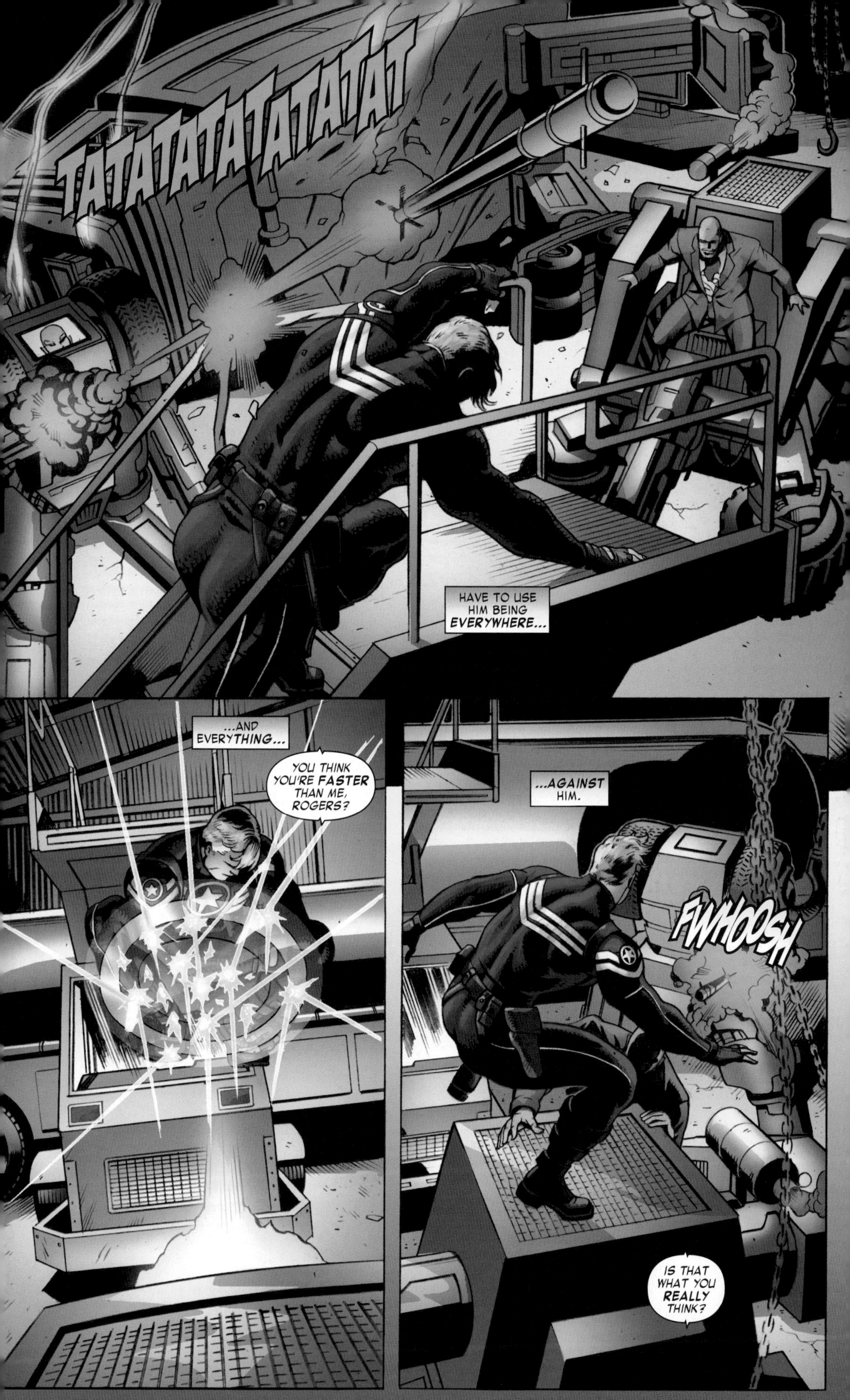
TATATATATATATAT
HAVE TO USE HIM BEING EVERYWHERE...
...AND EVERYTHING...
YOU THINK YOU'RE FASTER THAN ME, ROGERS?
...AGAINST HIM.
FWHOOSH
IS THAT WHAT YOU REALLY THINK?

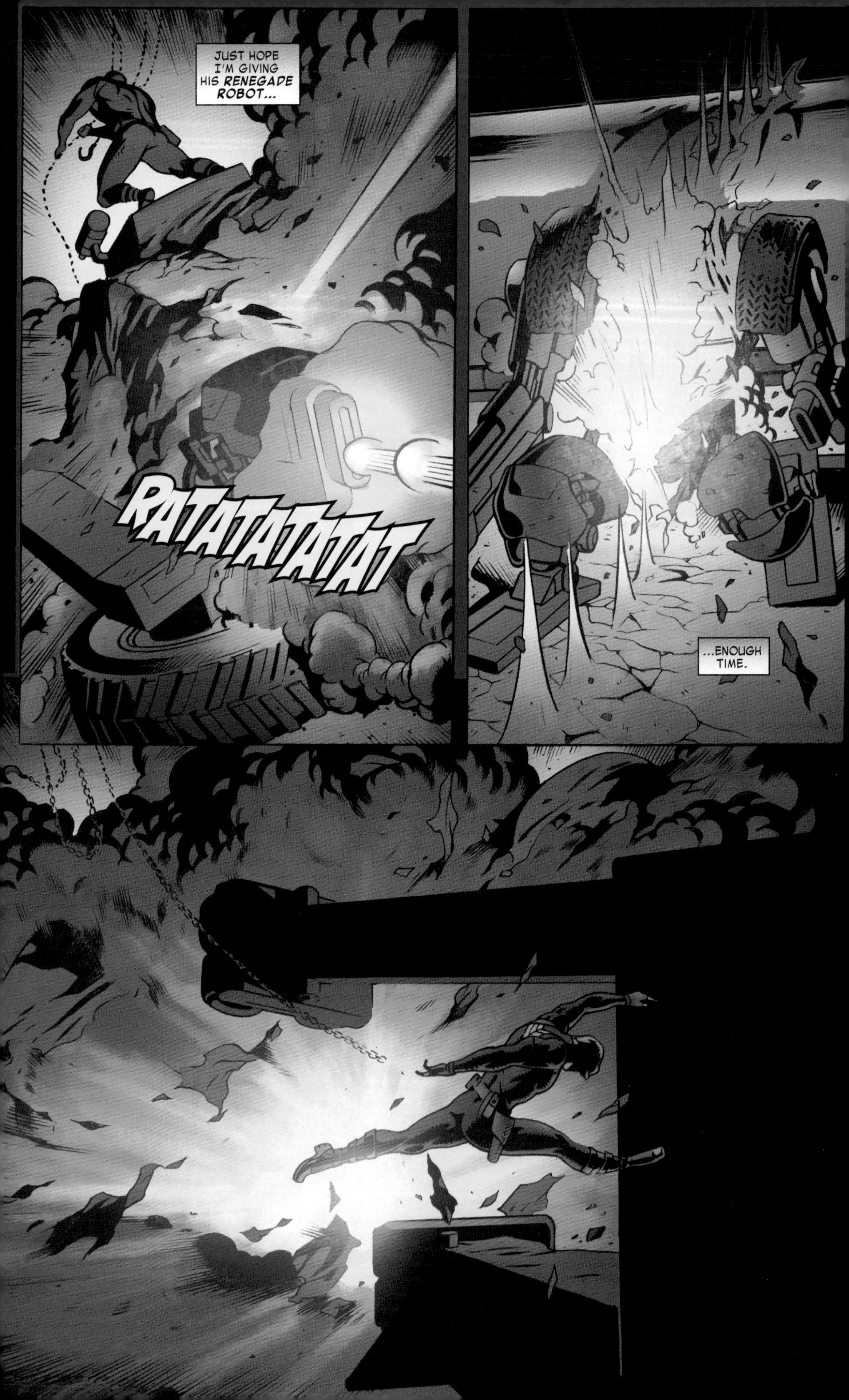
JUST HOPE I'M GIVING HIS RENEGADE ROBOT...
RATATATATAT
...ENOUGH TIME.

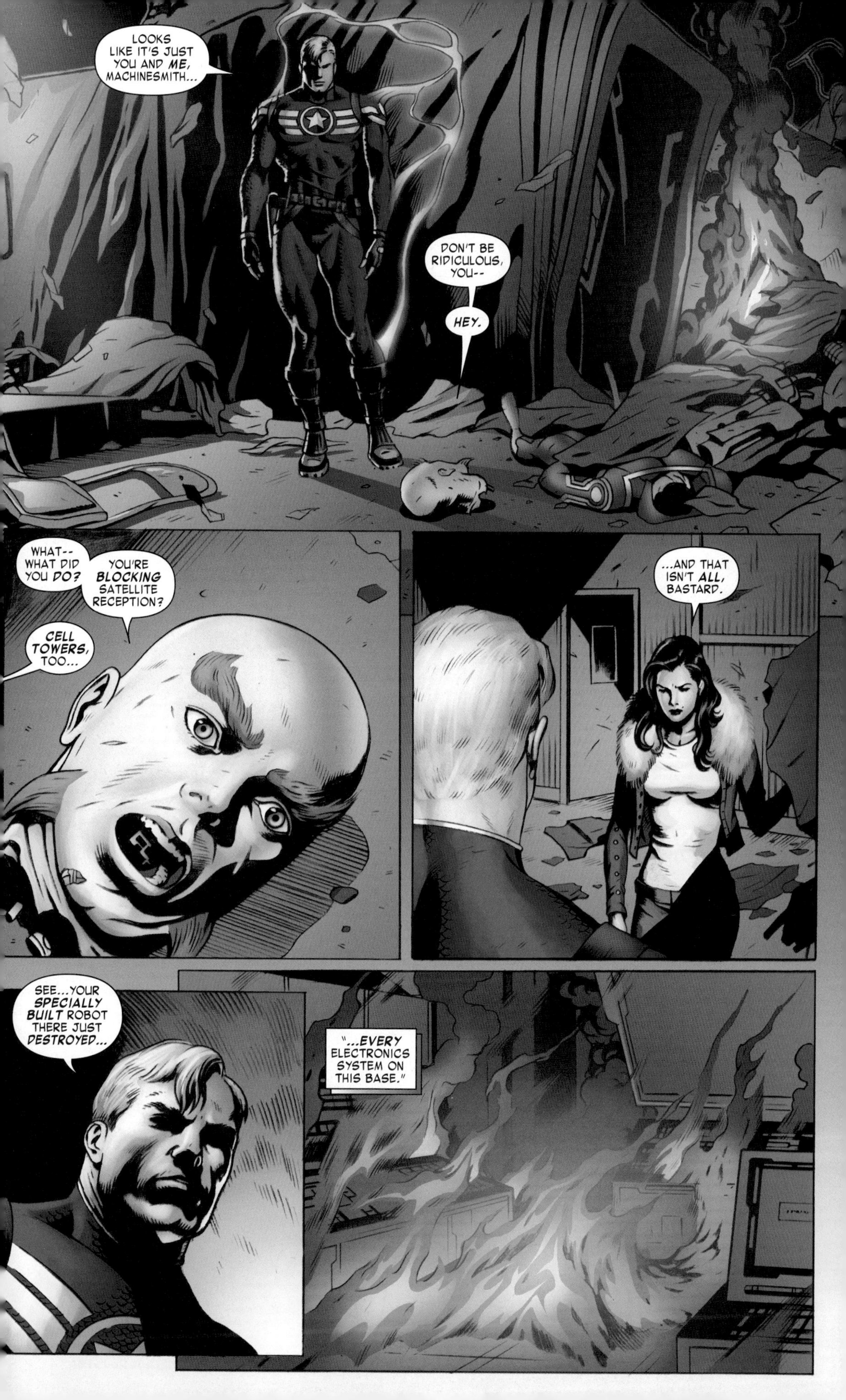

LOOKS LIKE IT'S JUST YOU AND ME, MACHINESMITH...
DON'T BE RIDICULOUS, YOU--
HEY.
WHAT-- WHAT DID YOU DO?
YOU'RE BLOCKING SATELLITE RECEPTION?
CELL TOWERS, TOO...
...AND THAT ISN'T ALL, BASTARD.
SEE...YOUR SPECIALLY BUILT ROBOT THERE JUST DESTROYED...
"...EVERY ELECTRONICS SYSTEM ON THIS BASE."

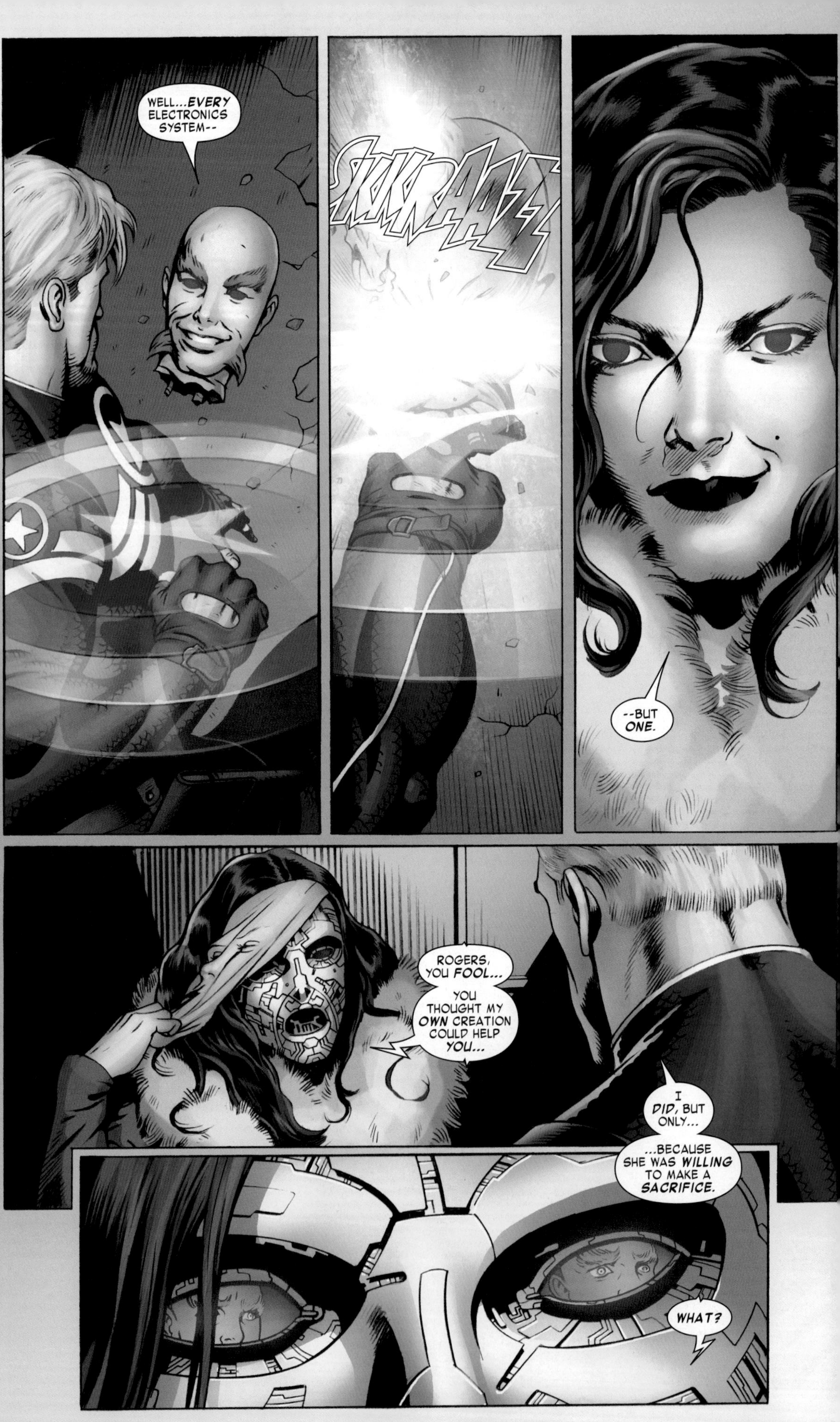
WELL...EVERY ELECTRONICS SYSTEM--
SKKRAAZZ
--BUT ONE.
ROGERS, YOU FOOL...
YOU THOUGHT MY OWN CREATION COULD HELP YOU...
I DID, BUT ONLY...
...BECAUSE SHE WAS WILLING TO MAKE A SACRIFICE.
WHAT?

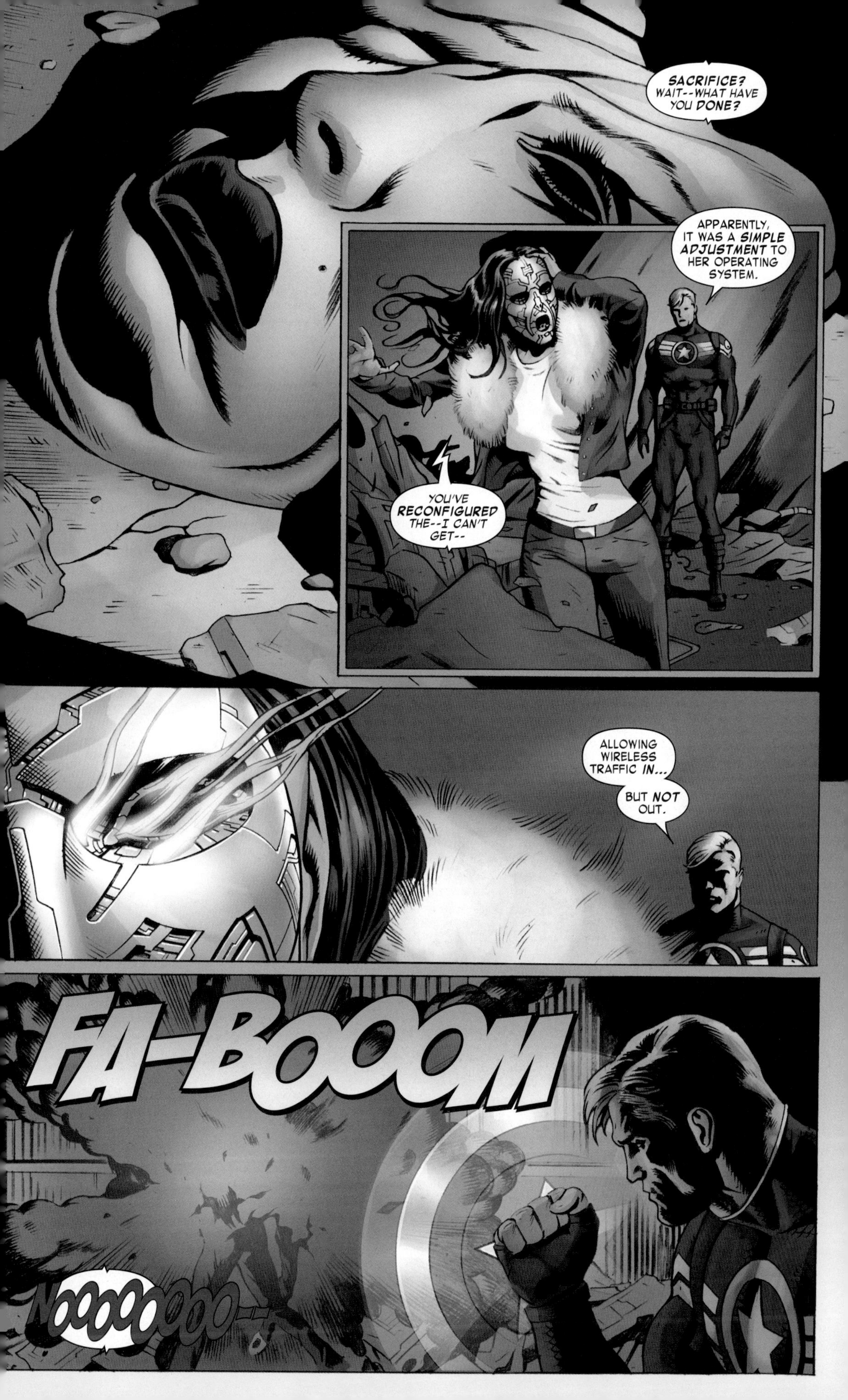
SACRIFICE? WAIT--WHAT HAVE YOU DONE?
APPARENTLY, IT WAS A SIMPLE ADJUSTMENT TO HER OPERATING SYSTEM.
YOU'VE RECONFIGURED THE--I CAN'T GET--
ALLOWING WIRELESS TRAFFIC IN...
BUT NOT OUT.
FA-BOOOM
NOOOOOOOO

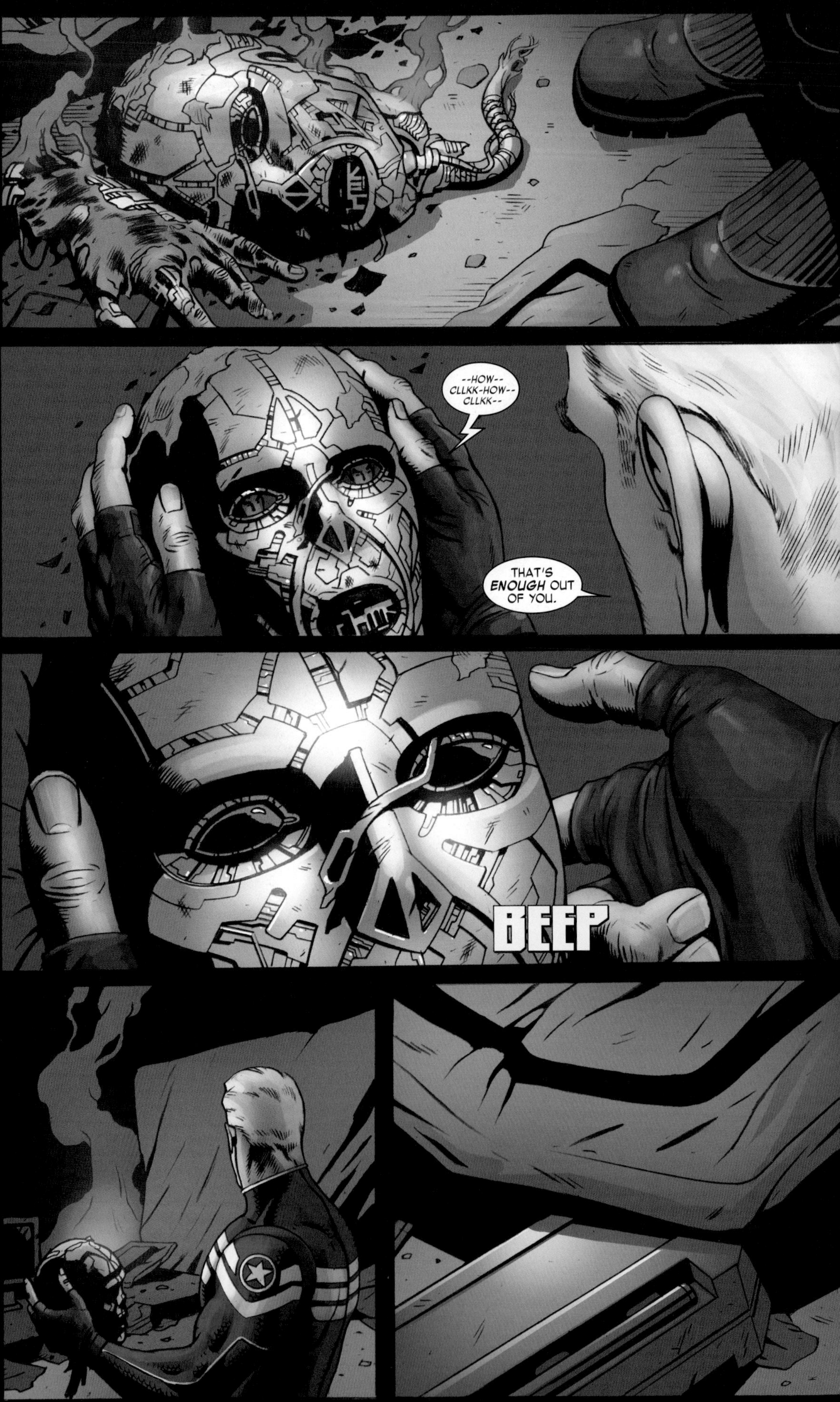
--HOW--
CLLKK-HOW--
CLLKK--
THAT'S ENOUGH OUT OF YOU.
BEEP

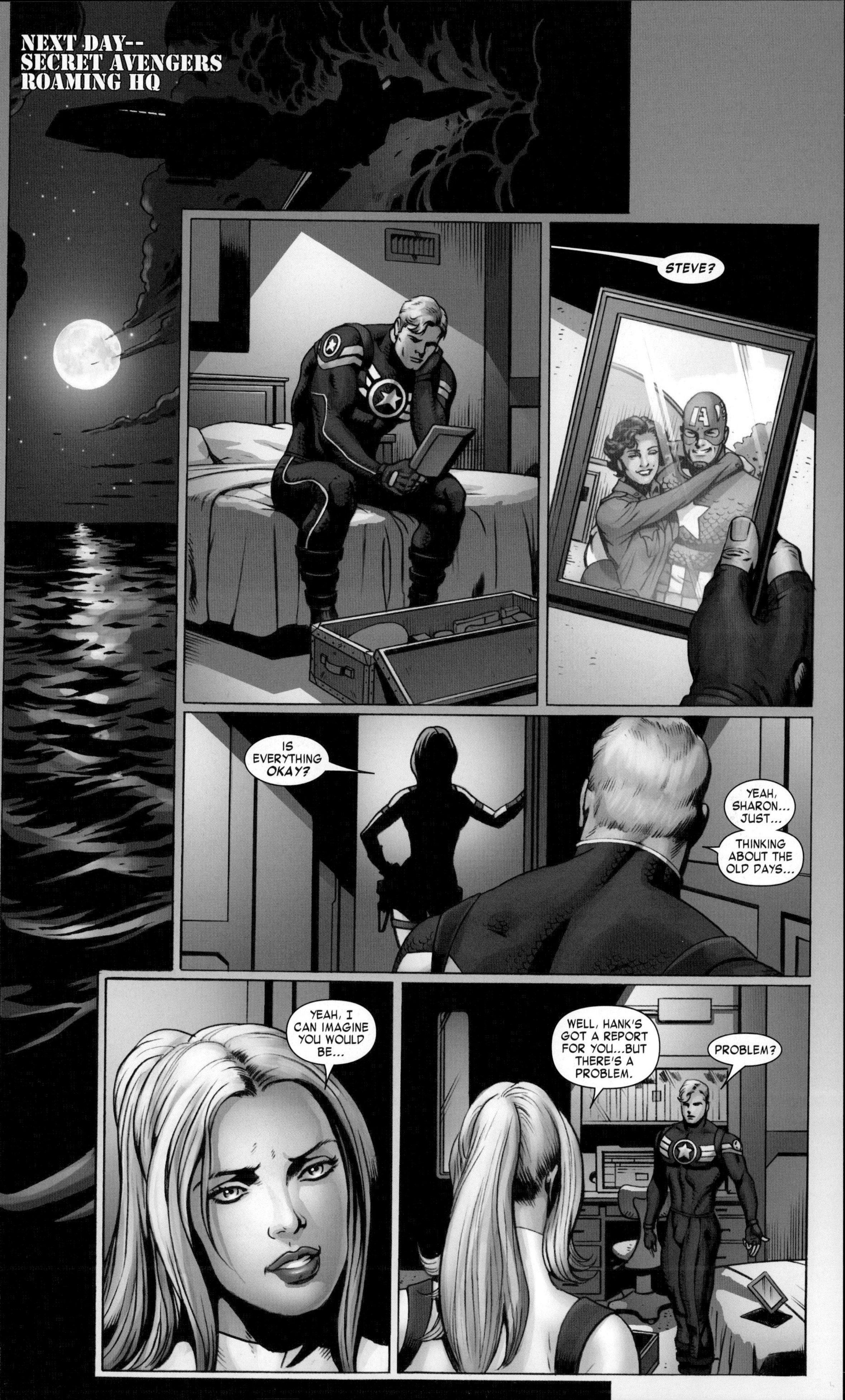
NEXT DAY--
SECRET AVENGERS
ROAMING HQ
STEVE?
IS EVERYTHING OKAY?
YEAH, SHARON... JUST...
THINKING ABOUT THE OLD DAYS...
YEAH, I CAN IMAGINE YOU WOULD BE...
WELL, HANK'S GOT A REPORT FOR YOU...BUT THERE'S A PROBLEM.
PROBLEM?

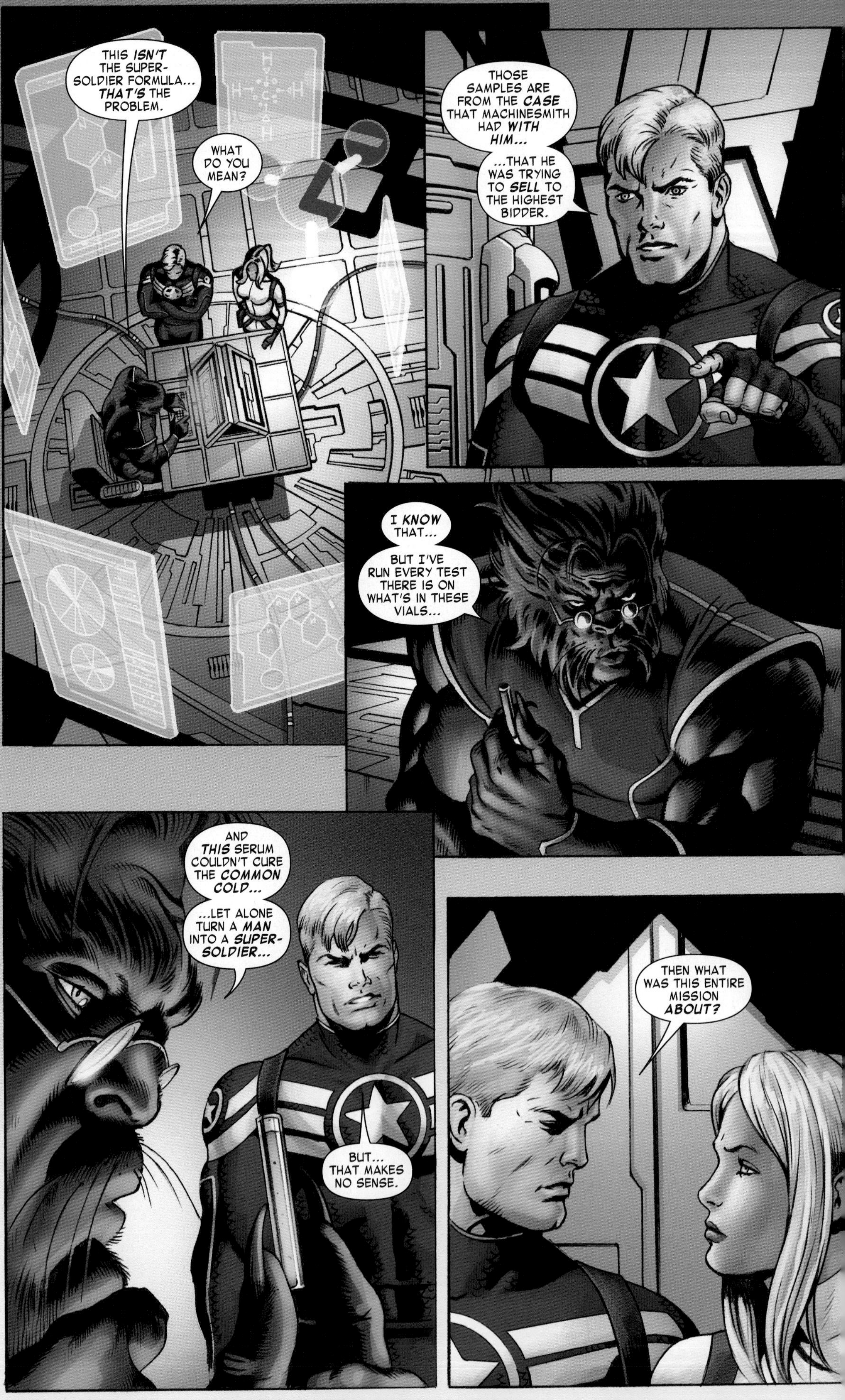
THIS ISN'T THE SUPER-SOLDIER FORMULA... THAT'S THE PROBLEM.
WHAT DO YOU MEAN?
THOSE SAMPLES ARE FROM THE CASE THAT MACHINESMITH HAD WITH HIM...
...THAT HE WAS TRYING TO SELL TO THE HIGHEST BIDDER.
I KNOW THAT...
BUT I'VE RUN EVERY TEST THERE IS ON WHAT'S IN THESE VIALS...
AND THIS SERUM COULDN'T CURE THE COMMON COLD...
...LET ALONE TURN A MAN INTO A SUPER-SOLDIER...
BUT... THAT MAKES NO SENSE.
THEN WHAT WAS THIS ENTIRE MISSION ABOUT?

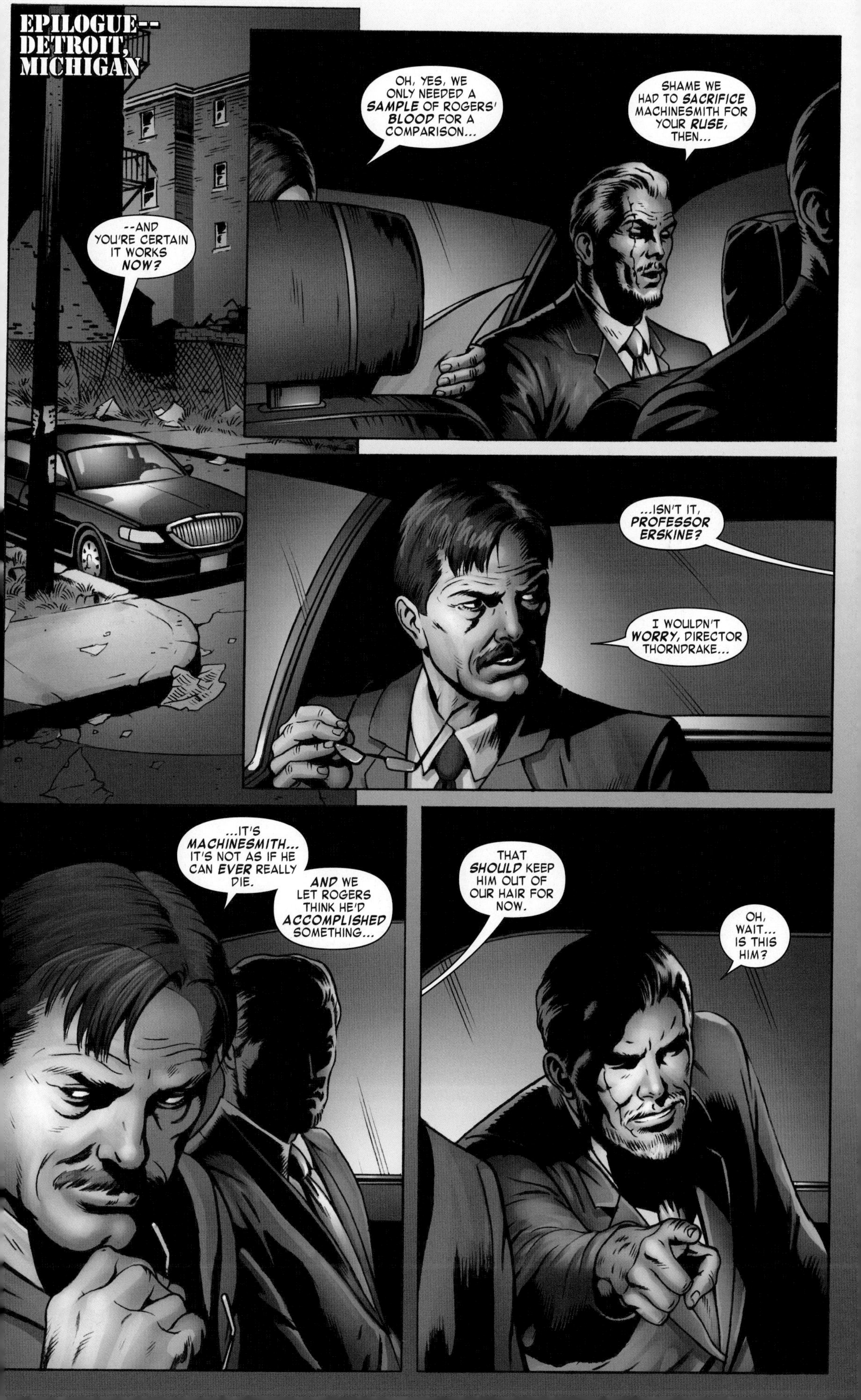
EPILOGUE-- DETROIT, MICHIGAN
--AND YOU'RE CERTAIN IT WORKS NOW?
OH, YES, WE ONLY NEEDED A SAMPLE OF ROGERS' BLOOD FOR A COMPARISON...
SHAME WE HAD TO SACRIFICE MACHINESMITH FOR YOUR RUSE, THEN...
...ISN'T IT, PROFESSOR ERSKINE?
I WOULDN'T WORRY, DIRECTOR THORNDRAKE...
...IT'S MACHINESMITH... IT'S NOT AS IF HE CAN EVER REALLY DIE.
AND WE LET ROGERS THINK HE'D ACCOMPLISHED SOMETHING...
THAT SHOULD KEEP HIM OUT OF OUR HAIR FOR NOW.
OH, WAIT... IS THIS HIM?

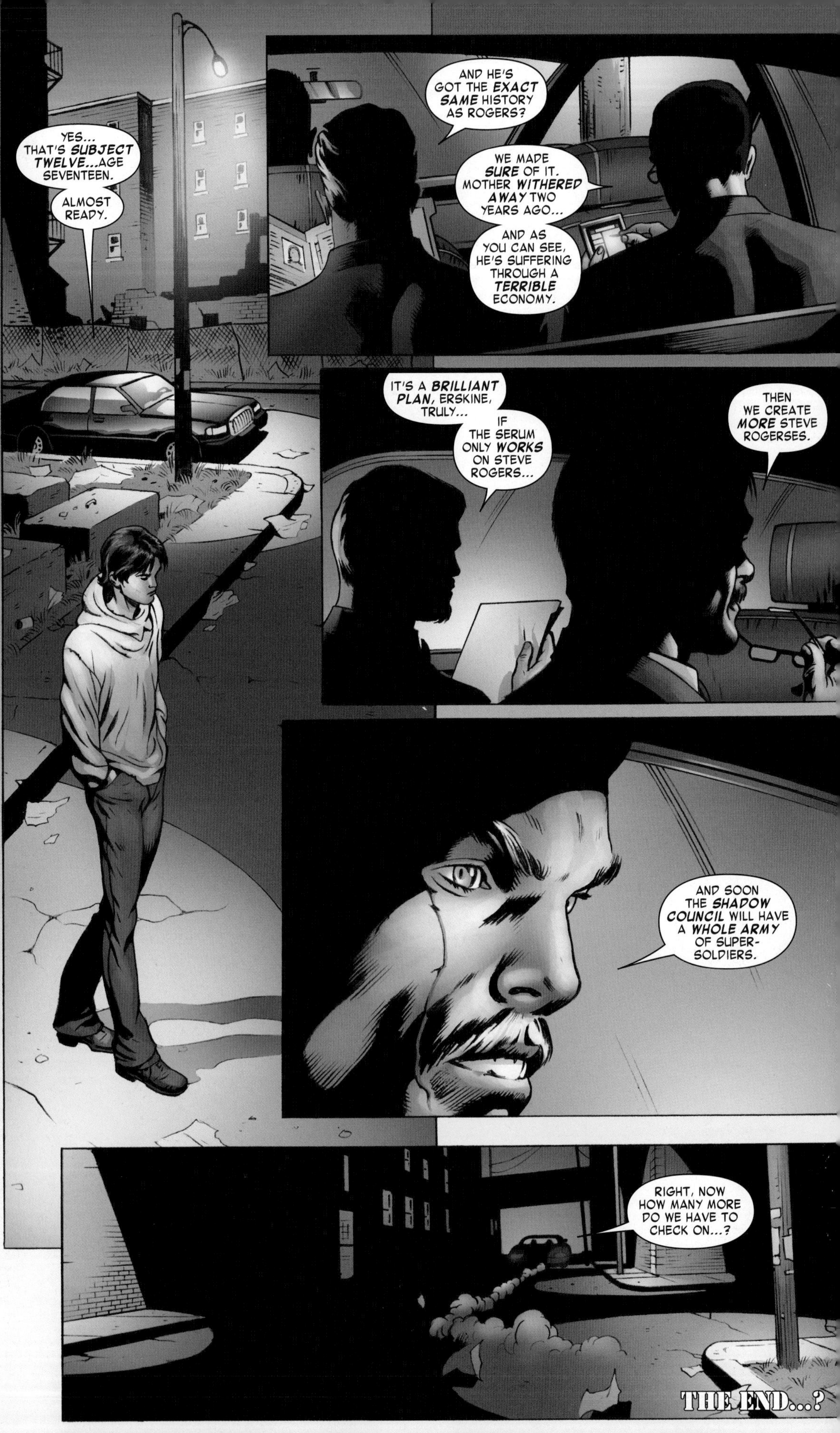
YES... THAT'S SUBJECT TWELVE...AGE SEVENTEEN.
ALMOST READY.
AND HE'S GOT THE EXACT SAME HISTORY AS ROGERS?
WE MADE SURE OF IT. MOTHER WITHERED AWAY TWO YEARS AGO...
AND AS YOU CAN SEE, HE'S SUFFERING THROUGH A TERRIBLE ECONOMY.
IT'S A BRILLIANT PLAN, ERSKINE, TRULY...
IF THE SERUM ONLY WORKS ON STEVE ROGERS...
THEN WE CREATE MORE STEVE ROGERSES.
AND SOON THE SHADOW COUNCIL WILL HAVE A WHOLE ARMY OF SUPER-SOLDIERS.
RIGHT, NOW HOW MANY MORE DO WE HAVE TO CHECK ON...?
THE END...?

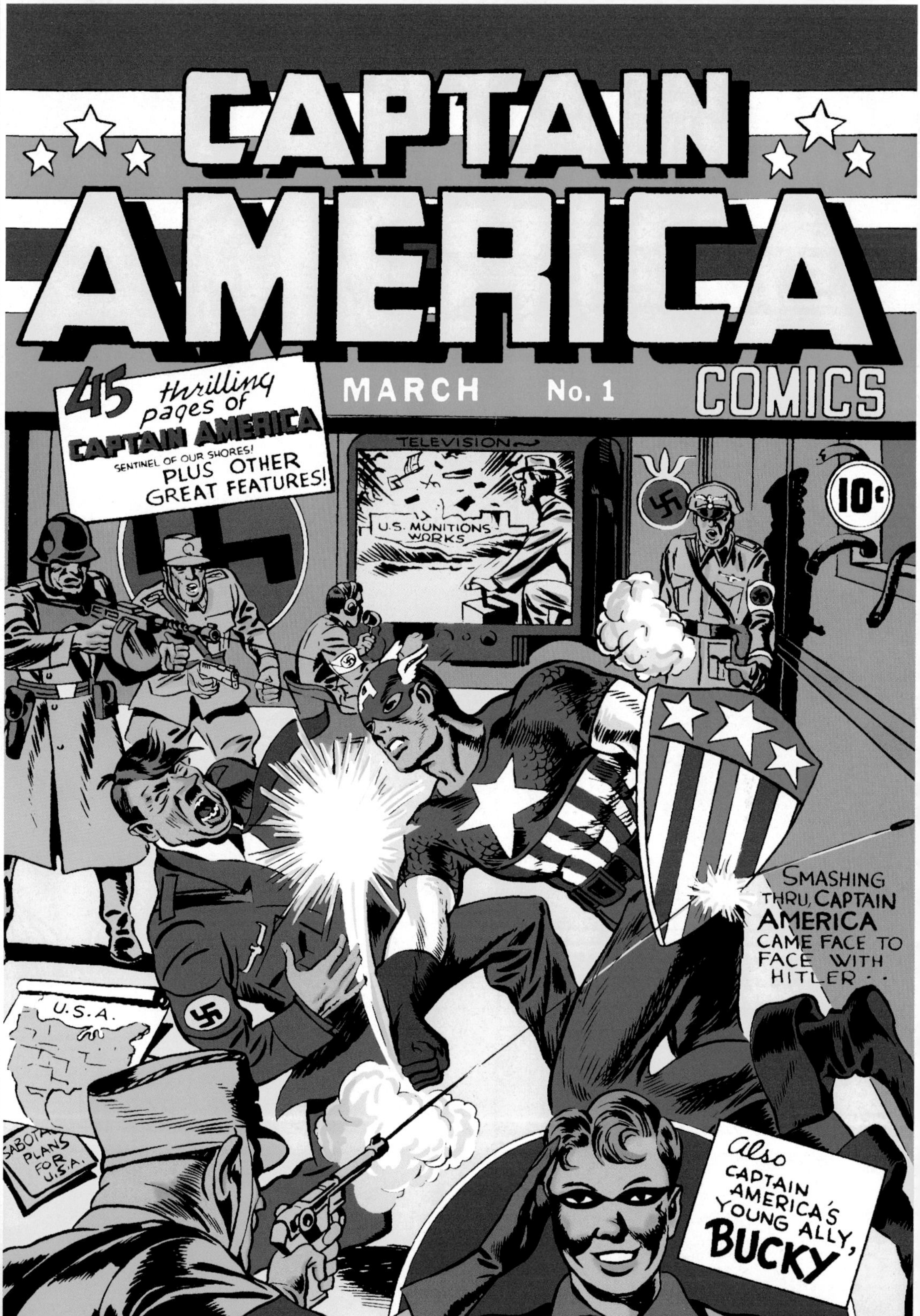
CAPTAIN AMERICA
COMICS
MARCH
No. 1
45 thrilling pages of
CAPTAIN AMERICA
SENTINEL OF OUR SHORES!
PLUS OTHER GREAT FEATURES!
TELEVISION
U.S. MUNITIONS WORKS
10¢
SMASHING THRU, CAPTAIN AMERICA CAME FACE TO FACE WITH HITLER . .
U.S.A.
PLANS FOR U.S.A.
also
CAPTAIN AMERICA'S YOUNG ALLY, BUCKY

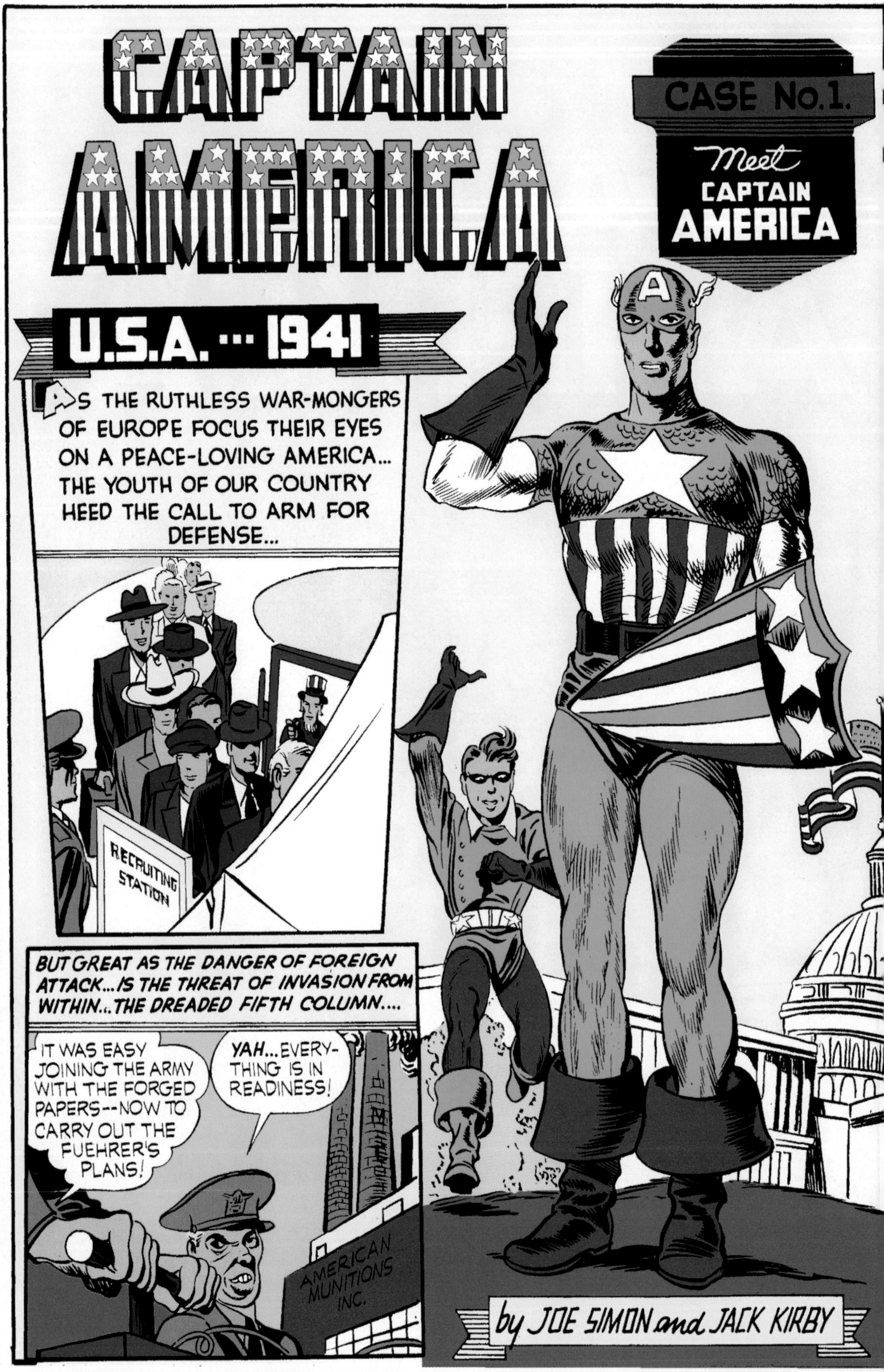

CAPTAIN AMERICA
CASE No. 1.
Meet CAPTAIN AMERICA
U.S.A. ... 1941
AS THE RUTHLESS WAR-MONGERS OF EUROPE FOCUS THEIR EYES ON A PEACE-LOVING AMERICA... THE YOUTH OF OUR COUNTRY HEED THE CALL TO ARM FOR DEFENSE...
RECRUITING STATION
BUT GREAT AS THE DANGER OF FOREIGN ATTACK... IS THE THREAT OF INVASION FROM WITHIN... THE DREADED FIFTH COLUMN....
IT WAS EASY JOINING THE ARMY WITH THE FORGED PAPERS--NOW TO CARRY OUT THE FUEHRER'S PLANS!
YAH... EVERY-THING IS IN READINESS!
AMERICAN MUNITIONS INC.
by JOE SIMON and JACK KIRBY

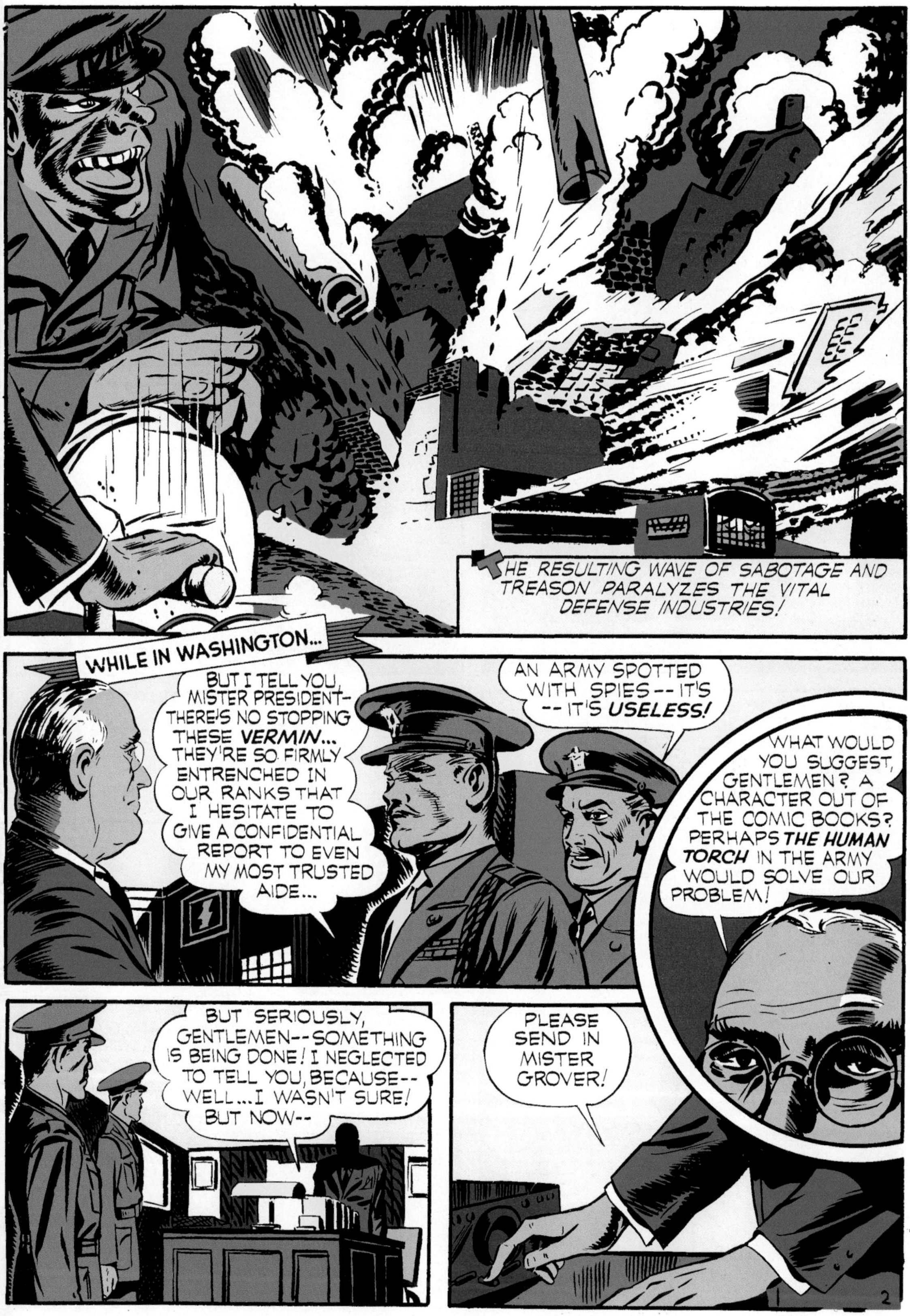
THE RESULTING WAVE OF SABOTAGE AND TREASON PARALYZES THE VITAL DEFENSE INDUSTRIES!
WHILE IN WASHINGTON...
BUT I TELL YOU, MISTER PRESIDENT-- THERE'S NO STOPPING THESE VERMIN... THEY'RE SO FIRMLY ENTRENCHED IN OUR RANKS THAT I HESITATE TO GIVE A CONFIDENTIAL REPORT TO EVEN MY MOST TRUSTED AIDE...
AN ARMY SPOTTED WITH SPIES -- IT'S -- IT'S USELESS!
WHAT WOULD YOU SUGGEST, GENTLEMEN? A CHARACTER OUT OF THE COMIC BOOKS? PERHAPS THE HUMAN TORCH IN THE ARMY WOULD SOLVE OUR PROBLEM!
BUT SERIOUSLY, GENTLEMEN--SOMETHING IS BEING DONE! I NEGLECTED TO TELL YOU, BECAUSE-- WELL...I WASN'T SURE! BUT NOW--
PLEASE SEND IN MISTER GROVER!
2

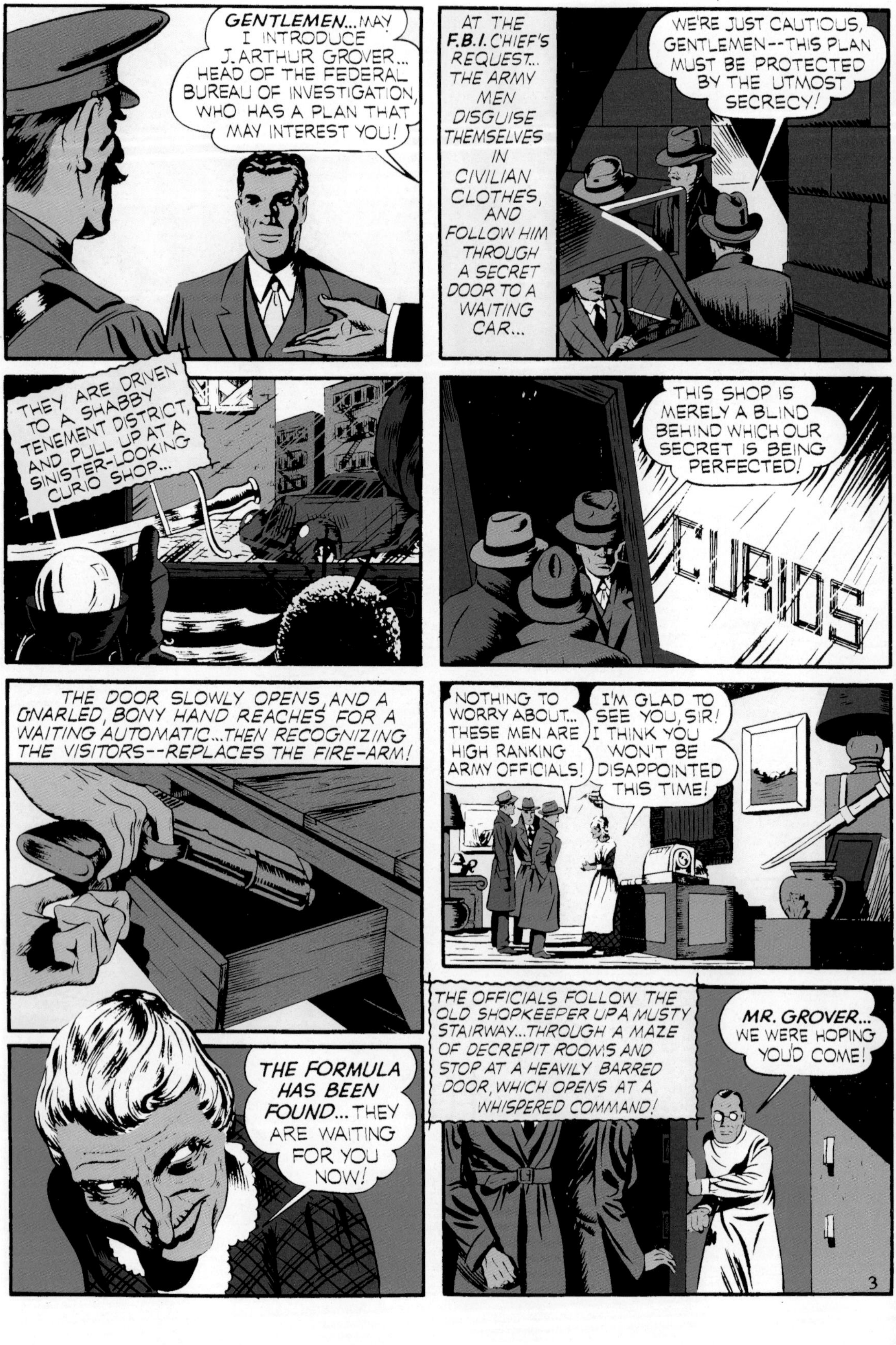

GENTLEMEN...MAY I INTRODUCE J. ARTHUR GROVER... HEAD OF THE FEDERAL BUREAU OF INVESTIGATION, WHO HAS A PLAN THAT MAY INTEREST YOU!
AT THE F.B.I. CHIEF'S REQUEST.. THE ARMY MEN DISGUISE THEMSELVES IN CIVILIAN CLOTHES, AND FOLLOW HIM THROUGH A SECRET DOOR TO A WAITING CAR...
WE'RE JUST CAUTIOUS, GENTLEMEN--THIS PLAN MUST BE PROTECTED BY THE UTMOST SECRECY!
THEY ARE DRIVEN TO A SHABBY TENEMENT DISTRICT, AND PULL UP AT A SINISTER-LOOKING CURIO SHOP...
THIS SHOP IS MERELY A BLIND BEHIND WHICH OUR SECRET IS BEING PERFECTED!
CURIOS
THE DOOR SLOWLY OPENS, AND A GNARLED, BONY HAND REACHES FOR A WAITING AUTOMATIC...THEN RECOGNIZING THE VISITORS--REPLACES THE FIRE-ARM!
NOTHING TO WORRY ABOUT... THESE MEN ARE HIGH RANKING ARMY OFFICIALS!
I'M GLAD TO SEE YOU, SIR! I THINK YOU WON'T BE DISAPPOINTED THIS TIME!
THE FORMULA HAS BEEN FOUND... THEY ARE WAITING FOR YOU NOW!
THE OFFICIALS FOLLOW THE OLD SHOPKEEPER UP A MUSTY STAIRWAY...THROUGH A MAZE OF DECREPIT ROOMS AND STOP AT A HEAVILY BARRED DOOR, WHICH OPENS AT A WHISPERED COMMAND!
MR. GROVER... WE WERE HOPING YOU'D COME!

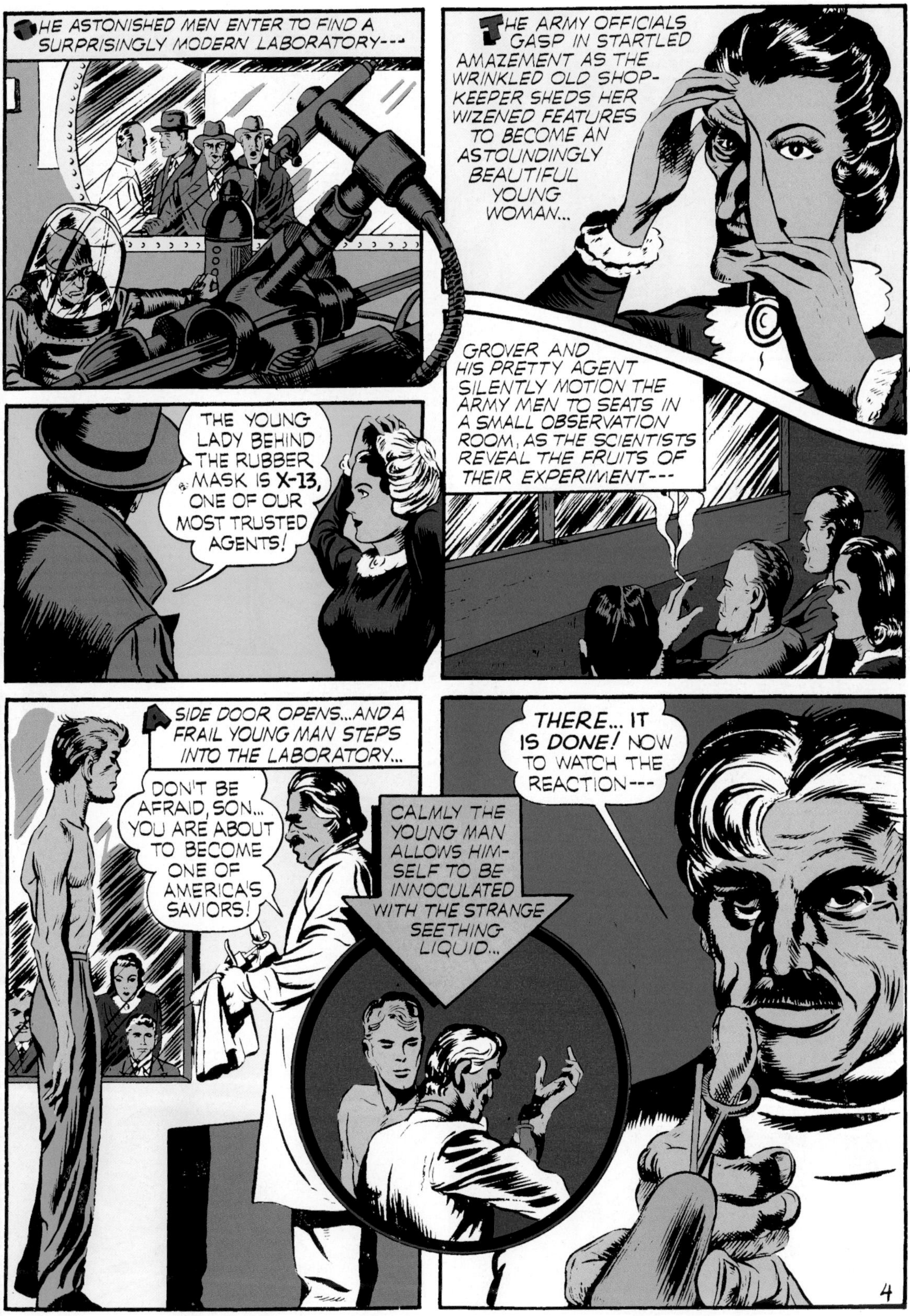

THE ASTONISHED MEN ENTER TO FIND A SURPRISINGLY MODERN LABORATORY---
THE ARMY OFFICIALS GASP IN STARTLED AMAZEMENT AS THE WRINKLED OLD SHOP-KEEPER SHEDS HER WIZENED FEATURES TO BECOME AN ASTOUNDINGLY BEAUTIFUL YOUNG WOMAN...
THE YOUNG LADY BEHIND THE RUBBER MASK IS X-13, ONE OF OUR MOST TRUSTED AGENTS!
GROVER AND HIS PRETTY AGENT SILENTLY MOTION THE ARMY MEN TO SEATS IN A SMALL OBSERVATION ROOM, AS THE SCIENTISTS REVEAL THE FRUITS OF THEIR EXPERIMENT---
A SIDE DOOR OPENS...AND A FRAIL YOUNG MAN STEPS INTO THE LABORATORY...
DON'T BE AFRAID, SON... YOU ARE ABOUT TO BECOME ONE OF AMERICA'S SAVIORS!
CALMLY THE YOUNG MAN ALLOWS HIM-SELF TO BE INNOCULATED WITH THE STRANGE SEETHING LIQUID...
THERE... IT IS DONE! NOW TO WATCH THE REACTION---

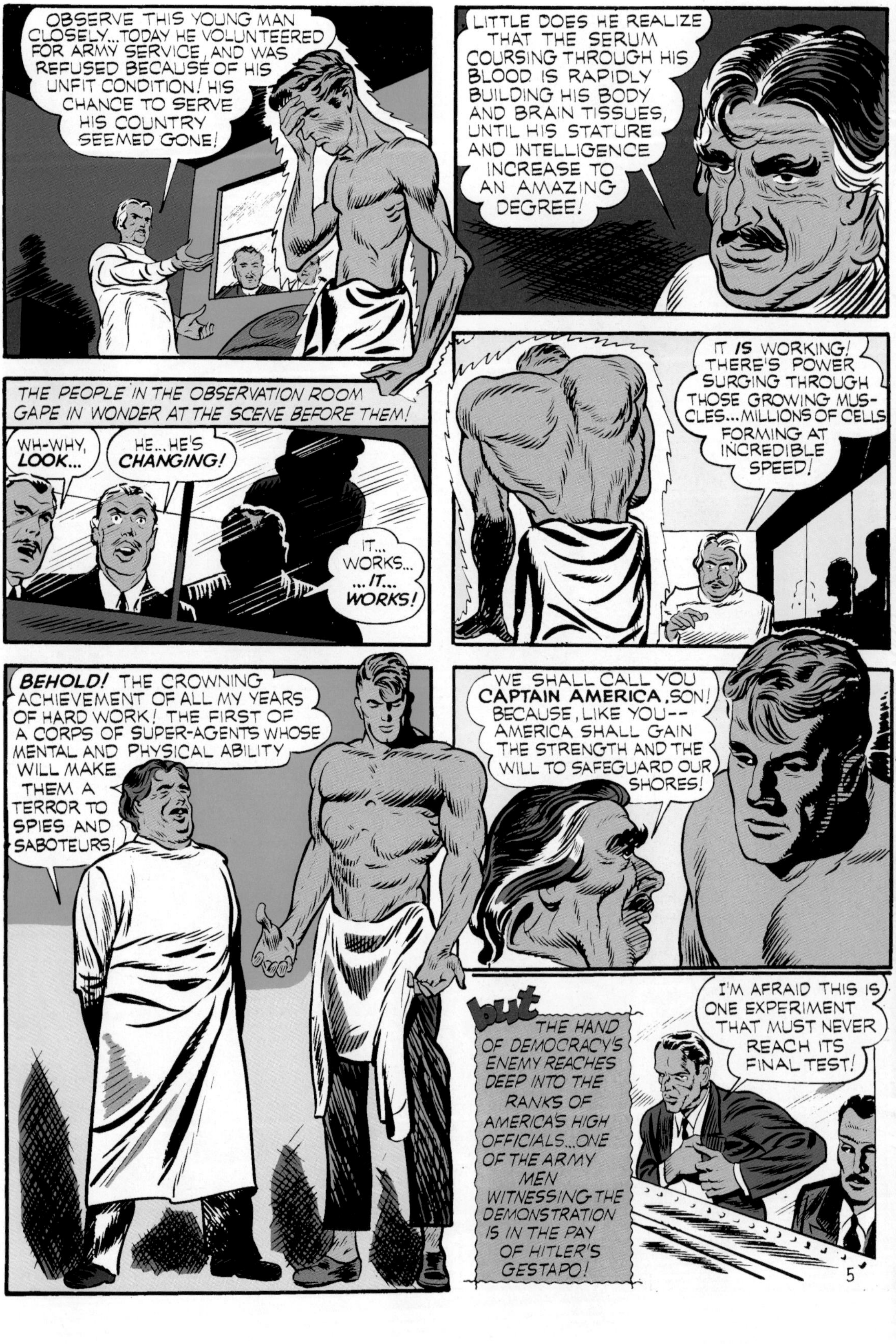
OBSERVE THIS YOUNG MAN CLOSELY...TODAY HE VOLUNTEERED FOR ARMY SERVICE, AND WAS REFUSED BECAUSE OF HIS UNFIT CONDITION! HIS CHANCE TO SERVE HIS COUNTRY SEEMED GONE!
LITTLE DOES HE REALIZE THAT THE SERUM COURSING THROUGH HIS BLOOD IS RAPIDLY BUILDING HIS BODY AND BRAIN TISSUES, UNTIL HIS STATURE AND INTELLIGENCE INCREASE TO AN AMAZING DEGREE!
THE PEOPLE IN THE OBSERVATION ROOM GAPE IN WONDER AT THE SCENE BEFORE THEM!
WH-WHY, LOOK...
HE...HE'S CHANGING!
IT... WORKS... ...IT... WORKS!
IT IS WORKING! THERE'S POWER SURGING THROUGH THOSE GROWING MUSCLES...MILLIONS OF CELLS FORMING AT INCREDIBLE SPEED!
BEHOLD! THE CROWNING ACHIEVEMENT OF ALL MY YEARS OF HARD WORK! THE FIRST OF A CORPS OF SUPER-AGENTS WHOSE MENTAL AND PHYSICAL ABILITY WILL MAKE THEM A TERROR TO SPIES AND SABOTEURS!
WE SHALL CALL YOU CAPTAIN AMERICA, SON! BECAUSE, LIKE YOU-- AMERICA SHALL GAIN THE STRENGTH AND THE WILL TO SAFEGUARD OUR SHORES!
but THE HAND OF DEMOCRACY'S ENEMY REACHES DEEP INTO THE RANKS OF AMERICA'S HIGH OFFICIALS...ONE OF THE ARMY MEN WITNESSING THE DEMONSTRATION IS IN THE PAY OF HITLER'S GESTAPO!
I'M AFRAID THIS IS ONE EXPERIMENT THAT MUST NEVER REACH ITS FINAL TEST!

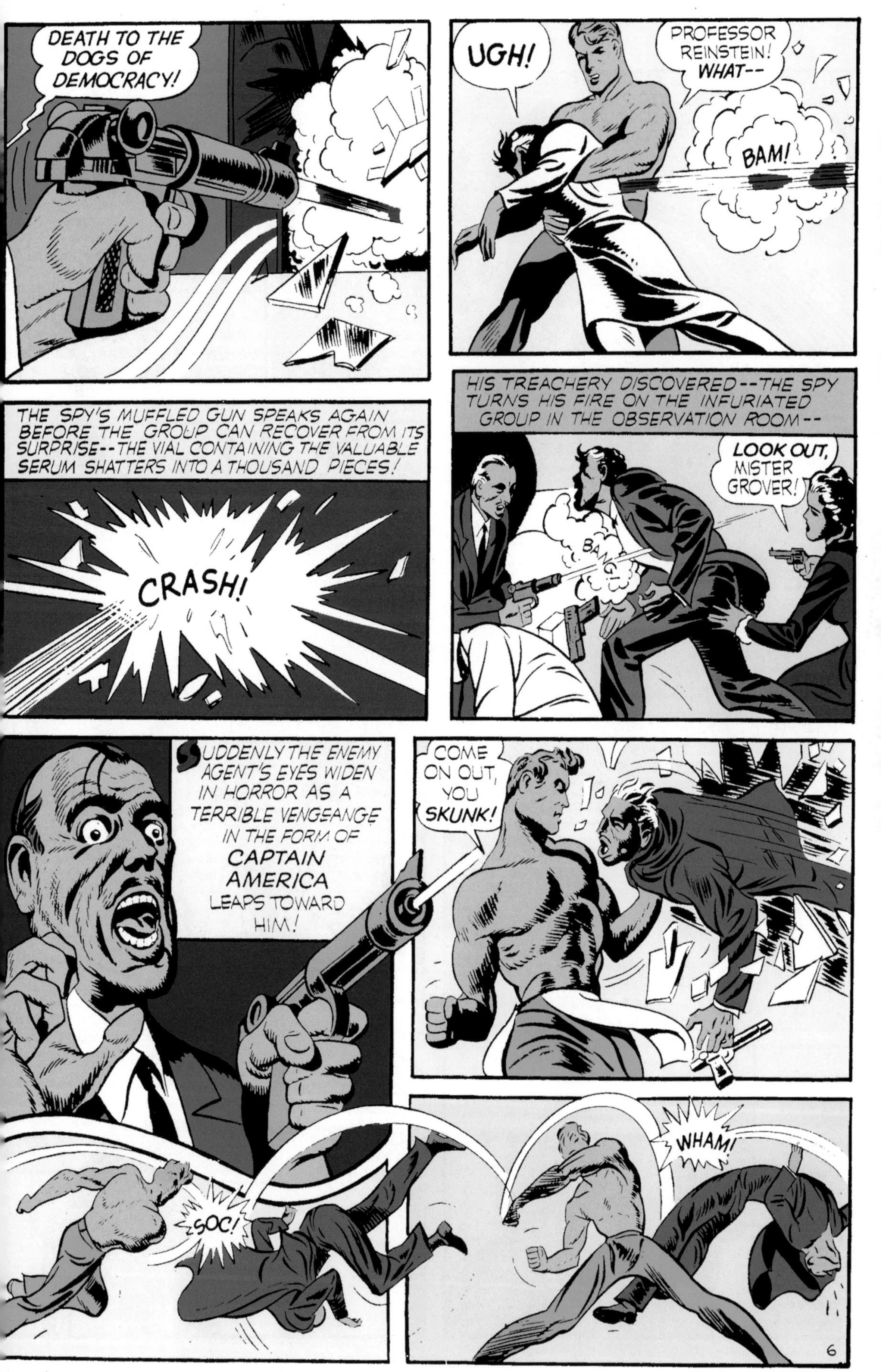

DEATH TO THE DOGS OF DEMOCRACY!
UGH!
PROFESSOR REINSTEIN! WHAT--
BAM!
THE SPY'S MUFFLED GUN SPEAKS AGAIN BEFORE THE GROUP CAN RECOVER FROM ITS SURPRISE--THE VIAL CONTAINING THE VALUABLE SERUM SHATTERS INTO A THOUSAND PIECES!
CRASH!
HIS TREACHERY DISCOVERED--THE SPY TURNS HIS FIRE ON THE INFURIATED GROUP IN THE OBSERVATION ROOM--
LOOK OUT, MISTER GROVER!
BANG!
SUDDENLY THE ENEMY AGENT'S EYES WIDEN IN HORROR AS A TERRIBLE VENGEANCE IN THE FORM OF CAPTAIN AMERICA LEAPS TOWARD HIM!
COME ON OUT, YOU SKUNK!
SOC!
WHAM!

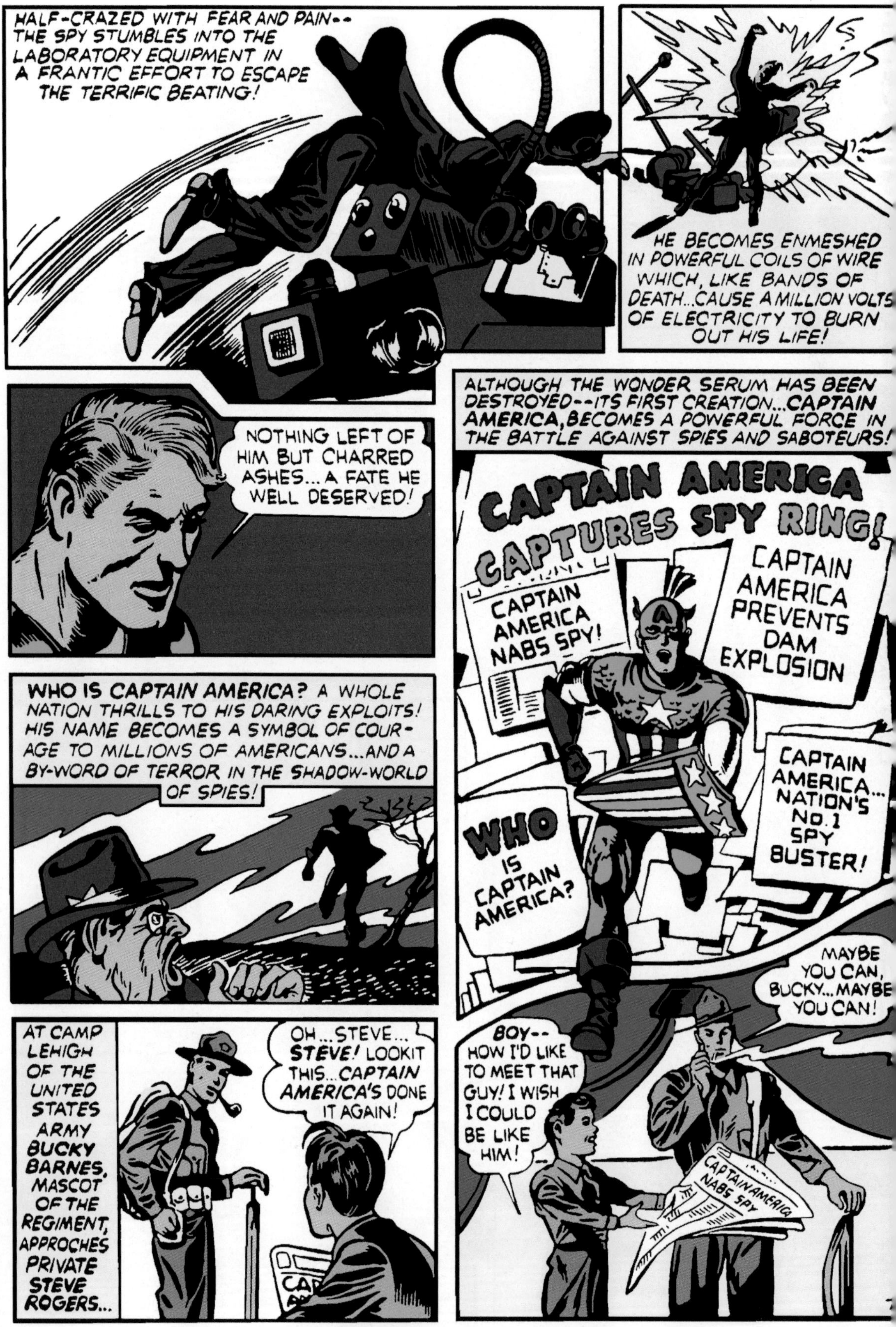
HALF-CRAZED WITH FEAR AND PAIN-- THE SPY STUMBLES INTO THE LABORATORY EQUIPMENT IN A FRANTIC EFFORT TO ESCAPE THE TERRIFIC BEATING!
HE BECOMES ENMESHED IN POWERFUL COILS OF WIRE WHICH, LIKE BANDS OF DEATH...CAUSE A MILLION VOLTS OF ELECTRICITY TO BURN OUT HIS LIFE!
NOTHING LEFT OF HIM BUT CHARRED ASHES... A FATE HE WELL DESERVED!
ALTHOUGH THE WONDER SERUM HAS BEEN DESTROYED--ITS FIRST CREATION...CAPTAIN AMERICA, BECOMES A POWERFUL FORCE IN THE BATTLE AGAINST SPIES AND SABOTEURS!
CAPTAIN AMERICA CAPTURES SPY RING!
CAPTAIN AMERICA NABS SPY!
CAPTAIN AMERICA PREVENTS DAM EXPLOSION
CAPTAIN AMERICA... NATION'S No.1 SPY BUSTER!
WHO IS CAPTAIN AMERICA?
WHO IS CAPTAIN AMERICA? A WHOLE NATION THRILLS TO HIS DARING EXPLOITS! HIS NAME BECOMES A SYMBOL OF COURAGE TO MILLIONS OF AMERICANS...AND A BY-WORD OF TERROR IN THE SHADOW-WORLD OF SPIES!
AT CAMP LEHIGH OF THE UNITED STATES ARMY BUCKY BARNES, MASCOT OF THE REGIMENT, APPROCHES PRIVATE STEVE ROGERS...
OH...STEVE... STEVE! LOOKIT THIS...CAPTAIN AMERICA'S DONE IT AGAIN!
BOY-- HOW I'D LIKE TO MEET THAT GUY! I WISH I COULD BE LIKE HIM!
MAYBE YOU CAN, BUCKY...MAYBE YOU CAN!
CAPTAIN AMERICA NABS SPY

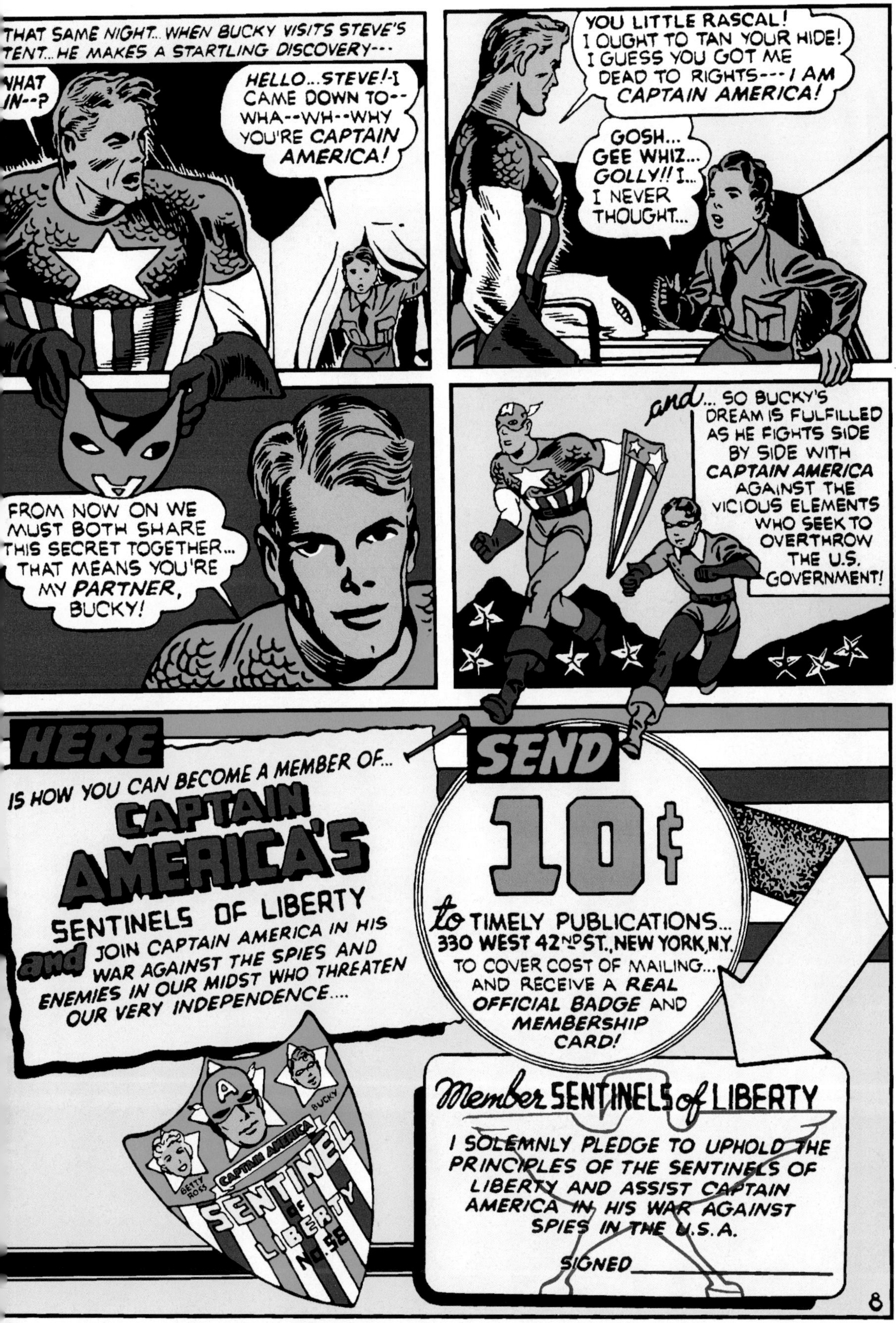
THAT SAME NIGHT... WHEN BUCKY VISITS STEVE'S TENT... HE MAKES A STARTLING DISCOVERY---
HELLO...STEVE!-I CAME DOWN TO-- WHA--WH--WHY YOU'RE CAPTAIN AMERICA!
YOU LITTLE RASCAL! I OUGHT TO TAN YOUR HIDE! I GUESS YOU GOT ME DEAD TO RIGHTS---I AM CAPTAIN AMERICA!
GOSH... GEE WHIZ... GOLLY!! I... I NEVER THOUGHT...
FROM NOW ON WE MUST BOTH SHARE THIS SECRET TOGETHER... THAT MEANS YOU'RE MY PARTNER, BUCKY!
and... SO BUCKY'S DREAM IS FULFILLED AS HE FIGHTS SIDE BY SIDE WITH CAPTAIN AMERICA AGAINST THE VICIOUS ELEMENTS WHO SEEK TO OVERTHROW THE U.S. GOVERNMENT!
HERE IS HOW YOU CAN BECOME A MEMBER OF... CAPTAIN AMERICA'S SENTINELS OF LIBERTY
and JOIN CAPTAIN AMERICA IN HIS WAR AGAINST THE SPIES AND ENEMIES IN OUR MIDST WHO THREATEN OUR VERY INDEPENDENCE....
SEND 10¢
to TIMELY PUBLICATIONS... 330 WEST 42ND ST., NEW YORK, N.Y.
TO COVER COST OF MAILING... AND RECEIVE A REAL OFFICIAL BADGE AND MEMBERSHIP CARD!
BETTY ROSS
BUCKY
CAPTAIN AMERICA
SENTINEL OF LIBERTY NO.56
Member SENTINELS of LIBERTY
I SOLEMNLY PLEDGE TO UPHOLD THE PRINCIPLES OF THE SENTINELS OF LIBERTY AND ASSIST CAPTAIN AMERICA IN HIS WAR AGAINST SPIES IN THE U.S.A.
SIGNED____________
8

FOR MORE OF CAP'S GOLDEN AGE ADVENTURES, CHECK OUT
MARVEL MASTERWORKS: GOLDEN AGE CAPTAIN AMERICA VOLS. 1-4!

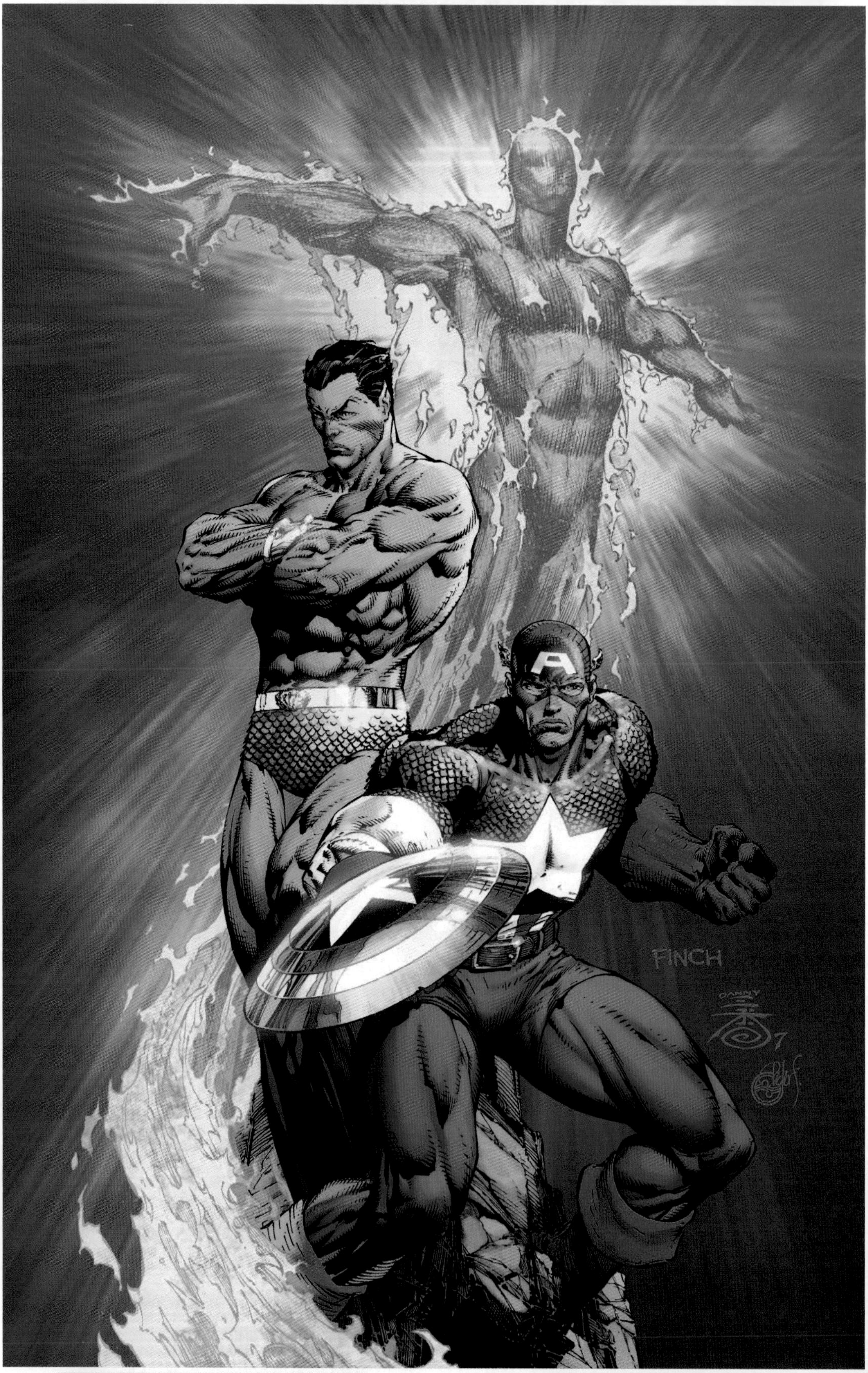
FINCH

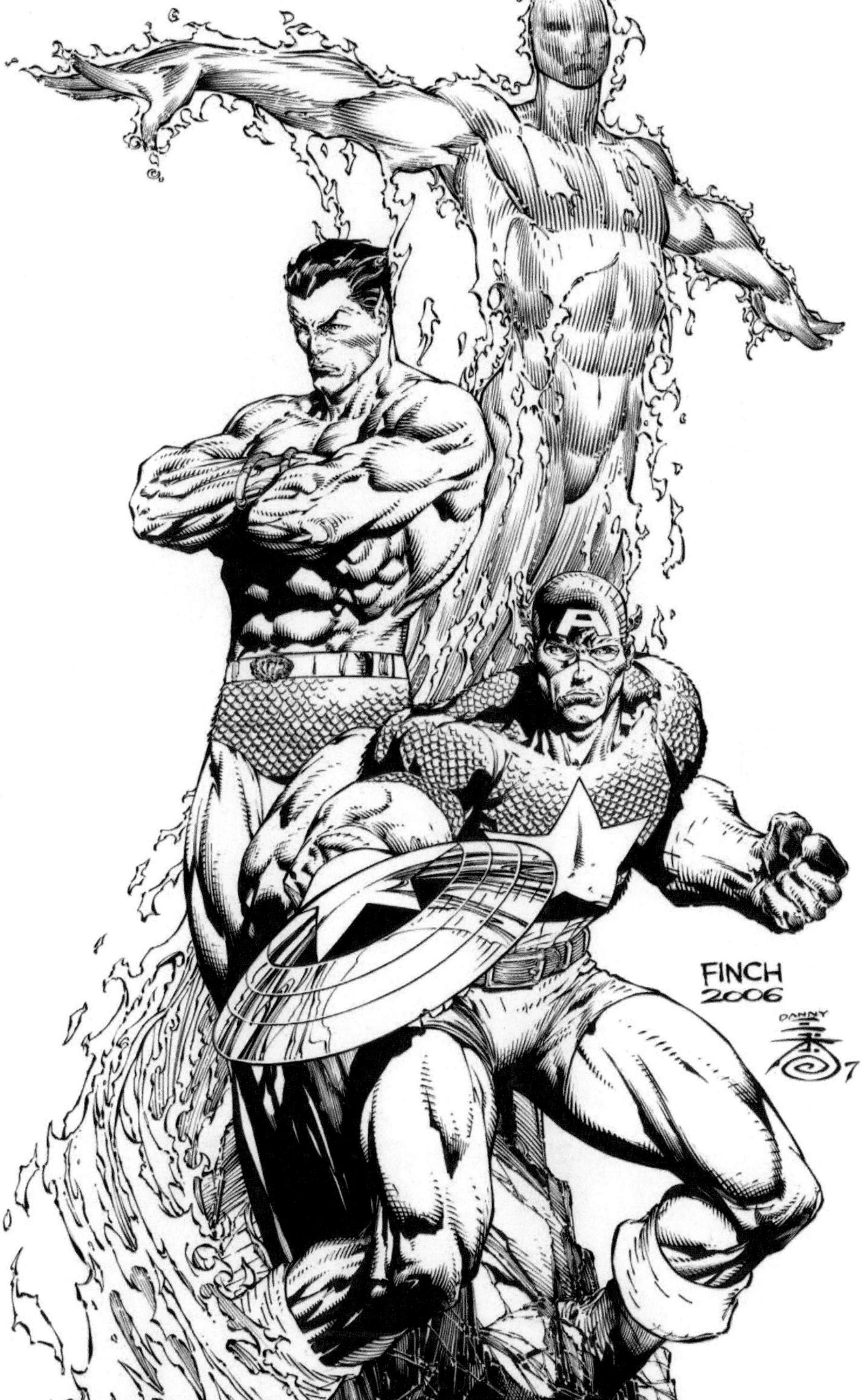
FINCH
2006
DANNY

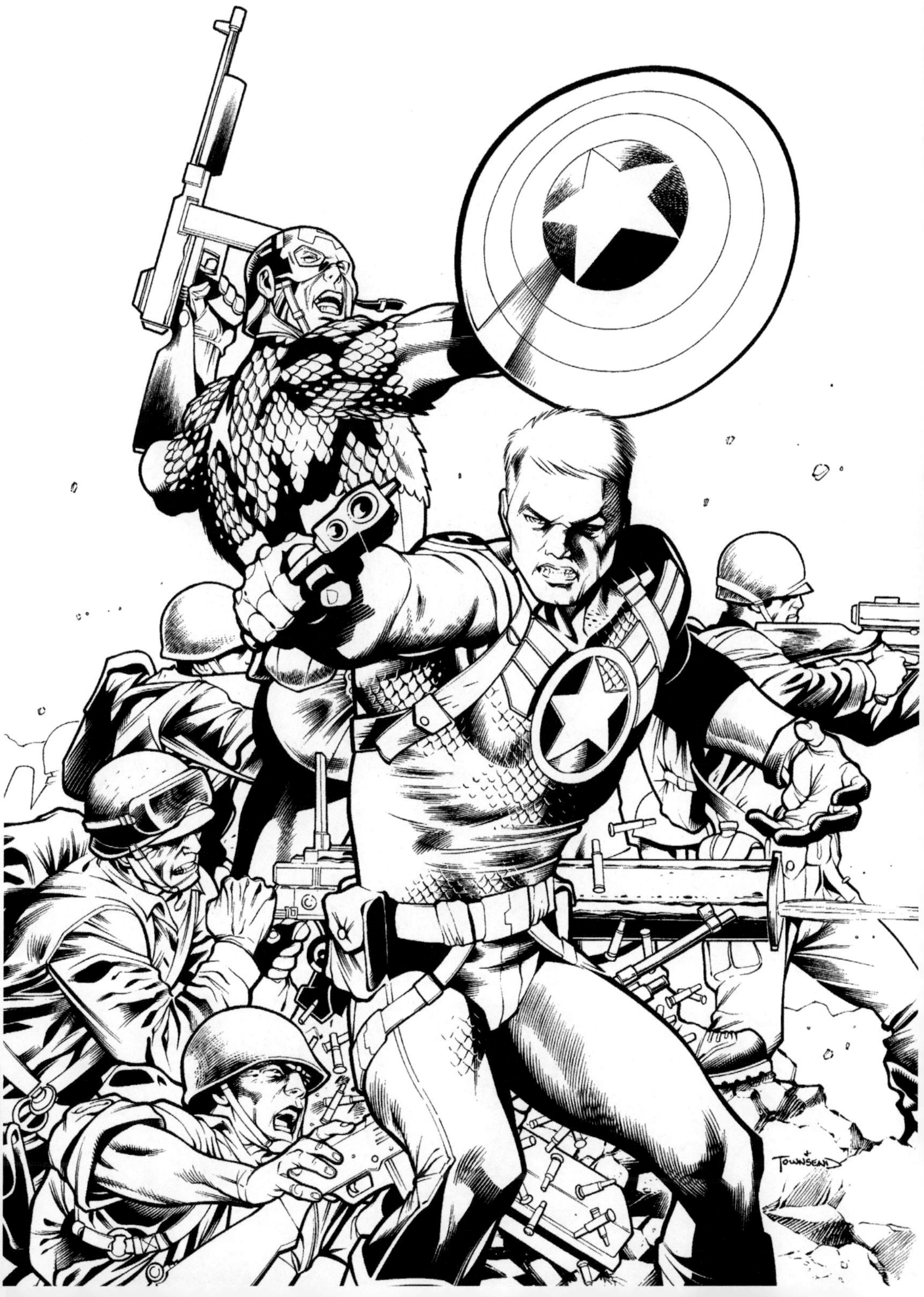
TOWNSEND

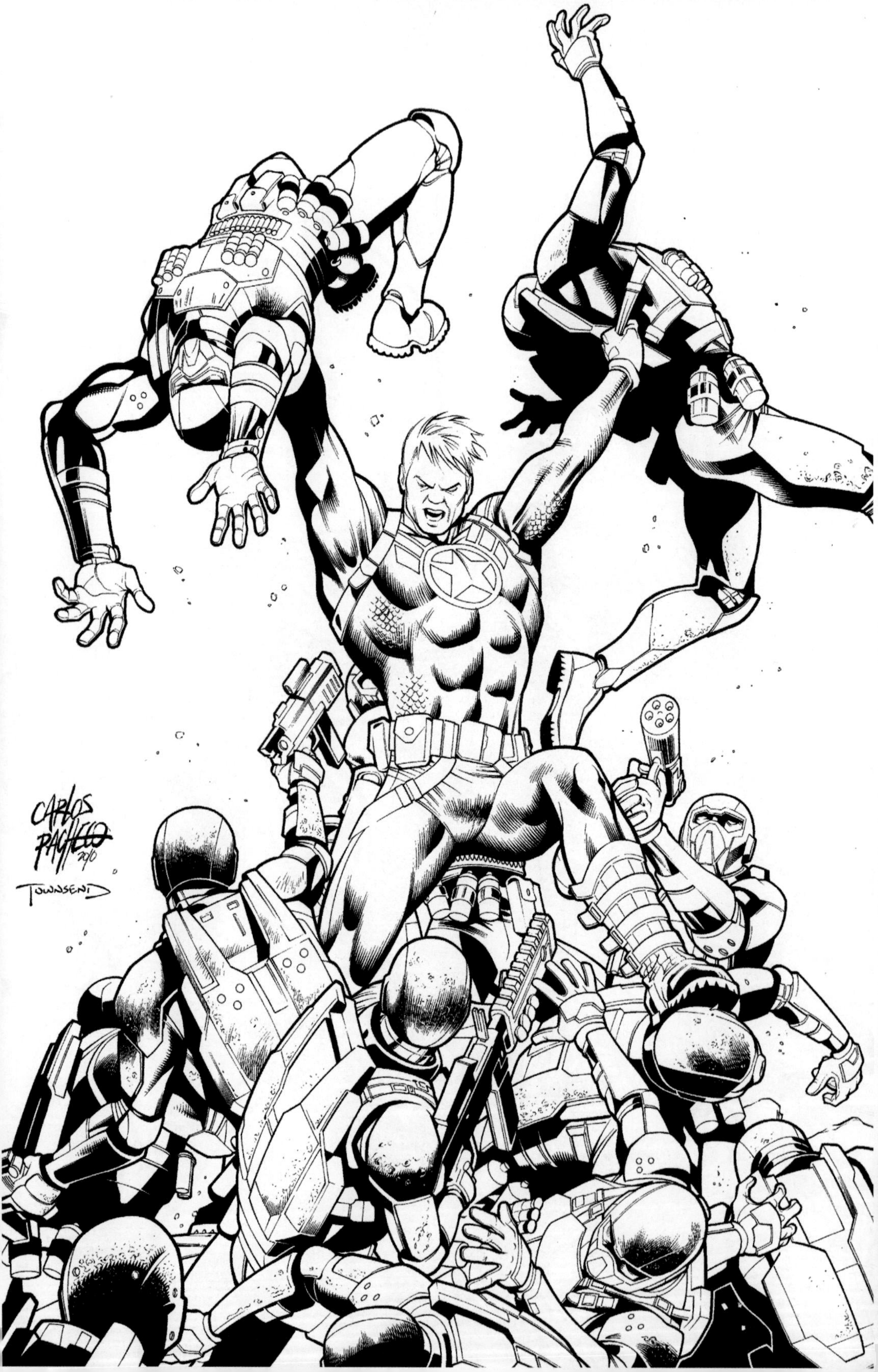
CARLOS PACHECO 2010
TOWNSEND

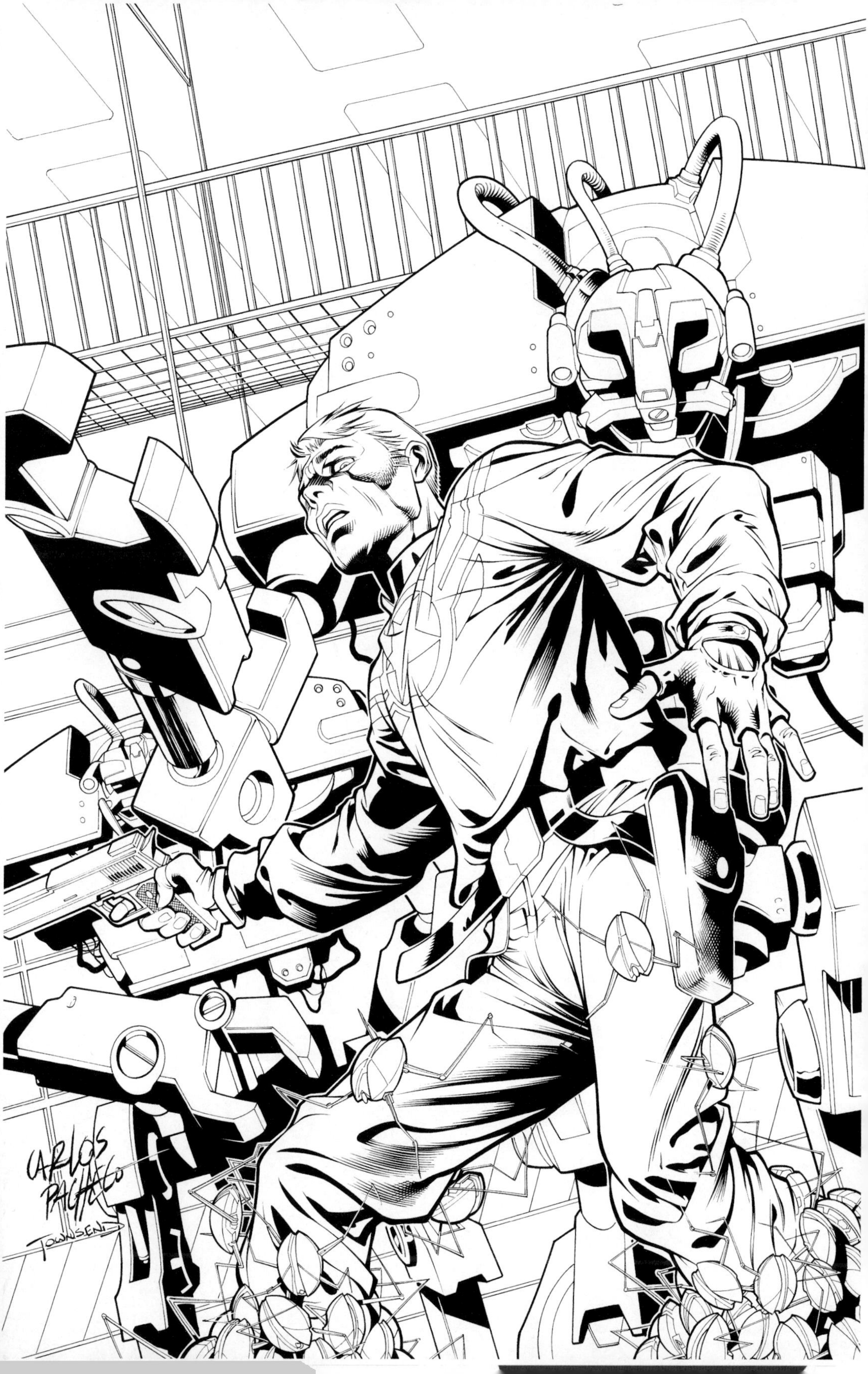
CARLOS PACHECO
TOWNSEND

#4 INKS
BY CARLOS PACHECO

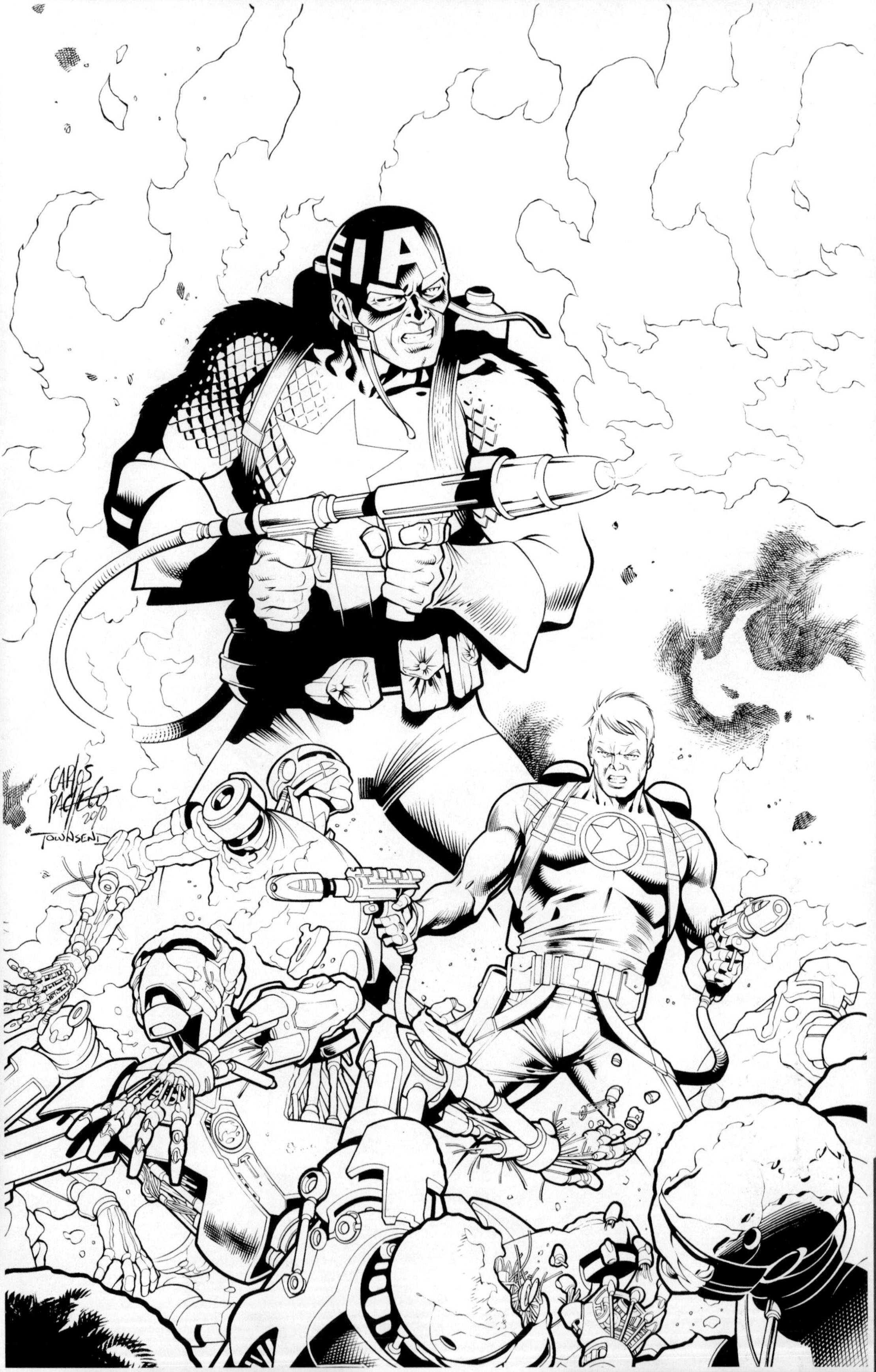
CARLOS PACHECO 2010
TOWNSEND